Mary and Archie Tisdall acquired their great love of travel during Archie's service in the Royal Air Force, when they lived in such diverse countries as Singapore, Jordan, Libya, Tunisia and Malta. After returning to live in England, they bought a motorcaravan and started to explore Europe. Gradually they began to write of their experiences for magazines.

They have travelled extensively in Spain, spending many winters in the Canary Islands. This resulted in 1984, in the publication of two guide books *Tenerife and the Western Canary Islands* and *Gran Canaria and the Eastern Canary Islands*, the latter of which is now published as two volumes, *Gran Canaria* and *Lanzarote and Fuerteventura*. Their affection for Spain has also taken them many times to the Balearic Islands. The outcome is a three title series: *Majorca*, *Menorca* and *Ibiza and Formentera*. Other books include guides to *Madeira and Porto Santo* and *The Algarve*.

The need to update and revise their books, and to look for new material, now keeps Mary and Archie Tisdall happily on the move for a large part of the year.

Our Lady of Lluc looks down on playas bright,
where once King Jaime fought.
Now aerial argonauts, to this treasure island of delight,
happy humanity have brought

Acknowledgements

The authors would like to thank the following people and organisations for their help, directly or indirectly, in the preparation of this book:

The Spanish National Tourist Office, London; Señor Eduardo Gamero, Director of Tourism, Majorca; Señor Jaime Rodriguez Caras of Ultramar Express; The Director of Sol Hotels in Majorca; Eve Hardingham, Majorca; Señor M.A. Bravo, Trasmediterranea, Barcelona; Gloria Ward and Julia Angrove, Thomson Holidays; Sharon Alexander, Brittany Ferries; The Director, Platja Blava Camping and The Director, Club San Pedro Camping.

Our thanks go to Yvonne Messenger, our helpful editor, and to our publisher, Roger Lascelles. Finally we acknowledge the interest and encouragement from friends and family.

Front Cover: Shades of Don Quixote combined with alternative energy. Windmills capturing the breezes to save animal power.

Majorca
A Traveller's Guide

Mary and Archie Tisdall

Roger Lascelles, Cartographic and Travel Publisher
47 York Road, Brentford, (Middx) TW8 0QP. Tel: 081 847 0935 Fax: 061 568 3886

Publication Data

Title	Majorca A Traveller's Guide
Typeface	Phototypeset in Compugraphic Times
Photographs	By the authors
Maps	John Gill, Chessington, Surrey
Printing	Kelso Graphics, Kelso, Scotland
ISBN	0 903909 59 6
Edition	First edition Aug 1987. Reprinted May 1988.
	Revised reprint Mar 1989. This new edition May 1992
Publisher	Roger Lascelles
	47 York Road, Brentford, Middlesex, TW8 0QP
Copyright	Mary and Archie Tisdall

Distribution

Africa:	South Africa	Faradawn, Box 17161, Hillbrow 2038
Americas:	Canada	International Travel Maps & Books, P.O. Box 2290, Vancouver BC V6B 3W5.
	U.S.A.	Available through major booksellers with good foreign travel sections
Asia:	India	English Book Store, 17-L Connaught Circus,P.O. Box 328, New Delhi 110 001
Australasia:	Australia	Rex Publications, 15 Huntingdon Street, Crows Nest, N.S.W.
Europe:	Belgium	Brussels – Peuples et Continents
	Germany	Available through major booksellers with good foreign travel sections
	GB/Ireland	Available through all booksellers with good foreign travel sections.
	Italy	Libreria dell'Automobile, Milano
	Netherlands	Nilsson & Lamm BV, Weesp
	Denmark	Copenhagen – Arnold Busck, G.E.C. Gad, Boghallen
	Finland	Helsinki – Akateeminen Kirjakauppa
	Norway	Oslo – Arne Gimnes/J.G. Tanum
	Sweden	Stockholm/Esselte, Akademi Bokhandel, Fritzes, Hedengrens.Gothenburg/Gumperts, Esselte. Lund/Gleerupska
	Switzerland	Basel/Bider: Berne/Atlas; Geneve/Artou; Lausanne/Artou: Zurich/Travel Bookshop

Contents

Foreword

Alternative Place Names

1 Introducing Majorca
Situation 14 – Climate 16 – Majorca at a glance 17 –
Important monasteries 21 – Beaches 22

2 Planning your holiday
When to go 23 – What to pack 23 – Budgeting for your
holiday 25 – Tourist information 25 – Package holidays
26 – Travel agents 29 – Taking the children 30 – Taking
pets 32

3 Getting there
By air 33 – By ferry from Europe 34 – By road to the
ferry ports 36 – By coach to the ferry ports 37 – By rail
to the ferry ports 38 – Inter-island services 38 – Cruises
39 – Yacht and boat facilities 40

4 Where to stay
What to expect 43 – Hotels and other accommodation
46 – Camping and motor-caravanning 54 – Property and
estate agents 57

5 Getting about
The road system 58 – Driving in Spain and Majorca 59
– Self-drive car hire 62 – Hire of scooters and mopeds
62 – Bicycles 63 – Taxis 63 – Bus services 63 – Horse
drawn carriages 64 – Coach excursions 65 – Island
railways 66

6 A – Z information for visitors
British Consul 67 – British American Club 67 – Churches 67 – Communications 68 – Currency and banks 70 – Duty free allowance 70 – Electricity 71 – Fire precautions 71 – Hairdressing 71 – Health 71 – Holidays and festivals 72 – Laundry and dry cleaning 75 – Markets 77 – Medical services 78 – Newspapers and books 79 –Police 80 – Problems and complaints 81 – Public conveniences 81 – Radio 81 – Shopping 82 – Souvenirs 83 – Television 83 – Time 84 – Tipping 84

7 Food and drink
Food on the menu 85 – Some local dishes 86 – Drinks 88 – Bars and cafés 89 – Restaurants 89 – A selection of restaurants in Palma 91

8 Leisure activities
Art galleries and museums 99 – Bull fights 101 – Nightlife 101 – Sea cruises 102 – Sports and pastimes 103

9 The country and its people
The history of Majorca 109 – Majorca today 116 – The Mallorquin way of life 119 – Language 120 – Music and dancing 121 – Folklore and handicrafts 122 – Fiestas and festivals 123 – Flora 125 – Wildlife 127

10 The city of Palma
Visiting the capital 130 – Tour 1: Cathedral and historic buildings 131 – Tour 2: Shopping expedition 136 – Tour 3: Saturday morning market 138 – Tour 4: The old city and museums 137 – Tour 5: Pueblo España 143

11 South-west from Palma to Sant Telm
Cala Major to Magalluf 145 – Inland excursion: Palma Nova to Galilea 149 – Portals Vells to Port d'Andratx 150 – Andratx and Sant Telm 152

12 The north-west coast: Andratx to Pollença
Andratx to Coll de Sa Bastida 155 – Valldemossa 156 –
Deiá to Port de Sóller 158 – Gorg Blau, Sa Colobra
and the Lluc Monastery 160 – Lluc to Pollença 164

13 The north-east coast: Port de Pollença to Cala Rajada
Formentor and San Vincenç 167 – Port de Pollença and
the Bay of Alcudia 168 – Sa Pobla, Cuevas de
Campanet and Muro 174 – C'an Picafort 175 –
Artá to Cala Rajada 176

14 The east coast: Caves of Artá to Cala Figuera
Cuevas de Arta to Porto Cristo 180 – Cuevas del Drach
and Cuevas de Hams 184 – Manacor 185 – Cales de
Mallorca, Felanitx and Campos 185 – Sanctuary of Sant
Salvadore and Santueri Castle 187 – Porto Colom to
Cala Figuera 187

15 The south coast: Cabo de Salinas to Bay of Palma
Cabo de Salinas to Banyos de Sant Joan 189 – Salinas
de Levante to Estanyol 191 – Capocorb Vell 193 – Cala
Pi to Bay of Palma 193

16 Excursions inland
Llucmajor, Randa and the monastery of Cura 196 –
Petra and Sineu 197 – Inca and Binissalem 202 – Santa
Maria, Alaró and Orient 203 – Bunyola for the Raxa
and Alfabia Gardens 205 – La Granja 206

Finale 208

Appendices
A Spanish/English vocabulary 209
B The Beaufort Scale 212
C Useful conversion tables, Imperial/Metric 214
D Bibliography 218

Index 219

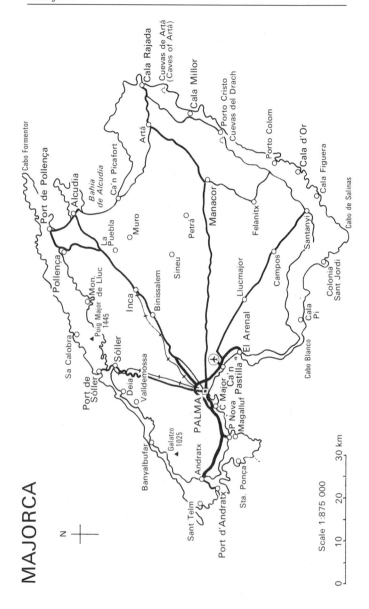

MAJORCA

Foreword

Majorca is the English name for the island the Spanish call Mallorca.

The aim of this guide book is to introduce the visitor to Majorca: where it is situated, how to get there, and when to go. Places of interest for all types of holidaymakers are described in detail. These include buildings of historic merit as well as the fine sandy beaches and quiet coves that abound round the island.

Much is written here to help the tourist have a pleasant stay. Types of accommodation are explained with local prices quoted, shopping areas and markets are described, souvenirs and good buys are suggested. The costs of car rental, taxis and coach excursions are detailed; also listed are the many and varied sports and entertainments that fill the resorts.

For those travellers who wish to explore the island beyond the glorious beaches and sunny climate, day drives are suggested. Away from the lively coastal regions lies a Majorca that still retains a fascinating charm and aura of bygone days. Old monasteries and ancient towns remain peaceful and law abiding; set in fertile green plains or colourful mountain scenery they are a delight to visit. The local inhabitants preserve their age old customs with a quiet dignity, yet accept the incursion of tourists as a way of life, offering a friendly welcome to their visitors.

Majorca has magical moments; we hope that this book will help you enjoy them.

Note: In this book heights and distances correspond with those on the Telegraph map of Majorca. Facts and information are as accurate as possible, but the authors wish to point out that where prices are given they must be taken as a guide only, considering today's ever increasing costs.

The spelling of place names

As in some other regions of Spain, in Majorca there is now a strong revival of the use of the native spelling, Mallorquin, which is derived from Catalan instead of Castilian Spanish. This affects tourists mainly when observing place names and street signs. In some instances road signs have been crudely altered or obliterated with spray paint.

To assist travellers, some of the more important alternatives are listed below:

	(new spelling)
Andraix	– Andratx
Banalbufar	– Banyalbufar
Banos de San Juan	– Banyos de Sant Joan
Bunola	– Bunyola
Cala Guya	– Cala Agulla
Cala Llombardo	– Cala Lombarts
Cala Mayor	– Cala Major
Cala Moreya	– Cala Moreia
Cala Ratjada	– Cala Rajada
Cala Romantica	– Cala Romaguera
Canamel	– Canyamel
Cap de Ferrutx	– Cabo Ferrutx
Colonia San Jordi	– Colonia Sant Jordi
Deya	– Deiá
Esporlas	– Esporles
Estellenchs	– Estellencs
Illetas	– Illetes
La Calobra	– Sa Calobra
La Puebla	– Sa Pobla
Lluch	– Lluc
Lluch Mayor	– Llucmajor
Magaluf	– Magalluf
Playa de Trench	– Platja d'es Trenc
Pollensa	– Pollença
Puerto Alcudia	– Port d'Alcudia
Puerto Andraitx	– Port d'Andratx
Puerto de Pollensa	– Port de Pollença
San Agustin	– Sant Augusti
San Juan	– Sant Joan
San Lorenzo	– Sant Lorenc D'es Cardassar

San Vicente	– Sant Vincenç
Santa Margarita	– Sant Margalida
Santa Ponsa	– Santa Ponça
San Salvador	– Sant Salvadore
San Telmo	– Sant Telm
Son Severa	– Son Cevera
Valldemosa	– Valldemossa

ONE

Introducing Majorca

Over many years Majorca has become the playground of Europe with visitors from all over the world making for its golden shores. Often called the Pearl of the Mediterranean and Island of Calm, the island more than justifies these titles. The pearl-like quality is easy to behold in the clear light and translucent waters found in a multitude of idyllic bays.

Some may query the legendary calm of the island as they wander along the bright and noisy streets of the tourist havens such as **Magalluf** and **Palma Nova** where music blares from every bar for much of the day and night. But drive inland some five or six kilometres from the coast towards **Capdella** and **Calvia** and you will find it – the tranquillity that goes hand in hand with an agricultural way of life that has changed little over the centuries. The sweetness of the pine-scented air and the silence combine to create a charm that few can resist.

Majorca offers everything you could want when on holiday. It has a generous climate which allows you to choose the brilliant hot sunshine of the summer or an agreeable mild temperature in winter. Spring and autumn bring fresh breezes that are health-giving and pleasant: this is an ideal time for walking and many sporting activities. It has warm seas with safe swimming and a myriad of sandy beaches, many bounded by low pinewoods. And by contrast there are craggy mountains and forest areas, to provide a delightful variety of landscape.

Accommodation ranges from luxury hotels, villas and apartments to simple guesthouses and two campsites. Visitors have a wide choice of the kind of establishment best suited to their requirements. If you like a bright and cheerful holiday with plenty of modern amusements then choose the coastal resorts used by the many package tour operators: places like **Palma Nova, Cala Major, Magalluf, C'an Pastilla** or **El Arenal** in the south.

Along the east coast the popular places are **Cala d'Or** and **Porto Cristo** where modern amenities and tourist shops provide interest and entertainment, while in the north the huge **Alcudia Bay** has many large hotels and apartments right by the sea. In the warm evenings the streets are well lit and busy with tourists who enjoy the shops, cafés and restaurants. Discos, barbecues and night spots stay open until the early hours of the morning.

Should your taste be for something quieter then you will find a whole range of small and very beautiful coves that offer tourist accommodation. Fishing ports, too, are friendly and colourful, often providing water sports. Yacht marinas are plentiful: **Port d'Andratx** on the south west coast has now a much sought after harbour and excellent mooring facilities; it also boasts varied restaurants. **Port de Sóller** on the west coast is another attractive venue for a quieter holiday, where you will find some quite sophisticated gourmet restaurants.

Those people who do not wish to be near a beach will enjoy the inland towns of **Deia, Sóller** and **Valldemossa.** They offer fantastic mountain scenery with the orange and lemon groves giving the air a sweet perfume. The smaller villages have modest accommodation in guesthouses that are clean and very Mallorquin in atmosphere.

Palma ranks with the finest cities of the world for the beauty of its setting. Lying beside a large and beautiful natural bay, its historic cathedral and ancient buildings are partially enclosed by the old city walls. These stand out clearly on the skyline as one approaches Palma from the sea. A long, attractive promenade with palm trees lines the seafront, where craft of all kinds are moored. Beautiful Moorish gardens lead to the busy and clean city. Modern shops mingle with old statues and stately buildings; the streets throb with a vitality that characterises this bustling and busy city. Roads lead out in all directions from Palma, which is very much the heart of the island.

One of the delights of Majorca is that tourism has, surprisingly, not spoilt the island; rather it has seemed to expand in the warmth with which it welcomes its visitors. Majorca takes pride in meeting the requirements of its guests. It is moving with the times by building up-to-date amenities, such as a modern music centre, casino, conference halls and amusement parks. The Tourist Council has set up a School of Tourism to make sure that international standards are maintained and that the island continues to be the most popular resort in the Mediterranean.

By containing the tourist growth in carefully planned areas of expansion, Majorca has allowed its inland plains and mountainous countryside to retain a true Mallorquin way of life. Yes, there is a place for everyone on the lovely island of Majorca.

Situation

Situated in the western Mediterranean, Majorca forms part of the Balearic group of islands, the others being Menorca, Ibiza, Formentera and Cabrera. All the islands belong to Spain, with Majorca being the largest and the capital island.

Majorca is two hundred and eleven kilometres from Barcelona, and one hundred and forty kilometres from Valencia in mainland Spain. Marseilles on the south coast of France is four hundred and sixty kilometres away and across in North Africa, Algiers is two hundred and seventy five kilometres distant.

The island has a population of around 600,000 inhabitants and its shape is likened to a sea (conch) shell. With an area of 3,640 sq kms, it is roughly the size of Cornwall.

Two mountain ranges divide the island. The Sierra Alfabia, known locally as the **Tramuntana,** is a rugged ridge which runs from the north to the southwest, thus protecting the island from cold north winds. Its highest peak is **Puig Major** (1445 m); this is a striking feature carved by erosion into fantastic shapes, which in winter can be snow-capped. In the extreme north east at the Formentor peninsula, the limestone sierras are said to be a continuation of the Spanish Levant. These white rock faces rise sheer from the sea, forming a dramatic and wild scenery. It is from these mountains that much of Majorca's water supply is drawn.

In the centre of the island is a vast agricultural plain called **Es Pla,** very fertile and well cultivated, which contributes to the economy of Majorca.

Along the east coast the **Sierra Levante** is a series of low mountains with average peaks of only 426 m, which in places give way to deep indentations that lead to the sea. These attractive small bays and coves are ideal for swimming and sunbathing. The three great caves of Arta, Drach and Hams are all in this area and within two kilometres of the sea. Two large bays, one in the north east, Alcudia Bay, and the Bay of Palma in the south, add to the island's character.

Majorca has a coastline three hundred and twenty kilometres long. Overland the longest distance from north to south is a little over eighty kilometres, which makes day trips very possible. The longest

The modern yacht marina in Palma is one of the largest in the Mediterranean, with excellent mooring facilities close to the city.

beach lies in the Bay of Alcudia, where twelve kilometres of golden sand and shallow waters make it a tourist paradise. The most unspoilt and quietest beaches of the island are either side of the town of Colonia Sant Jordi.

No wonder then that Majorca, with excellent communications by road, sea and air, has become such a popular holiday destination.

A tranquil island

In recent years Majorca has suffered from some bad press reviews. While some may be just, much has been exaggerated. The Ministry of Tourism and the police are aware of the situation. Tough action has been taken on the few incidents provoked by a minority of holidaymakers.

The police are empowered to arrest people who cause damage to property or persons. They can impose on the spot fines for noise disturbance. It is the intention of those in authority to ensure that visitors to Majorca will have a peaceful and enjoyable holiday.

Climate

The climate of Majorca is one of the most mild in the Mediterranean and very agreeable at all times of the year. In summer the temperature rarely goes above 36ºC, with sea breezes helping to make the high temperatures acceptable. Winter in Majorca is pleasant; average temperature in Palma is 14ºC, and frost is practically unknown.

Climatic chart		Air temp Max av	Air temp Min av	Sea temp Av	Sunlight hrs Av
Jan	ºC	15.1	4.6	13.7	5.2
	ºF	60.0	40.0	61.0	
Feb	ºC	14.9	3.0	13.8	6.4
	ºF	59.9	37.0	61.0	
Mar	ºC	17.3	5.4	14.6	6.3
	ºF	63.0	42.0	59.8	
Apr	ºC	19.2	7.6	15.7	6.8
	ºF	67.0	46.0	60.1	
May	ºC	23.7	11.0	18.1	9.6
	ºF	74.0	51.0	66.8	
Jun	ºC	27.9	14.9	20.6	10.7
	ºF	82.5	59.9	77.5	
Jul	ºC	33.3	17.7	25.8	8.9
	ºF	91.5	63.2	78.0	
Aug	ºC	31.2	17.0	27.6	11.1
	ºF	86.5	62.5	81.9	
Sep	ºC	28.0	16.1	25.3	8.0
	ºF	82.6	61.0	77.9	
Oct	ºC	23.2	12.4	23.7	6.4
	ºF	73.8	54.0	74.0	
Nov	ºC	18.4	9.7	18.7	5.5
	ºF	65.0	49.0	65.1	
Dec	ºC	17.2	7.0	16.0	4.0
	ºF	63.0	45.0	59.9	

Average Humidity – 70%

Based on information from the Spanish Tourist Office - Fomento del Turismo de Mallorca

The average humidity is 70 per cent and Majorca boasts about 300 sunny days a year, with about five hours sunshine a day in winter and ten hours in summer. Showers of rain can be heavy but skies soon clear and regain their brilliance. Local people will always talk of the "January calm" when the air is mild and warm; this leads to the wonderful flowering of the almond blossom at the beginning of

February. Then the almond trees, which cover nearly a third of the arable land, burst out in a great cloud of delicate white blossom. People travel great distances to see this beautiful scene and to enjoy the fragrance of the air.

Because Majorca has a variable landscape, whatever the weather one is always able to enjoy a pleasant day. Should the coast become too bright with sunshine, then an hour or so in the bus or car will take you to the higher mountains where the breeze is fresher. Likewise on a cooler day one side of the island will be sheltered from the wind.

Majorca at a glance

This summary of places of interest in Majorca is intended to give you a quick introduction to this lovely and varied island. All the places mentioned here are described more fully in later chapters of the book (the relevant chapter numbers are shown in brackets).

Palma
Majorca's capital is one of the most beautiful cities in the Mediterranean. Set at the water's edge in the Bay of Palma, its elegant palm-lined promenade leads to the old walled city clustering around the impressive cathedral. Other places to visit in the city (described more fully in Chapter 10) are:

Almudaina Palace: Residence of Arab kings and Royal House, now a museum. Flemish tapestries and portraits.

Arab Baths: Original site, in Calle de Serra 13.

Cathedral: Gothic style. Colourful and impressive rose windows. Tombs of Mallorquin kings in apse.

Diocesan Museum: Medieval paintings, jewels, ceramics and carvings.

El Consejo Insular de Baleares: Sea Consulate with seventeenth-century gallery.

La Lonja: Museum of Art, considered to be one of Spain's finest Gothic buildings.

Pueblo España: Reconstructed Spanish village, with houses and palaces, to form an unusual museum and tourist attraction.

Palacio Vivot: Magnificent residence now a national monument with sumptuous collection of paintings, silver, old maps and antique furniture. All family heirlooms.

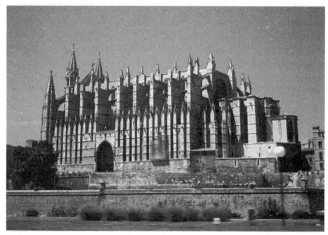

Palma's Gothic cathedral, La Seo, stands magnificently against Majorca's blue sky. Viewed here from the seafront at the Parque del Mar.

Beyond Palma

Wherever you stay in Majorca you are within easy distance of other places of interest. In this alphabetical list, approximate distances are given from the capital, Palma.

Alcudia 55 km: Roman name Pollentia. A walled town with an important port, situated in a huge natural bay. Nearby Roman theatre. Archaeological museum. (Chapter 13)

Alfabia Gardens 17 km: Beautiful shady gardens with roses, bamboos and palms. There is also a house, now a museum, with antique furniture, portraits and valuable library, originally built by Benahabet, a wealthy Moor. (Chapter 16)

Andratx 32 km: Old town with narrow streets that lies in a fertile valley which in the month of February is white with almond blossom. Thirteenth-century church. (Chapter 11)

Arta 71 km: Fine old village surrounded by mountain views. Museum. Nearby talayot settlement at Ses Paises. (Chapter 13)

Bellver Castle 5 km: Fourteenth century round castle set high in pine wood. Circular courtyard and museum. Extensive views of Palma city and harbour from ramparts. (Chapter 11)

Banyalbufar 30 km: Ancient terraced tomato cultivation near sea. Once the haunt of smugglers. (Chapter 12)

Binisalem 22 km: Noted for its vineyard and wine-making centre. Wine festival end of September with local costumes. (Chapter 16)

Bunyola 17 km: Small town on mountainside with twisting streets, panoramic views. (Chapter 16)

Capdepera 78 km: Ruins of fourteenth-century castle on top of steep hill. Scene of fiesta in December. (Chapter 13)

Capicorp Vell 37 km: Ancient hamlet that is said to have existed since 1000 BC. This Bronze Age settlement is now surrounded by a wall and locked gate. Gatekeeper lives in nearby interesting old farmhouse. (Chapter 15)

Cala Figuera 69 km: Known as the Venice of Majorca. Fishermen's families live on the edge of water with garages for their boats. Deep sea fleet at entrance to cove. Take your camera. (Chapter 14)

Caves of Artá 82 km: Near to town of same name and right on the coast, descend by a great flight of steps, 304 m into the earth. The caves have enormous limestone stalactites and stalagmites artistically lit. (Chapter 14)

Caves of Drach 65 km: Near Puerto Cristo. Caves discovered in 1896 include an underground lake more than two kilometres long. Music display. No photos allowed. (Chapter 14)

Caves of Ham 60 km: On road from Manacor to Porto Cristo. Underground lake called Sea of Venice. Outside is a large shaded picnic area, bar and toilets. (Chapter 14)

Deiá 30 km. Centre of writers and artists. Home of English author and poet Robert Graves until his recent death. Pretty village, cobbled streets, stone houses and colourful gardens. (Chapter 12)

Felanitx 51 km: Important agricultural town. Worth visiting on market day. Impressive thirteenth-century orange stone church. (Chapter 14)

Formentor 84 km. The most dramatic landscape of the island with cliffs, rugged rocks and lashing seas. Tremendous views from the mirador overlooking Pollença Bay. Look out for the wild goats on the way to the lighthouse. (Chapter 13)

Galilea 25 km: Surrounded by mountains and approached by narrow twisting roads. Pine trees. It is worth the drive and there is a bar and restaurant favoured by artists and writers. (Chapter 11)

Genova 7 km: Noted for its restaurants that specialise in Mallorquin cooking. Caves and panoramic view of coastline. (Chapter 11)

Inca 29 km: Industrial centre and third largest town. Tourist interest is leather factories that are open to the public for shopping. (Chapter 16)

La Granja 16 km: Near Esporlas. Country estate with gardens and fountain. House open, displaying country crafts. National costumes and dancers. (Chapter 16)

Manacor 50 kms: Important manufacturing town, especially for the famous cultured pearl factories. These are open to the public who may see the pearls being made and make purchases. (Chapter 14)

Orient 28 km: Picturesque village on mountain top, reached by steep and winding roads. (Chapter 16)

Petra 45 km: A quiet town well worth visiting to see where Fray Junipero Sierra, the founder of California, was born. Small museum and huge church. (Chapter 16)

Pollença 52 km: Ochre-coloured town with narrow streets and central market square. Music festival in August. Visit nearby Calvario church, climbing 365 steps or driving up a very steep winding road. Impressive and extensive views from the top. (Chapter 12)

Isla Dragonera

To the south west of Majorca, facing Sant Telm, lies the small green island of La Dragonera, lying like a sleeping dragon or lazy lizard basking in the sunshine. Its shape is elongated and rectilinear with steep cliffs on the west side, while to the east the slopes are more gentle. Its highest point reaches 310m. The island is privately owned; a small port, Punta Negra, near Cala Lladro allows the lighthousekeepers to land. There are 228 hectares of grassland, heather, rosemary, and wild olives, home for many wild birds including the osprey, Eleonora's falcon, shag, cormorant, storm petrel, Manx shearwater, puffin and robin. In 1983 the island was declared a Nature Reserve.

A path crosses inland to reach the two lighthouses. At Cabo Tramuntana the beam reaches for 32 kilometres, while in the south at Cabo Lieberg it extends seawards for 54 kilometres, an important warning light. An old watchtower stands on a high point and from there on a clear day you can see in the distance the island of Ibiza.

Boat excursions from Port d'Andratx and Sant Telm sail close to the island to see the many caves that were once the haunt of pirates.

Porto Colom 63 km: Quiet town, large natural harbour. Fish restaurants. Sea excursions to island of Cabrera. (Chapter 14)

Sà Calobra y Torrente de Pareis 67 km: Extraordinary natural marvel amid high rocks and gorge, then down to the sea. Very spectacular. Zig-zag road, only for good drivers! (Chapter 12)

Santa Maria 15 km: Quiet town with old Convent of Los Minimos, sixteenth century. Balearic costume museum. (Chapter 16)

Sant Telm 36 km: Most westerly point, facing sloping islet of Dragonera. Fishing village turning to tourism. Small restaurants by sea. Nearby Son Pou cave over 45 m deep, illuminated by sun. (Chapter 11) (Note: called Sant Elm on Firestone map)

Sineu 30 km: In centre of island, old market town. Get there early on Wednesdays to see cattle market including horses and donkeys. (Chapter 16)

Sóller 30 km: Valley of orange and lemon groves amid beautiful scenery. Journey there by small electric train from Palma. Tram car from Sóller to Port de Sóller a good experience. (Chapter 12)

Important monasteries

Lluc Monastery 47 km: Spiritual centre of Majorca. Large monastery, high in the mountains, which provides shelter for travellers. Church contains Virgin of Lluc. Museum. (Chapter 12)

Randa 28 km: Three monasteries are situated at various levels on this high peak. The drive is comparatively easy and view from top is very extensive. Slightly marred by radar station. (Chapter 16)

Sant Salvadore Monastery 57 km: Reached by a long and twisting road but the climb is rewarding. Unique buildings and monuments

---

Isla de Cabrera

The smallest of the major Balearic Islands is Cabrera, 17 sq km and lying 17 km off the most southern point of Majorca. It can be seen from Palma on a clear day. With steep cliffs, it is a wild and desolate place. At present it is a military base and visitors are not allowed without permission. However, it is proposed that the island becomes a Nature Reserve for birds and wild goats.

Once a week a ship leaves Palma for a sea excursion to Isla de Cabrera. Boat trips also go from Colonia Sant Jordi to visit the Blue Grotto, a cave where the translucent waters reflect the sunlight in a myriad of colours.

Near Cabrera harbour on the western side of the island is a fourteenth-century castle, once used by pirates. During the Spanish War of Independence in 1809, 9,000 French prisoners were deported to Cabrera and left with only one well of water. Most died of hunger and disease; when they were finally released in 1814 only 3,600 remained. In 1847 the French government erected a monument to their death.

Today, fortunate visitors will be able to enjoy the antics of a school of dolphins as their boat sails round the little island.

plus panoramic views in all directions. You need a good head for heights. Restaurant. (Chapter 14)

Valldemossa 19 km: Carthusian Monastery. Chopin and George Sand museum, church and old pharmacy. Despite many tourists it retains a peaceful atmosphere. (Chapter 12)

Beaches

Fine beaches abound in Majorca. Here are some sandy beaches within reach of main roads; distances are given from Palma, in kilometres. A full list can be obtained from one of the tourist Information offices in Palma.

Alcudia Bay	(55)	Colonia Sant Jordi	(56)
Arenal	(11)	Formentor	(72)
Cala d'Or	(63)	Illetes	(9)
Cala Fornells	(26)	La Calobra	(70)
Cala Major	(5)	Magalluf	(15)
Cala Mesquida	(84)	Mal Pas	(57)
Cala Millor	(71)	Peguera	(23)
Cala Murada	(68)	Palma Nova	(14)
Cala Rajada	(80)	Porto Cristo	(63)
Cala Santanyi	(55)	Port de Soller	(35)
Cala de Sant Vincenç	(56)	Santa Ponça	(20)
Camp de Mar	(25)	Sa Romaguera	(73)
Ca'n Pastilla	(6)	Sant Telm	(37)
Ca'n Picafort	(60)	Ses Salines	(56)
Canamel	(62)	S'Illot	(68)

Platja Mago (24km) is an official nudist beach, and the **Platja d'es Trenc** (50km) is unofficially accepted as nudist.

TWO

Planning your holiday

When to go

Because of its moderate climate Majorca has developed into an all-the-year-round tourist haven. No matter when you stay in Majorca you will feel invigorated and have a sensation of well-being. The peak period for visitors is from the beginning of July to mid September, with many hotels having regular bookings each year. Some families have used the same hotel for seven years and more, therefore early booking is necessary for the summer months in the popular resorts along the coasts.

Spring and autumn holidays are particularly beautiful in Majorca, with quieter roads and fewer tourists. Spring time is when the wild flowers grow in great profusion. Botanically-minded people will delight in the tiny wild marigolds, cowslips, violets and miniature cyclamen. Bird watchers, too, will want to visit the island in April and May for the spring migration, or in October, the main month for the autumn migration. The area around Pollença in the north provides the best habitat in superb scenery.

Of recent years, with the increase of package holidays, some of the larger hotels in the south remain open throughout the winter. In places like Peguera and El Arenal, special winter rates for long stay holidays can provide a good bargain. Programmes of entertainments and indoor sports are organised for any windy or cloudy days, so much is done to make a winter sojourn in Majorca a happy one.

What to pack

Depending on the time of year of your visit to Majorca, choice of clothes will vary from the lightest of summer wear to woollen garments. From June to September you can count on hot weather every day; you will need a cardigan or jacket only when visiting the mountain areas. The most comfortable clothing for hot weather is cotton or other natural fibres; if you use the easy care, manmade synthetics, then loose styles will feel more comfortable. The same applies to footwear; do not take tight fitting shoes, as feet will tend to swell in the warmth. However, for walking in woods and on the mountains strong shoes or boots are required, as the ground is very hard and stony.

Nowadays the wearing of bikinis, even topless, is becoming accepted on the quieter beaches. But when walking in the streets a shirt or cotton top should be worn over swim wear. Churches no longer require women visitors to cover their heads, but modesty and a decorous manner are expected.

Evening wear is mostly casual; in the four and five star hotels, men may be required to wear ties and jackets. When you go on an evening barbecue excursion, some sort of shawl or jacket may be needed as you will probably be eating outside.

Remember to take a sunhat and sunglasses (though these can be bought locally). Suntan oils and creams are a necessity unless you are already very tanned. Some anti-mosquito cream may be useful, too. No need to pack quantities of toothpaste, soap or shampoo, for plenty of brands are sold on the island, though prices can be higher at some resorts.

Even the most amateur of photographers will wish to pack a camera, for Majorca has a potential for marvellous holiday snaps. If you wish for something of better quality, remember that the strong light, the white-washed houses and sparkling seas will require a light density filter. All popular sizes of films are available, but with prices generally higher than at home. In the major resorts a twenty-four hour developing service is usual.

You may wish to take some reading matter. English paperbacks, newspapers and magazines can be purchased, though usually at double the UK price. A Spanish/English phrase book will be useful if you wish to make contact with the local Mallorquins, especially when visiting the inland towns. Travel into the mountains will be enhanced if you take your binoculars, for there are many opportunities for distant viewing. In the northern parts of the island, many wild birds can be observed in their natural habitat or migrating.

If you are a pipe smoker you may wish to take your own favourite brand as some imported tobaccos are hard to find; many foreigners feel that Spanish pipe tobacco is a bit on the rough side. Cigarette smokers will probably arrive with their duty free smokes, bought on the aircraft. Most Spanish cigarettes are made of strong black tobacco. Nearly all popular foreign brands are sold at twice the price of the domestic product.

Budgeting for your holiday

The cost of living should not prove higher in Majorca than in Europe or the UK. Generally speaking, package tour holiday-makers require spending money for entertainments, drinks and possibly additional meals, unless the package includes full board. You must allow for extra costs such as taking part in sports, excursions, the hire of sun umbrellas and chairs, laundry and tips *(propina)* for waiters, taxi drivers and porters (about 10% is sufficient); and maybe for some extra film for the camera and for buying souvenirs.

Prices in tourist areas will probably be a few pesetas higher than elsewhere but if one takes into consideration the extra cost of travelling to a non-tourist area to shop it will probably work out much about the same.

For the independent traveller, it is possible to live quite cheaply especially by buying local foods. Chickens, eggs, fruit, tomatoes, cucumbers and many drinks are less expensive than in the UK.

Bars and restaurants are less costly and generally give a cheerful and good service.

Tourist information

Visitors to Majorca require a valid passport. You do not require a visa for a stay of up to ninety days, but after this it may be necessary. Information can be obtained from: The Spanish Consulate, 20 Draycott Place, London SW3. Tel: 071-581 5921.

Up to date tourist information can be obtained from: The Spanish National Tourist Office, 57/58 St James's Street, London SW1. Tel: 071-499 0901.

Vaccinations are not normally needed for Majorca. Only in the case of an epidemic would they be required.

Visitors are allowed to bring in any amount of foreign or local currency, in notes or travellers' cheques. You may take out of the country 100,000 pesetas and foreign currency equivalent to 500,000 pesetas.

Tourist offices in Majorca

The Spanish Tourist Industry is organised through the Secretaria de Estado, part of the Ministerio de Transportes, Turismo and Comunicaciones and funded by the State. The Secretaria has a delegation in the capital, Palma. Public information offices are found there, as well as in the tourist complexes. They provide information free of charge. It is recommended that use is made of these facilities; they can supply lists of accommodation, island and town maps and literature often with good pictures. Although in some offices the staff may have only a limited knowledge of English, much effort is made to assist tourists. Open weekdays from 1000 to 1300 hrs and 1600 to 1930 hrs. Tourist offices in Palma are:

Conselleria de Turismo de Balears Montenegro 5, Palma. Tel: 71 20 22.

Information Office of the Secretary of Tourism Avenida Jaime III 10, Palma. Tel: 21 22 16

Fomento del Turismo de Mallorca Constituo 1, Palma. Tel: 72 53 96.

Municipal Tourist Information Office Santo Domingo 11, Palma. Tel: 72 40 90.

Information Office Aeropuerto de Son San Juan, Palma. Tel: 26 08 03.

Tourist information offices can also be found in:

– Cala d'Or: Avda. Cala Llonga. Tel: 65 74 63.
– Cala Millor: Parc de la Mar 2. Tel: 58 54 09.
– Cala Rajada: Placa dels Pins. Tel: 56 30 33.
– Ca'n Picafort: Pza. Igro. Gabriel Roca, 6. Tel: 85 03 10.
– Magalluf: Galeon. Tel: 68 11 26.
– Peguera: Placa Aparcaments. Tel: 68 70 83.
– Port d'Alcudia: Avda R Juan Carlos 1. Tel: 54 86 15.
– Port de Pollença: Miquel Capllonch. Tel: 53 46 66.
– Porto Cristo: Gual 31. Tel: 82 09 31.
– Santa Ponça: Puig de Galatzo. Tel: 69 17 12.
– Soller: Placa de Sa Constiticio 1. Tel: 63 02 00.
– Valldemossa: Cartuja. Tel: 61 21 06.

Package holidays

There are over fifty UK firms operating package holidays to Majorca. These provide a wide choice for selection and offer good value to holidaymakers with a limited amount of time. They also allow

Sea, sand and sun along the shore between Magalluf and Palma Nova, just the place for a suntan.

customers to budget in advance for most of their holiday expenses.

When you book a package holiday, the price of the air fare is included plus transport to and from your destination in Majorca, unless otherwise stated. Tour operators brochures will give details of flight arrangements, type of resort, entertainments and the star rating of the accommodation. These vary from five-star luxury hotels to modest guest houses and self-catering apartments.

In the larger resorts and holiday complexes like **El Arenal** and **Magalluf,** entire hotels are taken over by the tour operator and prove so popular that they are full for most of the year.

The Holiday Club International at **Mezquida, Capdepera,** is situated in the north east of the island, and offers the choice of staying in a hotel, apartment or chalet, all of which are set in a modern complex, right by the edge of a golden sandy beach. It is open from April to October.

Thomson Holidays Ltd., one of the leading tour operators in the Balearics, guarantee that once you have made your booking and paid a deposit, the cost of your holiday cannot be increased. They specialise in suiting the accommodation to their clients. For example some hotels are for couples without children, others cater especially for children, and there are hotels that have extra sports facilities. Very popular is their two resort package where holidaymakers can stay in different resorts, even on different islands, during the same holiday.

A pleasant budget holiday in the sun at **Camping Platja Blava** (see Camping, Chapter 4) is offered by Lotus Holidays, 9/5 Oxford Street, London W1R IFR. Tel: 071 734 4525. Modern tents equipped with camp beds, pillows, table, lamp and mirror are erected, complete with fitted ground sheet and lounge area. To reduce cost a catering pack can be hired that includes cooker, utensils, gas, crockery and cutlery. The camp is just three hundred metres from the sandy beach of Alcudia Bay and one kilometre from lively C'an Picafort. Wash rooms and toilets include hot showers, shaver points and laundry facility. Amenities include a self service restaurant, swimming pool, volley ball and tennis. On site entertainment is arranged. Another tour operator that offers good camping holidays is Club Cantabrica; for brochure and reservations call freephone 0800 202 202.

Classic Collection Holidays (9 Liverpool Terrace, Worthing, West Sussex, BN11 ITA. Tel: 0903 823088) is an independent specialist operator which gives a very personal service on a high level. Their package holidays are based on using scheduled flights so that holidays are totally flexible to meet individual requirements. With stays from three nights to three months, they can arrange two centre locations and explorer tours that include taxi or self-drive. In some instances their high class accommodation is exclusive to the UK market.

Travel agents

There are numerous travel agents *(viajes)* in the city of Palma and in the tourist areas of Majorca. Their services vary; they may be agents for hotels, apartments, ferries and flight bookings, self-drive car rental, coach tours and currency exchange. Usually opening hours are from 0900 to 1300 hrs and 1630 to 1900 hrs, Monday to Friday, 0900 to 1300 hrs on Saturday, closed Sunday and on public holidays.

Established firms such as Ultramar Express, Melia, Wagonlit Cooks and Barcelo have agencies in the main parts of Majorca, usually with English-speaking representatives. Ultramar Express is probably one of the best and runs excursions throughout the island in coaches that are modern and comfortable.

Some of the principal travel agents in **Palma** are:
– Aeromaritima, Es Born 27. Tel: 22 59 40.
– Airtour Palma, Avenida Jaime III 16. Tel: 22 79 45.
– Barceló, Avenida Alejandro Rosselló 34B. Tel: 46 05 90.
– Club de Vacaciones, Marq. de la Cenia. Tel: 23 82 62.
– Corte Ingles, Paseo Mallorca 26. Tel: 22 31 42
– Euroclub, Avenida Jaime III 5. Tel: 22 50 43.
– Hispan Travel, Es Born 15. Tel: 22 23 43.
– Jumbo Tours, Plaza de la Reina 13. Tel: 22 25 00.
– Kontiki, Paseo Maritima 15. Tel: 28 48 08.
– Mallorca Tours, Avenida Jaime III 4. Tel: 22 26 06.
– Meliá, Es Born 22. Tel: 21 53 11.
– Olimpia, Joan Miró 113. Tel: 23 07 40.
– Sidetours, Paseo Maritima 16. Tel: 28 39 00.
– Transglobal, Plaza de Espana 3. Tel: 21 09 43.
– Ultramar Express, Paseo Mallorca 32. Tel: 22 70 45.
– Wagon Lits Cook, Es Born 11. Tel: 22 21 29.

Some travel agents in resorts include:
C'an Picafort Aeromar Tours, Isaac Peral. Tel: 52 77 05.
Santa Ponça A.M.S., Edificio Deiá. Tel: 68 64 13.
Cala d'Or Credit Tours, Avenida Porto Petro 1. Tel: 65 72 20.
El Arenal Halcon, Maria Antonia Salvá 2. Tel: 26 57 30.
C'an Pastilla Hispano Balear, Avenida Riutort 18. Tel: 26 01 08.

Peguera Peguera, Carretera de Andratx. Tel: 68 69 68.
Magalluf Solitur, Edificio La Porrasa.

Taking the children

Children of all ages will really enjoy being in Majorca, because the island has just about everything for their pleasure and amusement. The Mallorquins are fond of children and spend much of their time looking after them; so they will be pleased to see visitors taking the same attitude.

Modern hotels and apartments generally provide cots and high chairs for infants, sometimes there is an extra charge. Dried milk, disposable nappies and baby foods are obtainable in all the supermarkets; plenty of toys, too, including things for the beach and warm weather clothing. Playrooms, paddling pools and baby sitting services (charges are about 400 pesetas per hour) will help to make life easier for parents with very small children. Courtesy buses will convey holidaymakers to the nearest beach – this is a very useful facility.

Package tour operators often have hotels that specialise in catering for families with youngsters. There you will find staff who are trained to look after children. Many hotels have Mini Clubs that have programmes designed to entertain and amuse their young members. Badges are issued, competitions organised and outings arranged. This allows parents some relaxation from their responsibilities and time to follow their own pursuits.

In Majorca young children are allowed into bars, cafés, restaurants and hotel lounges until very late at night, even on to the dance floors. So it is worth remembering not to let children become overtired. An afternoon or early evening rest is sensible, even if they protest it is worthwhile being firm, to keep the child from getting exhausted.

Care should be taken even with teenagers that they do not have too much sunshine, especially during the first few days. With the excitement of the change of surroundings and different foods, it is easy to be over indulgent. It is sensible to drink the bottled water (sold in hotels and supermarkets) and do wash well all salads and fruits before eating. However nice that bunch of grapes looks on the market stall do not be tempted to eat them without washing.

In Majorca the tourist areas provide many amusements. Playgrounds and sports places abound for youngsters. **Marineland** with dolphins is to be found between **Portals Nous** and **Palma Nova**.

Ideal for young children are the soft sands and shallow, clean water at Playa de Moro, between Alcudia and C'an Picafort. The low pines give shade.

The **Safari Park** is near **Cala Millor.** These are but two of the larger places that will appeal to both young and older children. The train and tram ride to **Port de Sóller** is an experience to be enjoyed. The caves, too, are exciting when reassurance is given that all is safe underground.

Young children go on coach excursions and most have a happy time. But remember to take some toys and games for the little ones who will not want to look at mountain scenery for long. When the coach makes a stop be sure to use the toilets, for it is not always possible for the driver to make other stops, especially on some of the narrow and winding roads.

For older children there are bicycles to hire and plenty of land and sea sports to enjoy. Video games and disco dances are plentiful. Boutiques, hairdressing salons and jewellery shops will be a temptation to lure the pesetas from the pocket of the teenager.

Of course the greatest attraction is the many lovely sandy beaches and the clear warm sea water. At those listed on page 22, safe swimming can be expected. However if a storm does blow up, watch out to see if a red flag is flying, this means that the seas are dangerous for bathing, even for the experienced swimmer – so leave it until the next day.

Please do not force any child into the sea, it is so easy to make them afraid. Use a little encouragement by sitting at the edge of the water, or just paddling. Making a sand castle, then asking for a bucket of sea water, will do a lot to gain the child's confidence. Be sure to provide a sun hat and some sun protection cream; even if it seems overcast the rays of the sun penetrate the clouds and can cause distress to a tender skin.

Taking pets

If you wish to take your cat or dog on holiday with you, a Health and Rabies inoculation certificate is required. This is stamped by the Spanish Consulate in your own country. Remember, however, that on returning to the UK, your pet will have to spend six months in quarantine.

There are the British Boarding Kennels and Catteries at Calle Santa Lucia, Manacor de Valle, tel: 50 19 24, and Lluch Major, tel: 660825 (between 1330 and 1430 hrs daily). A veterinary clinic is to be found in Palma: José Aguilo, Calle Beata Catalina 7. Tel: 71 25 50.

The larger supermarkets have good stocks of pet food.

THREE

Getting there

By air

The international airport in Majorca, **Son San Juan,** is about ten kilometres east of the capital, Palma. This is one of the busiest airports in Europe with the bulk of its passengers at week-ends during the summer. During the busy summer season the airport handles an incoming aircraft every two minutes. In June 1991 it celebrated the arrival of the 200,000,000th passenger. It is an efficient airport, connecting with all major Spanish and international cities; it also serves Ibiza and Menorca. There are no airports on Formentera or Cabrera.

The cost of a single flight by Spanish Iberia Airlines from Heathrow to Palma is about £129. British Midland operates daily flights from Heathrow to Palma with fares ranging from £119. Several charter companies, such as Falcon Flights and Thomson Air Fares, offer low cost return flights – your local travel agent will have the details. The flight time between London and Majorca is about two hours.

The airport has two terminals: terminal A handles scheduled flights, terminal B is used by charter companies.

City buses 17a and 17b link the airport with Palma, operating every half hour from 0700 hrs to 2330 hrs; it is a fifteen-minute ride. Many taxis eagerly await your custom; city taxis have meters. (See Chapter 5 – Taxis.) Plenty of car parking space includes an area for overnight and long stay. There is a left luggage office in terminal A, and a hotel reservation service.

Airport services include a bank, post office, souvenir shops, tourist office, and car rental firms. Porters are available and charge an official rate based on the number of pieces of luggage; so you may prefer to wheel your own trolley. An escalator takes you to the second floor where there is a large restaurant and bar. A duty free shop is well stocked but prices are not necessarily cheaper than elsewhere on the island. Toilets include one with special facilities for the disabled. Public telephones are on the ground floor.

During July and August renting a car at the airport can be difficult. Europcar, Avis S.A. and Hertz will take advance bookings through European offices. Rates may be higher than those of Majorca's car rental firms in tourist resorts.

Inter island flights

There are flights daily from Majorca to Ibiza and Menorca, operated by Iberia and Aviaco. The flights take about thirty minutes and the single fare is 3,650 pesetas. There is no airport on Formentera or Cabrera.

By ferry from Europe

To visit Majorca by ferry ship from Europe you will need to depart from one of these ports: Barcelona or Valencia (Spain), or Sete (France).

• From Spain

The Trasmediterranea Shipping Company runs a regular car and passenger service from mainland Spain to the Balearic Islands. An inter-island service is operated throughout the year. All Trasmediterranea ferries are drive-on/drive-off, from either the end or the side of the ship. Sometimes it may be necessary to reverse your vehicle through the car deck; this is generally carried out with assistance from the ship's crew. Frequency and duration of services are as follows:

– Barcelona to Palma Majorca	daily, 8-9 hours
– Barcelona to Ibiza	3 times a week, 10 hours
– Barcelona to Mahon Menorca	twice a week, 9 hours
– Valencia to Palma Majorca	daily, 8-9 hours
– Valencia to Ibiza	twice a week, 7 hours

During April (Easter) and from the 15 June to 15 September, the frequency of all these services is increased.

The UK agents for Trasmediterranea are Melia Travel, 273 Regent Street, London W1. Tel: 071-409 1884. Approximate cost of the single fare including a cabin from either Barcelona or Valencia to Palma Majorca for two adults with car is £190.

There are no ferries that go directly to the island of Formentera. You

Port d'Andratx is a beautiful natural harbour, which has developed from a small fishing village into a smart, modern yachting centre.

must take an inter-island ferry from Majorca or Ibiza, see page 38.

Ferry reservations can be made in Spain through travel agents. In addition Trasmediterranea have offices in a number of the larger Spanish Towns. Their head office is at Plaza Manuel Gómez Moreno, Apartado de Correos 982, Edificio Bronce, Madrid 20. They have offices at the operating ports: Via Layetana 2, Barcelona; Avenida Manuel Soto Ing 15, Valencia; and Muelle Viejo 5, Palma Majorca. Tel: 22 67 40.

• From France

Trasmediterranea operates a return car and passenger ferry from Sete (near Marseille, France). The service operates from mid June to mid September, there being no service during the rest of the year. The ferry leaves Palma at 1700 hrs on Fridays and Sete at 1700 hrs on Saturdays. In addition to the UK Agents (Melia Travel, see above) reservations can be made through the SNCM agent at 4 Quai d'Alger, Sete. Tel: 747055. The approximate cost of the single fare, Sete to Majorca, for two adults and a car is £358.

The ferry ports can be reached by car, coach or rail as detailed in the following sections.

By road to the ferry ports

Travelling by road to these points of departure listed in the previous section presents no problem beyond choice of route. But remember that it is essential to book the ferry well in advance during the summer months.

Route 1 – Calais to Barcelona and Valencia (1,714 km)

If you wish to travel quickly by road from the UK, it is suggested that you cross the English Channel from Folkestone or Dover to Boulogne or Calais, then take the RN1 to Paris. Join the Périphérique (fast ring road), looking for the sign Est (east). You then follow the signs *Autoroute Sud* (south) A6, and then the signs, Lyon Autoroute A6. Continue on Autoroute, leaving at Orange. You then take the A9 to Narbonne. From there you follow the coastal route to Barcelona N11, or the Autopista A17.

To reach Valencia you continue south from Barcelona on the coast road N340, or the Autopista A7, for 248 km.

Route 2 – Plymouth (Devon) via Santander (N. Spain) to Barcelona and Valencia (1,023 km)

Brittany Ferries operate a regular car and passenger ferry (from Millbay Docks, Plymouth) throughout the year. The crossing takes 24 hours in a fully stabilised ship. Driving into the car deck is a simple operation. The ships are comfortable, with air-conditioned two- and four-berth cabins, some with showers and toilets. There are sun decks, restaurants, lounges with bars and dance floor, electronic games, shops, cinema and children's room. Single fare for two persons and car, between £205 and £264.

From Santander one can join the toll motorway at Bilbao which goes right past Zaragoza to Barcelona (740 km). There are frequent service areas, some are not open 24 hours, but ample notice is given of this. It is a quiet and pleasant motorway, toll costing £20, Bilbao to Barcelona.

The shortest route from Santander to Valencia (671 km) is through Burgos and Madrid. There is no motorway and it is quite a stiff climb to Burgos over the Puerto de Escudo (1,011 m), which should be considered if one is travelling between November and April because of the snow. If motorway driving is desirable it would be necessary to take the route Santander, Zaragoza to Barcelona and thence to Valencia, which would make the distance 1,023 km.

Route 3 – Calais to Sete (1,100 km)

Should you wish to travel via Sete (near Marseille, France) then take the French motorway, bypassing Paris and Lyon, all the way to Marseille. It is a toll motorway with service areas about every 30 km. This is about a ten-hour journey. Remember that the Sete to Palma Majorca ferry operates only from mid-June to mid-September.

By coach to the ferry ports

There are a number of coach services that pass through Barcelona. Eurolines, part of National Express operates from Victoria Coach Station. Tel: 071 730 3499. Information and reservations are at Luton. Tel: 0582 404 511. Coaches depart Monday, Wednesday and Friday, the return fare London to Barcelona being £104. Example timetable:

Day 1   London Victoria: train departs   1030 hrs

Day 2	Barcelona: train arrives	1245 hrs
Day 2	Barcelona Trasmediterranea ferry departs	2345 hrs
Day 3	Palma, Majorca: ferry arrives	0800 hrs

By rail to the ferry ports

Rail tickets to travel from London to Barcelona (where the Trasmediterranea ferry can be taken to Majorca) can be obtained from European Rail Travel Centre, Victoria Station, London SW1. Tel: 071 834 2345. The standard 2nd class adult fare is £144 return; return fare for a senior citizen (holding both a British and European Rail card) is £102. The example below illustrates the duration of the journey:

Day 1	London Victoria: train departs	1430 hrs
	Dover: ferry departs	1630 hrs
	Calais (France): train no. 10400 departs	1940 hrs
Day 2	Port Bou (France/Spain border): arrives	1105 hrs
	Port Bou (change to train no. 2554) departs	1155 hrs
	Barcelona: train arrives	1456 hrs
	Barcelona: ferry departs	2345 hrs
Day 3	Palma Majorca: ferry arrives	0800 hrs

It is necessary to change trains at the Spanish border because the Spanish Railway (RENFE) has a wider track gauge than the French Railway (SNCF). It is advisable to confirm that the number of the train you are boarding is correct. The railway station *(estación de ferrocarril)* in Barcelona is near the docks, about a twenty-minute walk; look for the high monument to Christopher Columbus. You will pass near the Trasmediterranea Ferry Office at Via Layetana 2 if you walk to the docks from the railway station.

Inter island services

The Trasmediterranea Shipping Company operates a car passenger ferry service directly from Palma (Majorca) to Ibiza and Palma to Menorca. The frequency and duration are as follows:

- Palma – Ibiza   twice a week, five hours
- Palma – Menorca   once a week, six hours

The approximate cost of the single fare, without cabin, from Palma Majorca to either Ibiza or Menorca, for two adults with car is £86. It is not possible to travel directly from Ibiza to Menorca and vice versa:

A regular ferry service between Majorca and Ibiza takes five hours and usually is a smooth crossing.

you must first return to Palma. There is a daily hydrofoil service between Palma and Ibiza, operating from June to September. The single fare is £22. Departing from Palma at 0800 hrs and from Ibiza at 1800 hrs, the journey taking two hours.

From Ibiza, there is a service to Barcelona or Valencia; and from Menorca a service to Barcelona. From Ibiza it is possible to get a local ferry to Formentera.

There are occasional small ferry excursions operating from Colonia Sant Jordi in the south of Majorca to the island of Cabrera. The sea journey takes about one and a half hours. It is not permitted to stay on Cabrera overnight. A daily service from Port d'Alcudia to Menorca operates during the summer, sailing time is two and a half hours. Details from Lineas Maritimas del Sur. Tel: 21 15 26.

Cruises

The following companies operate inclusive luxury liner cruises in the Mediterranean calling at Palma Majorca.

– Cunard Line Ltd., 8 Berkeley Street, London W1X 6NR. Tel: 071-491 3930.

– CTC, 1 Regent Street, London SW1Y 4NN.

– P and O Canberra and Sea Princess, Beaufort House, St Botolph Street, London EC3A 7DX. Tel: 071-377 2551.

– Equity Travel Ltd., 10 Goswell Road, London EC1M 7AA. Tel: 071-253 6156.

Plenty of moorings at Port d'Andratx. Here a small pleasure craft is about to set sail to Isla Dragonara.

The Trasmediterranea Shipping Company offer weekend cruises from Barcelona, visiting Ibiza and Majorca: three nights in a veritable floating hotel with swimming pool, disco and entertainments. An example of the programme is:

Friday	2100 hrs	Arrive on board ship
	2300	Drinks party and dinner
Saturday	0900	Arrive at Ibiza: free day, coach excursions or on board entertainment
	2345	Sail for Majorca
Sunday	0800	Arrive Palma (Majorca): free day, coach excursions or on board entertainment
	2345	Sail for Barcelona
Monday	0800	Arrive Barcelona and disembark

The cost per person is about £167 inclusive of cabin and meals.

Yacht and boat facilities

Majorca possesses some of the finest yachting facilities found in the Mediterranean. King Juan Carlos and his family take their yacht to Majorca every year. The exclusive Club de Mar in Palma has an

Yacht and boat facilities

Arenal	**E of Palma Bay**	Club Nautico, fuel
Bonaire	**Harbour, NE**	Holiday resort
Cala Bona	**Small harbour, NE**	Hotels and water
Cala Calobra	**Sandy, some swell, jetty, NW**	Hotel
Cala Codolar	**Rocky creek, NW**	No facilities
Cala Deiá	**Anchor only, NW**	Deiá
Cala d'Or	**Good yacht moorings, NW**	Club Nautico
Cala Estancia	**Palma Bay, harbour, E**	Hotels
Cala Figuera	**Sheltered harbour, SE**	Water
Cala Gamba	**E of Palma Bay, harbour**	Club Nautico
Cala Millor	**Small harbour, NE**	Hotels
Cala Murta	**Anchor only, N**	No facilities
Cala Pi	**Anchor only, N**	Hotel
Cala Rajada	**Harbour, NE**	Hotels, Boatyard
Cala Santafly	**Anchorage, SE**	Hotels
Cala Santa Ponça	**Anchorage, SW**	Club Nautico
Cala Sant Vicenç	**Anchorage N**	Hotels
Cala Tuent	**Some shelter, NW**	Holiday resort
Ca'n Pastilla	**Harbour, E of Palma Bay**	Holiday resort
Ca'n Picafort	**Harbour, NE**	Holiday resort
Isla Dragonara	**W**	No facilities
Isla Ravena	**Alcudia Bay, harbour, N**	Club Nautico
Molinar	**Palma Bay E, harbour**	Hotels
Palma	**Yacht harbour, SW**	Boatyard
Palma Nova	**Palma Bay W, harbour**	Club Nautico
Portixol	**Palma E, harbour**	Club Nautico
Port Nou	**Harbour NE**	Hotels
Porto Colom	**Harbour, E**	Club Nautico
Porto Cristo	**Harbour, jetty, rocky, E**	Club Nautico
Porto Petro	**Harbour, moorings, SE**	Water provisions
Port Vey	**Small harbour, NE**	Hotels
Port d'Alcudia	**Harbour, N**	Fuel, Water
Port d'Andratx	**Good moorings, SW**	Boatyard
Port Campos	**Small harbour, S**	Fishing
Port de Pollença	**Major yacht harbour, N**	Boatyard
Port de Soller	**Moorings and harbour, NW**	Boatyard
La Rapita	**Small harbour, S**	Club Nautico
Sa Foradada	**Shelter, NW**	No facilities
Sant Telm	**Anchorage, W**	No facilities
S'Estanyol	**Jetty, S**	Club Náutico

abundance of enormous yachts berthed there from all over the world. The club has the facilities of a luxury hotel and sponsors the "Hundred Days of Yachting" around the Balearic Islands.

Each year sees yet more yacht marinas being built, where the rent for berthing is determined by the facilities offered by the marina, the length of the vessel and duration of stay. From June to September the prices shoot up, and the more popular harbours are fully booked ahead of the season.

For further information contact the **Real Club Náutico Palma de Mallorca,** Muelle San Pedro 1, Palma. Tel: 22 68 48. The Tourist Office can supply a full list of nautical clubs around the island.

Examples of mooring fees during the summer at Port d'Andratx are 728 pesetas for a craft of five metres and 2100 pesetas for one of twenty metres, per day.

The Tourist Information Office in Palma issues a free booklet *Instalaciones Nauticas de las Baleares*, which gives comprehensive details of yacht and boat facilities available in the Balearic Islands.

FOUR

Where to stay

There are 300,000 beds available for tourists in Majorca and accommodation ranges from luxury hotels to self-catering apartments, simple guesthouses, monasteries and modern campsites. A number of hotels and apartments are fully booked by tour operators, therefore they do not have rooms available for the independent traveller.

Great concentrations of hotels and apartments are to be found in the tourist complexes. In the city of Palma in particular besides hotels and apartments one finds numerous established guesthouses *(hostales)* that are simple, quaint, and sometimes old-fashioned – many of them existed before most of the hotels were built.

All accommodation has to be registered with, and is inspected by, the Tourist Board who give it a star rating. An up-to-date list of accommodation available, with current prices, can be obtained from tourist information offices (see Chapter 2).

It is recommended that you choose accommodation approved of by the Tourist Board and that you make reservations through property or travel agents. It is unwise to seek unlisted places where proprietors may not observe security and hygiene standards.

What to expect

Hotels

Hotels *(Hoteles* – H) are classified from 1 to 5 stars. A hotel always displays its rating outside by H, plus the appropriate number of stars. Hotels provide rooms and meals, as required, in their own restaurant. The larger hotels usually have outdoor swimming pools, tennis courts, shops and entertainment. Many have courtesy buses to take visitors to the beach. Those with three stars or more provide rooms with private bathrooms and toilets. Most of these rooms would have balconies, often with sea views. Maid service and laundry service should be available.

It is advisable to book accommodation in advance, particularly at the time of festivals and at tourist resorts. Reservations in writing can be sent direct to hotels. Letters sent to five, four and three star hotels can be written in English. For lower categories it is advisable to write in Spanish to avoid misunderstandings.

Hotel Apartments

Hotel Apartments (Apartamentos Hoteles – HA) are similar to hotels but are self-catering flats, bungalows or chalets with restaurant available. The star rating is shown after HA.

Resident Hotels

These hotels *(Hoteles Residencia* – HR) supply rooms but without restaurant facilities. They usually have less luxurious furnishings though often have private bathrooms and toilets. Shown as HR with star rating.

Guesthouses

Modest hotels and guesthouses (*Hostales* – HS) with a star rating of 1 to 3. They provide accommodation with or without meals. They do not have dormitories.

Pensions

Guesthouses (*Pensiónes* – P) with a small number of rooms, providing full board.

Residences

These establishments (*Residencias* – R) provide accommodation with a shared bathroom. Breakfast only available.

Inns

Inns *(pousadas, tabernas)* are usually in country districts; the standard is mostly good, but can vary so it is best to view rooms before booking. Often in beautiful surroundings with local atmosphere.

Paradors

This is the name given to hotels *(Parador Nacionales de Turismo)* belonging to the Ministry of State for Tourism in Spain. Usually they are converted historic castles, palaces, convents and monasteries, generally in a location of special scenic beauty or interest. They offer every comfort. At present there are no Paradors in Majorca.

Monasteries

It is possible to obtain family accommodation in some of the island's monasteries; facilities vary, some being quite simple. The attraction of this type of accommodation is the peaceful setting, for all the monasteries are situated in the high and remote areas of the island. Three which can provide family accommodation are:

– Sanctuario Nuestra Señora Sant Salvadore, Felanitx. Tel: 58 06 56.

– Ermita de Nuestra Señora de Cura, Randa. Tel: 66 09 94.

– Sanctuario Nuestra Señora de Lluc, Lluc Tel: 51 70 25.

The following sanctuaries provide simple, clean rooms which are mainly used by pilgrims, walkers and climbers:

– Ermita de la Victoria, Alcudia.

– Puig de Alaró.

– Puig de Maria, Pollença.

– Sanctuary of Montesion, Porreres.

There is no accommodation at Valldemossa.

Apartments and villas

Self catering accommodation is becoming more popular in Majorca, and new *urbanizaciones* (modern villages) are being built.

These purpose built areas are usually self contained, with supermarkets, hairdressers, bars, restaurants, shops, sports centres, discos, boat storage and car parks. Basic equipment in apartments will include bed linen, towels, kitchen equipment, cooking facilities, crockery, cutlery and glasses. Most have maid service and if there is a garden it is tended. A central reception will have information on display and offer excursion bookings and currency exchange facilities.

Costs

The cost of non-package accommodation varies according to the season. The high season is July to the end of September.

Charges range as follows for a double or twin bedroom in the high season per night. However, the charges quoted are to give an idea of costs – we wish to emphasise that the present trend is for prices to increase.

• **Hotel** ***** from 22,900 pesetas; **** from 8,000 pesetas; *** from 7,000 pesetas; ** from 6,000 pesetas; * from 4,000 pesetas.

• **Hotel Residencia** (HR) *** from 6,500 pesetas; ** from 5,000

pesetas; * from 3,000 pesetas.
• **Pensions, Hostals** (Hs) *** from 3,500 pesetas; ** from 3,000 pesetas; * from 2,500 pesetas.
• **Residential Apartments** (RA) **** from 6,000 pesetas; *** from 5,000 pesetas.
• **Apartments** (HA) **** from 11,000 pesetas; *** from 6,000 pesetas; ** from 4,500 pesetas; * from 2,500 pesetas.
• **Monastery accommodation** about 1,250 pesetas for two adults.

Hotels and other accommodation

For easy location on a map of Majorca, hotels are listed in a clockwise direction round the island, starting with Palma city and going westwards, therefore matching our description of tours. Under each town, accommodation is listed alphabetical in order of star rating.

Palma
***** Hotel **Melia Victoria** Avenida Joan Miro 1. Tel: 23 43 42. 167 rooms including suites. Open all year. Situated to the west of Palma overlooking the sea. Smart modern luxury hotel, offering first class comfort. All rooms have video and 24-hour service. Convenient for city centre, car park.
***** Hotel **Son Vida Sheraton** Urbanizacion Son Vida. Tel: 79 00 00. 166 rooms including suites. Open all year. Eight kilometres inland from capital. Prestigious converted thirteenth-century castle, with luxury facilities and high class service, quiet position close to the Son Vida Golf Course. Carpark.
***** Hotel **Valparaiso Palace** Francisco Vidal. Tel: 40 04 11. 138 rooms and suites. Open all year. Set in a tropical garden on hilltop, a kilometre from most shops and amenities. Three restaurants, two swimming pools, one indoors. Hairdressers and soundproof disco.
**** Hotel **Bellver Sol** Pol Ing Gabriel Roca 11. Tel: 23 80 08. 393 rooms including suites. Open all year. Central location for city, opposite seafront, elegant decor, convention halls, fully airconditioned. Facilities for the disabled. Satellite TV, night club.
**** Hotel **Palas Atenea - Sol** Pol Ing Gabriel Roca 29. Tel: 28 14 00. 370 rooms and suites. Open all year. Located on sea front with fine panorama of the Bay of Palma, and walking distance of city centre. Established luxury and courteous service. Facilities for the disabled, night club, carpark.

*** Hotel **Costa Azul** Pol Ing Gabriel 7. Tel: 23 19 40. 126 rooms. Open all year. Quiet and modest in prominent position along harbour. Heated swimming pool, restaurant overlooks the sea. Lifts and air conditioning.

*** Hotel Residencia **Almudaina** Ave. Rey Jaime III 9. Tel: 24 03 92. 80 rooms. Open all year. Quiet hotel in centre of city, mainly used by business people. Comfortable and simply furnished. Central heating.

*** Hotel **Mirador** Paseo Maritimo 10. Tel: 23 20 46. 78 rooms. Open all year. A fine view from the terrace of the Cathedral and waterfront, this Spanish style hotel has low ceilings and a quiet atmosphere, central heating and TV.

*** Hotel **Reina Constanza** Paseo Maritimo. Tel: 40 07 11. 97 rooms and suites. Open all year. Usefully situated in a central position opposite the Yacht Club. Well established with sedate atmosphere. Money change, bingo room, airconditioned public rooms.

** Hostal **Montmari** Jaime Ferrer 15. Tel: 71 39 79. 14 rooms. Open all year. Located behind the Longa de Mar and Naval Museum and close to the Apuntadores with its colourful restaurants. All bedrooms have running water. Dining room and Mallorcan cooking. Excursions to all parts of the island arranged.

** Hostal **Apuntadores** 8. Tel: 21 59 20. 27 rooms. Open all year. Right in the heart of the city, road leading west from the Plaza de la Teina. Many *tipico* restaurants nearby. Lift, money change.

** Hotel Residencia **Archduque** Calle Archduque Luis Salvador 22. Open 1 July to 1 October. This beautiful old mansion is full of faded glory. Situated conveniently near the bus station. Breakfast only, and check that the beds are comfortable before booking.

South west of Palma
• **Sant Augusti**

*** HA **Atalaya** Cabo Matorell Roca. Tel: 23 06 40. Apartments with well equipped kitchenettes and bathrooms. Small roof-top pool and terrace. Some traffic noise.

Hostal **Mimosa** Calle Sueca 5. Modest accommodation, bed and breakfast, evening barbecue, swimming pool.

• **Illetes**

***** Hotel **Melia de Mar** Illetes 7. Tel: 40 25 11. 140 rooms and suites. Open all year. In quiet, attractive residential area in the Bay of Palma. This elegant and luxurious hotel has terraces that overlook the sea. Beautiful gardens contain a large swimming pool; inside is a heated pool. Facilities for the disabled and children's play park.

• Magalluf
*** Hotel **Barbados Sol** Notario Alemany 7. Tel: 68 05 50. 428 rooms. Open all year. Adjacent to its sister, the **** Hotel **Antillas Sol**, both are just 150 metres from a sandy beach, shops and buses. Used by tour operators. Indoor heated pool and pools outside for adults and children. Full entertainment programme, disco and special winter activities.

• Peguera
**** Hotel **Villamil** Ctra Andratx 22km. Tel: 68 60 50. 125 rooms. Open all year. Long established Trusthouse Forte Group hotel. All rooms have satellite TV. Indoor and outdoor pools, watersports, sauna, jacuzzi, bars and discos. Early meals for children, baby sitting. Close to shops.
*** Hotel **Beverley Playa** Urb. La Romana. Tel: 68 60 70. 443 rooms . Open all year. In a well established busy resort, this large hotel is close to a long sloping beach and pinewoods. Buffet style meals and plenty of entertainment make it popular for all ages. Special prices for long stay winter holidays.

• Camp de Mar
*** Hotel **Playa Camp de Mar** Camp de Mar. Tel: 67 10 25. 286 rooms. Open April to 31 October. Set right by the edge of the tiny bay this large hotel has a friendly staff and pleasant decor. Swimming pool surrounded by terraces and gardens with views of pinewoods. Entertainment programme and tennis courts.

• Port d'Andratx
** Hotel **Brismar** Almirante Riera Alemany 7. Tel: 67 16 00. 56 rooms. Open all year. With a splendid view over the picturesque harbour and yacht marina, this hotel is always busy. Telephone in all rooms. Lift. Sea excursions, buses nearby.

• Sant Telm
* Hotel **Aquamarin** Playa de Sant Telm. Tel: 67 10 75. Open from 1 May to 31 October. Situated right by the sea in the fast developing village. Although in a quiet part of the island it can become busy at weekends as the restaurant and bar are very popular. Lift, money change and garden.

* Hostal **Eolo** Punta Blanca. 15 rooms. Open from 1 April to 31 October. Set above the small bay in a quiet position. Simple clean rooms. Bar.

The west
• **Banyalbufar**
*** Hotel **Mar Y Vent** Mayor 49. Tel: 61 00 25. 32 rooms. In pretty village on slopes of mountains with impressive seaviews. Sun terrace and swimming pool. Peaceful situation. Car advisable.
* Hostal **Baronia** Calle General Goded 16. Tel: 61 01 21. 34 rooms. Open 1 April to 31 October. Country accommodation in typical small west coast village amongst terraces of tomatoes and olive trees, with views towards the coastline. Full board with friendly service.

• **Deiá**
**** Hotel **Es Moli** Ctra Valldemossa to Deiá. Tel: 63 90 00. Open from 16 April to 31 October. Converted stone mansion in splendid gardens with fine views of the mountains. Modern interior and courteous service. Quiet location. Mountain walks can be arranged.
**** Hotel **La Residencia** Deiá. Tel: 63 90 11. 20 rooms. Open all year. South west of Deiá, two country houses restored with antique furnishings and paintings, standing in tranquil gardens. Central heating in bedrooms. Tennis.

• **Valdemossa**
* Hostal **C'an Mario** By Placa de Cartoixi. 8 rooms. Open all year. Typical Mallorquin hostal, clean and full of old furniture, fine entrance hall, simple dining room. Friendly and family-run, with delicious home cooking. Close to monastery. 18 kilometres to Palma.

• **Port de Soller**
*** Hotel **Esplendido** Calle Marina Es Traves 23. Tel: 63 18 50. 104 rooms. Open 1 April to 31 October. Well established, old fashioned hotel on coastal road. Facilities for the disabled. Dogs allowed. Most rooms having seaviews and balconies.
*** HR **Eden Park** Calle Lepanto. Tel: 63 12 00. 54 rooms. Open 1 April to 31 October. Modern and comfortable with pleasant staff, fifty metres from sea. Lifts and garage. Shared facilities with Hotel Eden across road.
*** Hostal **Es Port** Antonio Montis. Tel: 63 16 50. 96 rooms. Open all year. Well established with good facilities, including for the disabled. Close to the waterfront, lifts, central heating, swimming pool, terrace,

garden, children's play park. Dogs allowed.

The north east coast
• Cala Mesquida
* Hotel **Cala Mesquida** 2 Cala Mesquida, Capdepera. Tel: 56 35 96. 81 rooms. This modern hotel is part of a Village Club in an isolated position close to a lovely beach. Many sports facilities. Capdepera 6 km.

• Port de Pollença
*** Hotel **Daina** Atilio Boveri 2. Tel: 53 12 50. 60 rooms. Open 1 April to 31 October. Overlooking the harbour and bay, this hotel has its own private jetty. Sun terraces and swimming pool. Airconditioned fifth floor restaurant. Close to shops, bars and restaurants.
*** Hotel **Illa d'Or Colon** 265. Tel: 53 11 00. 119 rooms. Open all the year. On the quiet eastern side of the lovely bay, five minutes from the main beach and fifteen minutes walk to the centre of town. Guests from the Illa d'Or apartments opposite share the facilities of this hotel. Entertainments, live music twice weekly, English videos and occasional concerts.
*** Hotel **Pollença Park** Urb Uyal. Tel: 53 13 50. 316 rooms. Open 1 April to 31 October. Close to beach and suitable for young children. Large tourist hotel with full programme of entertainment, bingo, disco and four floodlit tennis courts.
*** Hotel Residencia **Sis Pins** Anglada Camarasa 229. Tel: 53 10 50. 50 rooms, An older style hotel with a friendly atmosphere, offering bed and breakfast only. TV and card room. On tree lined promenade with sun terrace.
** Hostal **Luz del Mar** Mendez Nunez 12/14. Tel: 53 27 12. 12 rooms. Open all year. Pretty, English run and clean, bedrooms with washbasins, shared bathroom. Breakfast.

• Playa de Formentor
***** Hotel **Formentor** Tel: 53 13 00. 127 rooms. Open 26 April to 31 October. One of the oldest and most prestigious hotels on the island. Famous for its cuisine and magnificent semi-tropical gardens. Isolated position.

• Port d'Alcudia
**** Hotel Apartments **Princesa** Ave Minerva. Tel: 54 69 50. Open 1 April to 31 October. Comfortably furnished apartments in pleasant

surroundings, 100 metres from the sea. Nearby windsurf school and tennis. Plenty of entertainments. Children's play park.

*** Hotel **Bahia de Alcudia** Avenida de Playa. Tel: 54 58 00. Open 1 April to 31 October. Within easy reach of beach and port. Large modern tourist hotel with plenty of facilities, including for the disabled. Children's play park. Aviary of colourful exotic birds.

*** Hotel **Condesa de la Bahia** Urb Lago Esperanza. Tel: 54 53 16. 491 Rooms. Open 1 May to 30 October. Huge modern tourist hotel with facilities for the disabled. Rooms have inland and sea views. Plenty of entertainments and organised sports.

*** Hotel **Fortuna Playa** Urb L. Gaviota, Playa de Muro. Tel: 54 59 58. Open 1 April to 30 October. Modern, comfortable and suitable for family holidays. Near saltwater lagoon, Lago Esperanza and 150 metres from beach.

*** Hotel **Lago Monte** Urb Lago Menor. Tel: 54 60 05. Open 1 April to 31 October. Especially suitable for young families. Free bus to beach and supervised children's games.

*** Hotel **Platja D'Or** Playa de Alcudia. Tel: 89 00 52. 232 rooms. Open 1 April to 31 October. This four-year old hotel is clean, bright and gives excellent service. Many of its clients return. Five minutes walk across sand dunes is the splendid white beach. Attractive blue and white decor, airconditioned dining room. Entertainments, outdoor stage, sports, spacious gardens and pool, bicycles for hire. Used by Thomson Sun.

** Hotel **Panoramic** More Verney. Tel: 54 54 84. 155 rooms. Open 1 April to 31 October. Modern hotel by the sandy beach within easy reach of shops, restaurants and entertainments. Suitable for children. Tennis and automatic games.

* Hotel **Bocaccio** Calle Pedro Mas Reus. Tel: 54 53 75. 400m from sea, near Largo Menor. Suitable for young families. Buffet restaurant. Sports facilities.

● **Ca'n Picafort**

** Hotel **Playas de C'an Picafort** Tel: 52 72 26. 156 rooms. Open 1 May to 31 October. Family hotel 40 metres from clean sandy beach. Ideal for young children and water sport enthusiasts. Plenty of shops, restaurants and bars nearby.

* Hotel Residencia **Mar Y Paz** Isabel Garan 1. Tel: 52 72 88. 60 rooms. Open 1 April to 31 October. Small, family run hotel at eastern end of resort, right by sandy beach. All rooms have bath, simple decor. Sun terrace and pool overlooks the sea.

The east coast
• Cala Millor
*** Hotel **Iberhotel Playa Cala Millor** Urb Sa Maniga. Tel: 58 52 12. 242 rooms. Open 1 April to 31 December. Large and modern and close to the lovely sandy beach. Well furnished, providing good facilities for families and the disabled.

*** Hotel **Talayot.** Son Sard. Tel: 58 53 14. 94 rooms. Open all year. Set back off seafront road. Well established and friendly. Swimming pool. Early suppers for children. Five minutes from town centre.

• Cales de Mallorca
**** Hotel **Gran Hotel Tucan** Bulevard 4. Tel: 65 72 00. 155 rooms. Open from 1 April to 31 October. Elegant, modern and comfortable. Restaurant serves buffet meals. Some entertainment. Nine hole Vale d'Or golf course nearby. Buses to Palma.

**** Hotel **Los Chihuahuas Sol** Cales de Mallorca. Tel: 83 30 01. 216 rooms. Open 1 April to 31 October. Well established high rise hotel with cosmopolitan atmosphere, right by the sea and ten minutes walk to sandy beach. Plenty of entertainment for all age groups. Large pools, sports club, sauna, night club, cliff walks.

**** Hotel **Los Mastines Sol** Cale de Mallorca. Tel: 57 31 25. 260 rooms. Open 1 April to 31 October. Situated close to Los Chihuahuas, this huge high rise hotel caters for package holidays and offers similar facilities to its sister hotel. Good for families. It is some way from a large town.

• Cala d'Or
*** Hotel **Costa del Sur** Avda de la Playa. Tel: 65 71 51. 102 rooms. Open 1 April to 31 October. Modern whitewashed building close to a sandy cove, with shops, cafés and nightlife nearby. Satellite TV, table tennis, swimming pools for children and adults.

*** Hotel **Skorpios Marina** Calle Egos. Tel: 65 71 51. 163 rooms. Open from 1 April to 31 October. With its sister, Hotel Corfu, they offer family entertainments and special children's club. Eating is at Corfu and the fun at Skorpios. A few shops and bars. Close to pinewoods and beach. Buses to Cala d'Or, two kilometres away.

The south
• Campos del Puerto
*** Hotel **Balneario San Juan de la Font Santa** Ctra Campos del Puerto. Tel: 65 50 16. 19 rooms. Open 1 June to 30 September. Set in flat, agricultural countryside, caters mainly for clients who wish to

use the thermal showers, baths and remedial treatments. A gracious building within a large garden and on the edge of salt lakes. It has a tranquil atmosphere. Fifteen kilometres north of Colonia Sant Jordi.

• Colonia Sant Jordi
** Hotel **Sur Mallorca** Plaza Cristobal Colon. Tel: 65 52 00. 200 rooms. Open 1 April to 31 October. Pleasant and cheerful, in a quiet position by a rocky beach. Spacious sun terraces surround the swimming pool. Tennis courts, table tennis and children's playground. Thirty minutes drive to Platja d'es Trenc beach. Town has a sandy beach, harbour, and fish restaurants.

• Ses Covetes
* Hostal **Lavi** Close to beach of Platja d'es Trenc. Simple accommodation above a bar restaurant. TV. Run by friendly Majorcan family.

• Ca'n Pastilla
*** Hotel **Alexandra Sol** Calle Pineda 15. Tel: 26 23 50. 164 rooms. Open all year. A short walk to the beach and shops. This old style hotel is used by tour operators. Buffet meals, high chairs and cots, entertainments, dancing, swimming pools, mini club in high season.
*** Hotel **Calma** Horacio 5. Tel: 26 11 50. 190 rooms. Open all year. Well established and homely, simple decor, swimming pool, TV, billiards and cards. Easy walk to beach.
*** Hotel **Gran Hotel El Cid Sol** Ctra El Arenal km8. Tel: 26 08 50. 216 rooms. Open 1 April to 31 October. This is a traditional lively seaside hotel, right by the beach, with plenty of activities day and night. Buffet meals. Swimming pool and children's playground. Bus to Palma.
*** Hotel **Playa d'Or** Virgil 26. Tel: 26 01 62. 71 Rooms. Open 1 April to 31 October. Overlooking sandy beach and yacht harbour, a small quiet hotel, buffet meals. TV, dancing three times a week. Swimming pool.

Inland
• Orient
**** Hotel **L'Hermitage** Ctra De Sollerich km8. Tel: 61 33 00. 20 rooms. Closed 1 November to 14 December. Tucked away on the outskirts of this country village, a seventeenth-century house, furnished with antiques, has been transformed into an exclusive hotel. The restaurant is well known for its cuisine. Sun terrace, pool and

Plenty of sports and indoor entertainments as well as swimming pools at Camping Platja Blava. Opposite the entrance are low pinewoods, sand dunes and a sandy beach.

gardens make this a restful holiday place. Advance booking is suggested.

** Hostal **de Muntanya.** Bordoy 6. Tel: 61 33 80. 13 rooms. Open all year. A much sought after mountain retreat. This delightful hostal serves typical Majorcan cuisine; in good weather meals are served on the terrace.

Camping and motor caravanning

Camping rules that apply in mainland Spain also apply in Majorca. A copy of the camping regulations should be obtained by anyone intending to camp on the island. This can be had from: The Spanish National Tourist Office, 57/58 St James's Street, London SW1. Tel: 071-499 0901.

It is not necessary to have a Camping Carnet, but it is an advantage, particularly for those who camp outside official sites, as third party insurance is included. Camping Carnets can be obtained from camping organisations such as the AA, RAC and the Caravan Club, and cost approximately £3. A passport-size photograph is required.

Amongst the several campsites near Barcelona, **Camping International Barcino** is very convenient for those en route to Majorca. It is convenient for visiting the city of Barcelona, being on a frequent bus route to the centre, and convenient for the port where the ferry leaves for Majorca. But during the high season the camp can become very crowded and dusty, therefore it is best to regard it only as a transit site. You are advised to avoid street parking of unattended camping vehicles in Barcelona.

Majorca has two Class 1a campsites, both on the north coast near Alcudia. **Camping Platja Blava,** a modern campsite, lies on the inland side of the main road between Puerto Alcudia and Ca'n Picafort at km8, Municipo de Muro, 41km from Palma. Open all year it becomes very busy during the high season, July and August. Part of the camp is used by the Sun Club Picafort which is a separate holiday organisation, with their own swimming pool, tents and bungalows. Club Cantabrica (Holiday House, 146-148 London Road, St Albans, Herts AL1 1PQ. Tel: 0727 66177) also use the camp, having tents and mobile homes for hire.

Opposite this pleasant camp is a long sandy beach. The camp is well lit at night and has five hundred pitches taking tents, trailer caravans and motorcaravans. The site is level and enclosed with an entrance barrier and reception office; opposite is a well stocked shop that includes frozen foods, gifts and Camping Gaz.

The pitches are unmarked and lie alongside wide avenues lined with trees, whose shade is much sought after in mid summer. Some electric hookups are available and water taps, dustbins and fire points are in strategic position. The large, spacious toilet block, partially open air, has cold water basins, mirrors and shaver points. Hot shower cubicles need a 25 peseta coin to operate. There is a disabled facility. Toilets are British type and cleaned twice daily. A laundry room has modern washing machines and dryers, irons can be hired. Two swimming pools are for the special use of campers, with sun patios sheltered by hedges.

Amongst the amenities are tennis, table tennis, mini football, volley ball, a large playground, bar and restaurant. Other activities include live bands, disco, sports, TV lounge, horse riding, moped and bicycle hire, pedalos and windsurfing, all at reasonable cost. Just outside the camp are payphones and the bus stop. A taxi from the camp to the airport costs 3,800 pesetas, to Alcudia 850 pesetas and to Palma 3,400 pesetas. A ten minutes walk brings you into Ca'n Picafort.

This camp makes an excellent base for touring the island; should you wish, the management will make your ferry reservation from mainland Spain and rent you a tent or bungalow. The manager and his staff speak English. A booking form and illustrated brochure can be obtained from Camping Caravanning, Platja Blava, Carretera Puerto Alcudia Bahia, Alcudia, Majorca. Tel: 53 78 63. Reservations can also be made at Algebeli SA, Calle Antonio Marques 18, Palma. Tel: 20 38 61. Telex: 69509 Llafe. Alternatively at the Federacion Española de Empresarios de Camping YCU, Gran Via 88, Grupo 3, 10 - 8, Madrid 28013, España. Approximate cost for two adults and a motorcaravan, per night, £10 high season and £7 low; electricity according to power, 2 amps is 170 pesetas. Special discount can be given for long stays.

Another camp site, **Camping Club San Pedro,** is located off the main C712 road, Arta to Puerto Alcudia km7.5, and signed Camping, Colonia San Pedro. At a distance of about 5km along a narrow country road a turning westwards towards the sea leads to Club San Pedro.

Its isolated position close to a shallow pebble, rock and sand beach, and the splendid panorama of the mountains behind and the wide Bay of Alcudia, make this an ideal camp for a restful holiday (except in the high season, when it can be completely full). Attractively landscaped and laid out in a setting of banana trees and tropical plants is a pretty swimming pool surrounded by a terrace with tables and sunbeds. Reception, restaurant, bar, TV room and table tennis are also there. Behind are lines of wooden chalets (there are also tents for hire), while to one side are the unmarked pitches and some electric hookups. As yet the trees are not fully grown so there is little shade.

The clean modern tiled block has free hot water showers, wash basins, mirrors, shaver points, British type toilets, and a facility for the disabled. A small shop has essential necessities, including frozen foods. A larger supermarket in the village has fresh meat and vegetables, also Camping Gaz.

In the Reception are safe deposit boxes. Cars and bicycles can be rented. At present no bus reaches the camp but a taxi can be arranged. Tennis court, volley ball, windsurfing, *petanca* (bowls) and riding are some of the sporting activities. Many good walks can be enjoyed, including one to an isolated *ermita* (chapel) in the mountains.

The site director is Spanish with an English wife. They live with their children on the camp during the season, and they and their staff are very friendly. This is a pleasant camping park where you will feel well away from it all. It is open from May to the end of October. For further details write to Camping Club San Pedro, Colonia San Pedro, Majorca. Tel: 23 03 65.

Camping off site
It is possible to free park with a motorcaravan on Majorca, but it is not encouraged by the authorities. Overnight parking is allowed for 50 pesatas an hour on the large carpark in front of the ferry terminal, **Estación Marítimo** at Palma; there is no security guard.

Motorcaravans have been known to park in quiet places, like outside country bars, or near a beach. At all times it is necessary to be vigilant against petty thieving and to get permission from the owner of the land. We think that one of the most pleasant ways to see the countryside of Majorca is with a motorcaravan.

Property and estate agents

Majorca presents an appealing location for purchasers to invest in property. Many British people have owned property there for a long time now, but it is advisable to get specialist advice on the subject.

Selling apartments, bungalows and villas, the administration of property, letting, legal advice, repairs, technical services and insurance, are all transactions carried out by real estate companies in Majorca and the UK. Most of the firms employ English-speaking staff trained to assist clients.

Some addresses of estate agents in Majorca are:
– Mesquida and Reynes, Paseo Maritimo 12, Palma. Tel: 23 40 73. (Associated with Spratley & Co, and David Russell (Spain) Ltd. London.)
– Jonsel S.A. Avenida Joan Miro 354/356, Sant Agusti. Tel: 40 06 93.
– Spanish Estates, King Park, Santa Ponça. (Associated with Durrant Developments Ltd., 16 Church Lane, Christchurch, Bournemouth. Tel: 0202 49811.)

Luxury one and two bedroom apartments can be had from £18,000, in the Cala Nova Marina. A country house with three bedrooms, two bathrooms and about 1,000 sq m land costs about £57,000.

Those who require an English-speaking lawyer could contact Don Antonio Ques, Calle San Jaime 22, Palma. Tel: 21 20 89. For removals by road from the UK, contact White & Co, plc, Elliot Road, West Howe, Bournemouth, Dorset. Tel: 0202 576514 or Palma 40 02 59.

FIVE

Getting about

The road system

There are toll free motorways *(autopistas)* leading out of Palma in three directions: west to the airport and El Arenal for thirteen kilometres; east to Palma Nova for fifteen kilometres; and north for ten kilometres in the direction of Santa Maria. The main roads leading out of the city are generally straight, a legacy of the days of the Roman occupation; some are modern carriageways but in many parts the surface is poor with little or no shoulder to the road. Roads between villages are narrow but generally bituminised; an effort has been made to widen hairpin bends in the mountain regions. Because of the terrain some approach roads to isolated coves are steep and uneven, so care is needed especially from the dust of oncoming cars.

In Palma traffic is heavy and generally moves fast, with the help of traffic police control. The standard of driving outside of the city is good and drivers appear to respect the state of the roads. On Sundays the roads are usually busy with Mallorquin family traffic.

To park in Palma it is first necessary to obtain a ticket called ORA from tobacconists. There is also parking underground beneath Plaza Major, entrance off the Rambla; behind Galerias Preciados, Calle Rosellon and at Park de la Mar on the seafront, opposite the Cathedral.

Roads are not always clearly signposted, so a good road map is essential. Recommended is one from the series which includes all the Balearic Islands, published by Firestone Hispania and available in Majorca from petrol filling stations and bookshops, or direct by post from the publisher of this book whose name and address appear at the foot of the title page (Map T-26 Balearic Islands 1 : 125,000 in self cover); another good map is the Telegraph Map, Majorca (Spanish Leisure Map Series) 1:160,000.

Police patrol on motorcycles, particularly on main highways; traffic

---

Road accidents

In the case of a road accident where persons are injured you must inform the police as soon as possible. Main routes have SOS telephones. If you are in a rented car you must also inform the hire company, so be sure to have their telephone number with you. It is sensible to have a Spanish/English phrase book handy. Where possible take photographs of the accident scene and record the addresses of witnesses. This can be taken from their *carnet de identidad*. If you are involved with another car note down the registration number and make, and, if possible, the name and number of their insurance company. Generally the local population are sympathetic and will do all they can to assist tourists in accidents.

---

offences are fined on the spot, and can cost up to 10,000 pesetas. There is a 10 per cent reduction if you pay immediately, so it is advisable to carry some pesetas as well as your driving licence and passport. Amongst the traffic offences that you can be fined for are not wearing seat belts and illegal parking on white and yellow lines.

Driving in Spain and Majorca

If you are taking a car to Majorca – driving through Spain and taking the car ferry from either Barcelona or Valencia – you will require the following:
1. International Driving Permit
2. International Insurance (Green) Card (your insurance company issues this)
3. Bail Bond (from AA, RAC or insurance company: this is an indemnity if you are involved in an accident)
4. Vehicle Registration Document
5. Passport
6. A spare set of car light bulbs (Spanish law requirement)
7. A red triangle, for warning of breakdown obstruction
8. Means of changing direction of headlight dip
9. GB sticker

Up-to-date information on these subjects is best obtained from the AA, RAC or the Spanish Tourist Office.

It is important to remember the following points when driving in Spain and Majorca:
• Stop for pedestrians on crossings.

The western coastline has dramatic scenery, which can be viewed from a series of watch towers and viewpoints, known as miradors.

- Wear seat belts.
- Sidelights only are required in built-up areas.
- Do not cross the single white line (which is equivalent to the double white line in the UK).
- Observe "no overtaking" signs and speed limits.
- Maximum speed in built up areas is 40 km.p.h.
- Give way to traffic coming from the right, especially at roundabouts.

- Drive on the right hand side of the road.
- Sound your horn when overtaking.
- Three point turns and reversing into side streets are forbidden in towns.
- Motorcyclists must wear crash helmets and travel with lights on.

Road signs

Most road signs are international. One important traffic control is the *cambio de sentido* (change direction), generally controlled by traffic lights, which prevents vehicles turning across oncoming traffic or from doing a U-turn. Here are some road sign translations:

Aduana	customs post	*Estacionamiento*	
Aparcamiento	parking	*prohibido*	no parking
Atención	caution	*Izquierdo*	left
Blandones	soft verges	*Obras*	workmen
Cedo el paso	give way	*Pare, Parada*	stop
Despacio	slow	*Peligro*	danger
Desvio	diversion	*Peligroso*	dangerous
Derecha	right	*Paso prohibido*	no thoroughfare
Escuela	school	*Peatones*	pedestrians
		Salidas	exit

Petrol stations

In Majorca most petrol filling stations are closed on Sundays and Public Holidays. The location of stations opening on Sundays is published in the *Majorca Daily Bulletin* costing 75 pesetas. There are petrol stations open all night in Palma, Inca and Manacor. You can obtain lead free petrol at the Aeropuerto de Palma and in Palma.

Petrol stations do not provide car repair services; this is a separate service called *taller mechanico*. Toilets and water can be found at filling stations. Autoshops sell spares and sweets. Car wash services are similar to those in the UK. Petrol comes in three grades, Extra 98 octane, Super 96 octane and Normal 92 octane. Currently there are only a few petrol stations that sell lead free petrol *(sin plomb)*. At the time of writing Super petrol is 88 pesetas a litre. Do not confuse petrol *(gasolina)* with diesel *(gasoil)*.

Car servicing and repairs

There are numerous places for servicing and repairing cars, as there are many cars on the island. Palma has agents for most well known British and foreign cars. There could be some delay in obtaining a particular spare required from abroad. In country towns a small workshop *(taller mechanico)* which deals with local vehicles will assist. The standard is good and repairs are promptly effected. Costs are usually more reasonable than in the UK. Facilities for tyre fitting, battery charging and car washing are available.

Parking in Palma

If you wish to park in the centre of the city of Palma you will need to purchase an ORA card, which is sold in tobacconists. It costs 30 pesetas for half-an-hour's parking, 50 for one hour and 75 for the maximum time of one and a half hours. You are restricted to certain areas and need to mark your card with the time when you park; if the time overlaps into a free time your card is still valid when a restricted time recommences. You can be fined up to 3,000 pesetas for illegal parking. Parking is easier at the edge of the city where there are meters.

The ORA system operates Monday to Saturday 0930 to 1330 hrs and Monday to Friday 1700 to 2000 hrs. An ORA card is not required between 1330 and 1700 hrs and between 2000 and 0930 hrs.

Self-drive car hire

Car hire agencies in Majorca include international names like Avis S.A., Europcar and Hertz. There are numerous local firms and prices can vary. A more reliable way to hire a car is through your hotel reception or a travel agent. The rates for hire usually include third party insurance; this should be noted as it is an essential requirement. In the Balearic Islands free mileage is included in the contract.

Examples of car hire prices per day: Marbella 1,900 pesetas; Opel City 2,100 pesetas; Ford Fiesta 2,300 pesetas; Suzuki 4,500 pesetas; Opel Kadett 3,600 pesetas.

Hire of scooters and mopeds

Mopeds and scooters are a practical way to get about the island. Rates vary a great deal. Remember it is necessary to wear a crash helmet.

Examples of hire prices are: scooters 2,200 pesetas per day, mopeds 1,800 pesetas.

Bicycles

Bicycles *(bicicletas)* are available for hire at all the resorts and this is a very popular form of travel. In some places there are tracks at the side of the road reserved for bicycles. Cost for hire is from 500 pesetas per day.

Taxis

There is a good taxi service on the island and the cost is not considered to be high. Towns and resorts have taxis in individual colour. Palma taxis are black with a cream coloured roof and bonnet and they also have meters.

For journeys outside of Palma there are official price lists, and these prices should be agreed with the driver before hire. There are additional fees for each piece of luggage, for night and for Sunday travel. Taxi stations in Palma are marked with a white T on a blue sign.

Examples of normal day time fares from the airport, Aeropuerto Son San Juan:

to	Palma	1500 pesetas	
	Arenal	1255	"
	Peguera	2850	"
	Cala Millor	5320	"
	Alcudia	4865	"
	Palma Nova	2130	"
	Puerto Cristo	4790	"

Bus services

Public bus services are inexpensive and frequent in all the tourist areas, but at peak periods the popular routes from the beaches to Palma may mean standing room only. There is a city bus service in Palma, the terminal being in the **Plaza San Antonio.**

The main bus terminal *(estación de autobuses)* is in the **Plaza España** where you may leave luggage and purchase tickets. Destinations are usually marked on the front of the bus. You must always enter the bus from the front and buy your ticket from the driver or conductor, unless it has been previously purchased at the bus station. Useful is a book of 10 bus tickets. Remember to leave the bus by the rear door. Bus stops are generally marked with the word *parada*, meaning stopping place. Bus queues are usually orderly and people line up facing the direction in which the bus will travel. Buses run every day including public holidays.

Because there are several different bus companies, not all the buses start from the Plaza España; it is therefore recommended that, if your hotel or apartment reception is unable to assist, you go to the local tourist office for information and timetables. The tourist office in Palma will also be helpful.

Taking a ride on a country bus can prove a delightful experience, and on market days expect to have various young farm animals aboard too. It is a good way to observe the country folk, without being too inquisitive, and a friendly smile may provoke some conversation.

For example a regular bus service runs between Palma and Alcudia.

• Departing from Palma Railway Station:

Monday to Friday	0945, 1200, 1330, 1800 and 2000 hrs.
Saturday	0945, 1330 and 1800 hrs.
Sunday and holidays	0945, 1830 and 2100 hrs.

• Departure from Alcudia:

Monday to Friday	0745, 0915, 1100, 1515 and 1815 hrs.
Saturday	0745, 0915 and 1615 hrs.
Sunday and holidays	0745, 1415 and 1900 hrs.

Horse drawn carriages

Horse drawn carriages *(tartanas)* are numerous in Palma and in some of the resorts. These gaily decorated open carriages allow you to view the sights at a pleasant pace. The drivers will ask you about 2,000 pesetas for a drive around the city of Palma. The price is a little higher than that recommended by the Tourist Office. However, do agree the cost before starting off.

Donkey carts, too, are available in the resorts – a hilarious drive so long as you are not in a hurry; children will love these forms of travel.

(Opposite): *The Saturday morning Flea Market in Palma, the Rastrillo, brings crowds from all over the island, looking for a bargain.*

A drive in a horse drawn carriage is a relaxing way to do some sightseeing in Palma; seen here in Avendia Jaime III passing the arcaded shops.

Coach excursions

There is no doubt that if your holiday on Majorca is for a limited period, then the easiest way of enjoying the sights of the island is to join a coach excursion. These outings are well advertised in travel agents *(viajes)*, hotel receptions and in the local newspapers. Half day, whole day and evening trips, plus visits to neighbouring islands, can be booked in advance. Prices vary according to routes and start points.

You may wish to make sure that your coach has an English-speaking guide and whether the cost includes a meal. Remember to take sunglasses and a hat, camera and jumper; possibly flat shoes and a towel if a beach visit is included. Your tour is sure to stop at a souvenir shop so some extra pesetas may be required. It is normal practice to tip the coach driver about 100 pesetas. You will feel it is well worth this when you have experienced some of the twists and bends on the mountain roads.

(Opposite): *Outside the parish church, Nuestra Señora de Los Angeles, stands the Lion of Sineu, erected by councillors to honour St Mark, their patron saint.*

Among the excursions offered are a visit to the pearl factory at Manacor; the caves at Arta and Drach; Marineland; the Safari Park; the market at Inca; and boat trips. Evening excursions include dinner and dancing, barbecues and a visit to a night club. Tours of the island including Palma city are very popular.

There are many travel agents from whom you can obtain tickets for excursions. **Ultramar Express** is a firm that has comfortable modern coaches and careful drivers. We recommend that your sightseeing includes the north and west of the island. Examples of coach excursion prices are:

• From C'an Picafort:

Caves of Drach	1,800 pesetas
Around the island	4,520 pesetas
Majorca markets (1/2 day)	1,950 pesetas
Pirate ship, sea trip	3,200 pesetas
Barbecue	3,300 pesetas

Children between two and twelve years are half price. Infants are carried free.

Island railways

There are two train services in Majorca, operating between Palma and Sóller 28km, 55 mins, 914mm gauge and Palma and Inca 29km, 36 mins, 915mm gauge. Each company has its own station in **Plaza España,** Palma. Tel: 75 22 5l. The trains are electric and of 1912 vintage; there were more extensive services once but these have fallen into disuse with the advent of the car.

There are five trains a day to Sóller, which is a scenic ride through the mountains taking about half an hour. At Sóller there is a tram that goes on to Port de Sóller. The return fare, including the tram, is 540 pesetas. More details of this journey are given in Chapter 12. Soller Railway, Tel: 75 20 51.

The train service to Inca is more frequent, fourteen times a day. This is because Inca is a busy town and the Mallorquins use the train, which stops on the way at Santa Maria, Consell and Binissalem. The return fare to Inca, from Palma, is 350 pesetas. Palma (F.E.V.E.) to Inca, Tel: 75 22 45.

SIX

A-Z information for visitors

British Consul

In case anything untoward should happen, like losing your passport, it is useful to know the whereabouts of the British Consul, Mr. Peter Cross. His office is situated in the Plaza Mayor, Number 3D, Palma (at the northern end of the Plaza, through an archway). Tel: 75 22 45. Opening hours are: Monday to Friday, June to October 0900 to 1300 hrs; and November to May 0900 to 1300 and 1600 to 1800 hrs.

The police headquarters and the town hall will also assist. Information notices and books in hotels are handy places for finding such addresses.

British American Club

The British American Club is at Soldado Marroig 8, Son Armadams, Palma. Tel: 23 13 33. This club is for members and their guests. Visiting membership can be taken out for one, two or three weeks. A restaurant provides lunch and dinner daily. There is a "Happy Hour" on Monday from 1830 to 1930, when drinks are at half price. There is dancing on Sunday at 1930 hrs, with Ron Marriner at the piano. Other amenities include bridge, kalooki, darts, billiards, video films, fashion shows and a thrift shop. The club is closed on Thursday.

Churches

Most Mallorquins are Roman Catholics and there are Catholic churches throughout the island. Visitors are always welcome. Times of Mass are displayed at the church entrance. In Palma confessions are heard in French, Italian, German and English at the Cathedral, the

Montesión Church and the Capilla de la Imaculado Church.

There is an Anglican Church, San Felipe and San Jaime, at Nunez de Balboa 6, Son Armadans, Palma. At the same address there is a Swedish Lutheran Church. There is an Evangelist Church at Murillo 16, Palma; Christian Science is to be found at Calle Ribera 4, (off Jaime III) Palma.

Services in English are held on Sundays at 1130 hrs, at the Parish Church, Parroquia de San Fernando, Balneario 6, El Arenal. Tel: 26 28 93. Jewish communities can attend at the Hotel Santa Ana, Cala Major on Fridays at 1900 hrs. Tel: 40 10 52. Jewish community Sabbath Eve services are held Fridays at 1900 hrs, at Calle Monsenor Palmer 3, Palma. The Salvation Army holds services in English at Avenida Joan Miro 285, Cala Major. See local press for times.

Communications

Post

Post offices *(correos)* similar to those in the UK are in all towns and most villages. They are generally open from 0900 to 1400 and 1600 to 1900 hrs, Monday to Saturday, closed on Sunday and public holidays. The main post office in Palma is in Calle Constitució 6. Tel: 72 16 67. Open 0900 to 1300 and 1600 to 1900 hrs.

You may have parcels and letters sent to a local post office for you to collect. They should be addressed to you (surname first, then initials) at Lista de Correos, in the appropriate town or village (e.g. *Lista de Correos,* Port d'Andratx, Majorca, Spain). There is no charge for this service. When you collect your mail from the post office you will be required to show your passport for identification. In shops where you purchase postcards, stamps *(sello)* are usually sold. Tobacconists *(estanco)* also sell stamps.

At the time of writing, postage to the UK for a letter or postcard costs 45 pesetas. All mail goes by air; parcels and packets can be registered.

In Majorca post boxes are painted yellow, and are similar in shape to those in the UK. The exception is at main post offices where posting boxes are in the wall of the building. Sometimes they are marked *extranjero* (for addresses abroad) and *insular* (for addresses within Spain). Small rectangular yellow boxes, may be attached to houses in remote country villages.

Telephones

Telephoning from Majorca to the UK, or other countries, is simple, provided the coin box is not too full to accept further coins. This happens quite frequently in busy tourist resorts. Look for a public telephone marked *international*; those marked *urbano* are for local calls only. You can use 100, 25 and 5 peseta coins, and directions for use are displayed in several languages near the telephone. In hotels, the switchboard operator will dial your number and call you as soon as the connection is made. Some hotels have telephones in the bedroom. A small charge is made for this service. *Cabina telefonica* is a phone mainly found in tourist resorts, where an operator obtains the number for you and payment is made after the call.

When using the public telephone, first dial 07 for international calls. Wait for a high pitched continuous sound then dial the code of the country required (for UK this is 44) followed by the subscriber's code and number. Note that in cases where the code starts with 0, this is omitted – for example, for London (071), just dial 71.

International country codes from Majorca are, Austria 43, Denmark 45, Germany 49, Holland 31, Italy 39, Portugal 351, Sweden 46 and UK 44.

Cost indication to UK: between 0800 and 2200 hrs, 175 pesetas per minute; 2200 and 0800 hrs, 140 pesetas per minute. Cheaper rates are between 2200 and 0800 hrs. It is possible to reverse the call charge by dialling an operator on 9398 and asking for *cobra revertido* but this can only be done on telephones that can accept incoming calls. It is not possible with public payphones.

Telegraph

Cable messages can be passed day or night, by way of the main telephone exchange. Dial 222000, 222001 or 222002.

Telex

For teleprinter service, dial 222005. For emergency remittances of money, one's own bank at home can do this by telex to a Spanish bank. This service can be granted very quickly. If necessary, ask permission to use a travel agent's telex number. Fax is now superseding telex.

General information on all these communication services can be had on 222003.

Currency and banks

Majorca is a part of Spain and therefore the currency is the peseta. The coins in use are: 1, 5, 10, 25, 50, 100, 200 and 500 pesetas. Notes are: 500, 1000, 2000, 5000 and 10,000 pesetas. The "high street" banks are the same as in Spain and have names like Banco de Bilbao, Banco March, Banco de Credito Balear and Banco de Santander. Opening hours do vary slightly but generally are 0930 to 1400 hrs daily, closing at 1300 on Saturdays. They are closed all day on Sundays and public holidays, and all day on Saturdays from July to October. Most Spanish banks accept Eurocheque encashment cards, Visa or equivalent, and these display the appropriate sign. Be sure to check with your bank that your cheque card is valid for use in Majorca, Spain. British National Girobank account holders, with postcheques and an international card, can draw the equivalent of £65 at a time in Spanish banks.

When you go to the bank you will need to take your cheque book, cheque card or travellers cheques and your passport; they will probably wish to know where you are staying. One can also cash travellers cheques and exchange currency in travel agents and hotels. The currency exchange rate is displayed in most banks and travel agents. A small charge is made for the transaction. The larger hotels will have deposit boxes or small safes for guests to lock up their valuables. The Mallorquins generally are law abiding but in busy plazas, markets and at fiesta time it is sensible to take precautions against pickpockets.

Duty free allowance

When you are returning to the UK from Spain, your duty-free allowance (adults only) is as follows:
– 300 cigarettes or 75 cigars **or** 400 grms of tobacco
– 5 litres of still wine
– 1½ litres of spirits over 22% **or** 3 litres below 22%
  (eg fortified or sparkling wine)
  or a further 3 litres of wine
– 90 cc perfume
– 375 cc toilet water
Other goods to the value of £420, but no more than 50 litres of beer, or more than 25 mechanical lighters.

Electricity

Electric current voltage is 220 to 225 AC; plugs are the round, two-pin variety.

Fire precautions

Fire precautions are observed in Majorca, with public buildings being inspected for adequate fire escape equipment. Details of emergency exits are shown in each hotel room. Modern fire fighting equipment is located in all places of population.

The Fire Brigade is located at Gremio Albaniles, Poligona La Victoria, Palma. Tel: 75 12 34.

Hairdressing

Men's barbers are called *barberia*, and ladies' salons *peluqueria*. Many hotels have their own salons, with prices varying according to the class of establishment. Average price for a shampoo and set in a town shop is 1000 pesetas while a man's haircut is 600 to 800 pestas.

Health

There are no dangerous animals or poisonous reptiles in Majorca, not too many flies, and mosquitoes are only a nuisance when there has been rain, which is rare. The Mediterranean climate is generally a healthy one, sea breezes move the air on most days, even during the summer months. In winter it is never extremely cold except in the high mountain regions. Usually the greatest health problem to visitors is caused by over indulgence of food and drink, coupled with sitting too long in the hot sunshine.

Care must be taken to ensure that salads and fruit are quite clean before being consumed. Water fit for drinking is *agua potable; agua non potable* is unsuitable. It is suggested that if your stay is of short duration you buy the bottled water to drink. Available at all supermarkets it is cheap and pleasant; this *agua mineral* is either aerated *(con gas)* or still *(sin gas)*.

Cases of upset tummies or diarrhoea are not to be expected but should these occur avoid alcoholic drinks and salads. Take a suitable medication such as Salvacolina, a Spanish product that is available from any chemist *(farmacia)*.

Be careful to avoid too much exposure of the body to the sun; beware especially of falling asleep whilst sun bathing. The wearing of sunglasses, hats and the early use of a suntan lotion or cream is sensible. Do not wait until the skin is turning red, that may be too late.

Sunstroke can be very distressing. Symptoms are a severe headache, vomiting and much discomfort. Mild cases require a cool shaded room with plenty of liquid to drink ("Seven-Up" is helpful). Apply calamine or similar cream to affected parts. If the skin is blistered or symptoms are not improving, do not hesitate to consult a chemist or doctor. Hotels have the addresses and telephone numbers of the nearest doctor or clinic.

Holidays and festivals

Remember that shops, offices, post offices, banks and petrol filling stations are closed on public holidays and fiesta days. Spanish national holidays are as follows:

January	1	– New Year's Day
January	6	– Epiphany
March	19	– San José
(variable)		– Good Friday
		– Easter Monday
May	1	– Labour Day
(variable)		– Corpus Christi
(variable)		– Ascension
June	24	– San Juan
June	29	– San Pedro and San Pablo
July	18	– National Day
July	25	– Santiago Apostal
August	15	– The Assumption
October	12	– Día de la Hispanidad
November	1	– All Saints
December	8	– Immaculate Conception
December	25	– Christmas Day

Calendar of Majorcan fiestas and festivals

January	6	– Palma: Cavalcade of the Wise Men of the East.
	15	– La Puebla: San Antonio Abad
	17	– Declared Day of Tourist Interest
February		– Almond trees in blossom, first ten days Carnival Procession in Playa de Palma
March		– Fourth Sunday in Lent, San Juan, Feast of Fish and Bread (Pan i Peix) Romeria (pilgrimage).
April		– Palma: Holy Week, religious processions.
		– Pollença; procession of tourist interest.
May		– Sóller: Christians and Moors fighting, Feast of the Virgin of Victory.
June		– Marratxi: Romeria San Marcial, market.
July	20	– Valldemossa: Feast of Santa Catalina Thomas "La Beata", holiday cart procession.
		– Sa Calobra and Torrente de Pareis, Escora: choral concert.
August	24	– Montuiri: Feast of the Patron Saint.
		– Pollença: Santo Domingo Cloister, musical festivals.
September	30	– Villafranca: Feast of the Melon
		– Binissalem: Grape Harvest
October	7	– San Juan: "Butifarro" holiday.
		– Inca: Feast of Cattle and craftmanship exhibition.
	3	– Petra: Eating of Buns. Commemoration of founder of Missions in California, Fray Junipero Serra.
December	18	– Capdepera: Nuestra Señora de la Esperanza.
	31	– Palma: commemoration of the Conquest by Jaime I, market of Bethlehem figures in Plaza España.

(Some of these festivals and fiestas are described in Chapter 9)

Fiestas of special interest to tourists

16 July, Virgin of Carmen. The Patron Saint of fishermen and sailors: port towns celebrate with decorated boats and fancy dress parades.

Inside the house in Petra where Junipero Serra was born stands this antique desk with a visitor's book full of signatures from all over the world.

24 – 26 July, Algaida. Devil and Dame in shabby rags and fearful masks. He with horns and cattle bell around his neck. The Dame represents good and triumphs over evil. This event is re-enacted at different times in other villages.

28 August, Falanitx. A prosperous inland farming town has a fair and fiesta. A medieval dance is performed by six children about the age of twelve. They are dressed as cardboard horses and perform a fertility dance around a Dame.

7 October, Festa d' Es Butifarro. The feast first started in 1960. After the finish of the Automobile, Motorcycle and Tractor Contests, there was much celebration and the eating of sausages, called Berenada de Butifarro i Llonganissa. Nowadays the jollification includes typical folk dancing, the playing of bagpipes *(xeremies capsgrosso)*, and the eating of a vegetable pie called Coca Amb Trampo. Increasingly popular, this fiesta takes place in several parts of the island, when the cooking of sausages over a bonfire is the highlight of the evening.

31 October, Witches and Warlocks. To celebrate All Saints (All Souls, All Hallows) pumpkins are replaced by a necklace made of sweets as an imitation rosary. Pastry and sweet shops are full of these decorations in all lengths and sizes from simple to expensive. The Spanish decorate graves with chrysanthemums while Majorcans take tools in donkey carts to freshen up the cemeteries.

24 December, midnight Mass. In Palma Cathedral, when a young Mallorcan choirboy or girl sings an ancient song called *Sa Sibla* (about the end of the world). After the Mass the usual custom is to go to a café for a hot chocolate drink, in which one dunks an *ensaimada,* the rich breakfast pastry in the shape of a snail.

5 January, Arrival of the Three Kings. They arrive at night in Palma by sea, amid great excitement, especially for the children. The harbour is a blaze of lights and decorations, with brilliant fireworks to brighten the sky. The Kings go in procession to the Plaza de Cort, where they distribute sweets and toys. Next morning the children awake hopefully to find their long desired presents at the end of the bed. Tradition says their shoes should be filled.

Laundry and dry cleaning

If you wish to have clothes cleaned and laundered it is probably easier to use the services of your hotel or apartment. Maids collect laundry and a list of charges is usually put in each room. There are self service launderettes *(lavanderia)* where you can wash and dry clothes. Cost is about 1,200 pesetas for seven kilos. Make sure that you are getting the service you require: dry cleaning is *tintoreria.* You will be delighted with the quick drying speed of clothes you hand wash, even if they are not put in the sun, but left to drip dry in the bathroom. There are plenty of washing powders and detergents available in shops.

*Amongst the many stalls at the Sunday morning market at Sa Pobla,
you will see a bright array of copper utensils.*

Markets

For fresh meats and vegetables you may like to visit the local markets *(mercados)*, where you will see fruit and vegetables arriving straight from the farms. Sometimes poultry will be killed as required. In Palma the *mercado* is located at Plaza Olivar from 0900 to 1300 hrs, weekdays.

Market days in Majorca are:

Alcudia	– Tue & Sun	Inca	– Thursday
Andratx	– Wednesday	Llucmajor	– Wed & Sun
Arenal	– Thursday	Manacor	– Monday
Arta	– Tuesday	Pollença	– Sunday
Binissalem	– Friday	Santanyi	– Saturday
Calvia	– Monday	Sóller	– Saturday
Felanitx	– Sunday	Son Cevera	– Friday

The market at Sineu, on a Wednesday, has preserved its traditional atmosphere by specialising in livestock. It is worth getting there early, by 0900 hrs, to see the cattle, sheep, goats and horses arrive for the sales.

Best known of all the markets in Majorca is the Rastrillo, or flea market, which is held in Palma on a Saturday morning; going on until about 1400 hrs. This is not a meat and vegetable market but there you will find everything from antiques to buttons. This market is fully described in Chapter 10.

Hypermarkets

On the outskirts of Palma are two large hypermarkets; both are well worth a visit for all types of shopping and car parking is no problem. **Continente** is the name of the hypermarket located just off the main autopista to the airport, near Coll d'en Rabassa. It is about six kilometres east of Palma. Here you can use Visa supported by your passport. As with all modern hypers you will find a large selection of electric and household goods, toys, clothes and footwear. Camping equipment, including Camping Gaz is stocked and used cylinders can be exchanged. Prices of most fresh, frozen and tinned foods are competitive, though sometimes the large packaging is not suitable for the short stay visitor. Restaurant, bars and toilets are added facilities. Smaller hypermarkets have recently been opened on the outskirts of towns.

To locate the **Pryca** hypermarket you will need to drive through the centre of Palma, it is advisable to look at a map of the city roads first.

Briefly, the way to reach it is to drive northwards on the route leading to Esporles and Establiments.

Both these hypermarkets are open from 1000 to 2200 hrs, closed on Sundays and public holidays.

Medical services

Spain has now joined the EEC and reciprocal medical services (Form Elll) apply in Spain, but you should assume that medical and hospital expenses have to be paid for. In the case of hospitals, operations usually have to be paid for in advance or guaranteed, so it is wise to take out insurance to cover this eventuality before leaving the UK. Emergency services are covered by the following:

– Hospital, Cruz Roja, Pons y Gallarza, 150, Palma (Tel: 28 91 00).
– Casa de Socorro, Plaza Santa Eulalia, Palma (Tel: 22 21 79).
– Centro Médico, Paseo Maritimo, 16, Palma (Tel: 23 00 23).
– Centro Médico, Gran Via, 50, C'an Pastilla (Tel: 26 41 41).
– Medical Centre of Majorca, Po del Mar, Palma Nova (Tel: 68 11 86).
– Emergency Medical Centre, Juan 23, 52, Port de Pollença (Tel: 53 25 64)
– Ambulancias (Ambulances), J. Mendez, Palma (Tel: 23 83 83).
– Ambulancias Urgencias. (Tel: 72 22 22).

Doctors

Doctors *(médicos)* have clinics which are run in a business-like manner. In tourist resorts, there would be an English-speaking receptionist. You usually get immediate attention and pay about 5000 pesetas for a visit or consultation. They will give you a receipt for insurance purposes. It is advisable to keep some pesetas available in case you should need emergency treatment at a time when the banks are not open, as payment is always required when medical treatment is given. If you are given a prescription you take it to a chemist *(farmacia)* whose sign is a green Maltese Cross. Unlike in the UK, where chemists also sell toiletries and cosmetics, the *farmacia* sells only medications but the staff are also able to give advice and first aid.

There are also first aid posts *(Casa de Socorro),* which are a national service. These posts are often in the country and the buildings are marked with a red cross and a road sign.

Our personal experience with doctors, dentists and opticians is of a kindly and qualified service, given with every consideration being made for the fact that one is a tourist in a foreign land.

Dentists

Dentists *(dentistas)* are fully qualified, their service is good and they use modern equipment. There are private practices and clinics *(clinicas)* where the group work is done. Generally as a tourist you can call at a surgery and take your turn. Not all dentists will speak English, but in tourist areas the receptionist will be used to dealing with holidaymakers. Make sure that your holiday insurance covers emergency dental treatment. As with doctors, treatment has to be paid for when received.
– Clinica Dental, Calle Fco Suav 2, Palma (Correr Calle 31 Diciembre) (Tel: 75 31 0).

Opticians

Opticians *(opticas)* provide a good service. In towns and tourist centres they are able to test your vision, without charge, and supply spectacles in about forty-eight hours. Generally charges are lower than in the UK, with a very good choice of frames.
– Doctor Herrero, Policlinica Miramar, Palma. (Tel: 28 76 00)
– Optica Moreno, Calle 31 Diciembre, Palma. (Tel: 29 08 08)

Newspapers and books

English daily and Sunday papers can be obtained in Palma, at the airport and in the major tourist complexes, usually on the day of publication. The cost is about three times the UK price. Some English and American periodicals are available. There is a wide choice of English paperbacks if you are prepared to pay the higher price. The Universal Bookshop, Ctra. Andratx 26, Portals Nous, has a selection of new and used books in English. Majorca has one daily English language newspaper, the widely distributed *Majorca Daily Bulletin* costing 75 pesetas. The office publishing this paper is at Sanfelio 17, Palma (Tel: 21 61 10.) Printed Tuesday to Saturday inclusive, it is useful for day-to-day news of the island, with local advertisements, entertainments, restaurants, sports and events; it includes some world news.

There is also an English language magazine called *Welcome to Majorca* which costs 200 pesetas. The office is at Lloyds Publications, Plaza Mayor 4, Palma. It is a two monthly edition, with very helpful information and ideal for the first time visitor and for those who want to know about island happenings; a really handy reference for the holidaymaker, it includes bus and train timetables, details of radio programmes, restaurants, sport, church services and even a map of the island.

The *Mallorca Tourist Info* is a newspaper published quarterly in four languages and costs 375 pesetas. There is also the *Mallorcan Reader*, published fortnightly, costing 100 pesetas and providing local news, information and light entertainment.

Security

Although the Spanish police have increased their vigilance, as elsewhere, petty crime is still prevalent, especially in the tourist resorts. It is always wise to use the hotel safe deposit boxes provided for your passport, jewellery and traveller's cheques. Lock your room door and the door leading to the balcony or terrace. Avoid carrying large sums of money. Your handbag should be carried away from the road side to avoid it being snatched by a motorcyclist. Do not put your wallet in your back trousers pocket, and be alert when leaving a bank. Cameras are a prime target, crowded markets and fiestas are places to be extra careful. Never leave valuables in a car. It is suggested that you make a photocopy of the relevant information on your passport and that you record details of credit cards, driving licence and airline tickets, to facilitate replacement in the event of loss. Keep these separate from the originals.

Always report incidents of loss to the police. You will need evidence of having done this if you are going to make a claim on your insurance. It is helpful to have a witness. There is a Lost Property Office in all major Spanish towns; stolen items have turned up in this way if not of marketable value. If the worst comes, do not offer resistance. It is not worth being heroic. Your safety is surely more important than possessions.

Police

There are several types of police in Majorca. The **Guardia Civil** wear a green uniform with a shiny black hat (this is now being replaced by a soft peaked cap). They are armed law enforcement officers. It is advisable not to get involved in a misunderstanding with them; they rarely admit to speaking English and have a great deal of power. The **National Guard** wear a brown uniform with a beret and are an anti-crime force. The **Municipal Police** wear a blue uniform; their duties are local and general. Finally the **Traffic Police,** besides controlling traffic, give assistance with breakdowns and accidents.

Their patrol cars are marked *Tráfico Policia* and they also use motorcycles.

All types of police are approachable and helpful, especially the Traffic Police. Telephone numbers in Palma: Police – 091 and 092; Guardia Civil – 46 51 12; Traffic Police – 22 50 40.

Problems and complaints

Complaints about accommodation should be made on official complaint forms *(hojas de reclamaciones);* tourist establishments should have these, but usually the hotel receptionist or the public relations person will sort out any problem you may have; they mostly speak English.

In extreme cases it may be necessary to go to the local police *(policia municipal)* or the town hall *(ayuntamiento)*. You will find officials pleased to assist, but be patient, the Mallorquin way of life is not to hurry.

Public conveniences

Public conveniences as known in the UK are not very often seen in Majorca. They can be found in market places *(mercado)*, petrol filling stations, bus and railway stations. Look for signs marked *aeso* or *servicios* and either *señoras* (ladies) or *caballeros* (gentlemen). Pictographs are often used; perhaps a fan and a Spanish sombrero, or a high-heeled shoe and a boot; some imagination is required! Generally the public use the facilities of a bar, café, restaurant or hotel. It is not necessary to be a customer but they prefer it when you are.

Radio

There are local radio stations in Majorca. Radio Antenna 3 broadcasts on FM, 103.2 mHz in English, times of programmes are given in the local papers. It is possible to hear Radio 4 on Long Wave and Radio 2 on Medium Wave when atmospheric conditions allow and a good aerial is used. The World Service of the BBC can be heard on Short Wave.

Shopping

Shopping in Majorca is very much the same as in the UK and Europe; though shops are open from 0900 to 1300 hrs and 1600 to 1900 hrs, on Saturdays they close at 1300 hrs and are generally closed all day on Sundays and public holidays. An abundance of supermarkets can be found in all the towns, and increasingly in small villages now. Prices are marked on most goods; remember that weight is by kilogramme (2.2 lb) or part thereof. Measurement is by the metre (there is a conversion table at the end of this book). Shopping baskets and trolleys are available in some of the larger stores, any personal parcels may have to be deposited at the entrance and a numbered tag is given as a receipt.

In tourist areas the shop assistants will understand English and generally are pleasant and helpful. In some shops you are expected to select your own vegetables, but in others an assistant will serve you. At the delicatessen, meat, fish and cheese counter you will be served. It may be necessary to take a numbered ticket to get your place in the queue for service. A good selection of frozen foods is always available; local fish and meat are prepacked and frozen at reasonable prices.

Buying clothes locally

The main tourist resorts have a good selection of clothes shops, including a great number of boutiques which stock very modern styles. Prices range widely. Many of the Paris and international fashion names have shops, often in the larger hotels. In Palma the big stores have whole floors of clothing to suit all ages and styles. Bargain counters with sales good are marked *rebaja*. It is useful to check on your continental, metric size before going shopping as not all the assistants will understand the old-fashioned English sizes. When buying in open air village markets check that the goods are not shop-soiled or flawed. Children's and baby clothes are often very attractive and colourful. Beach and sportswear can be purchased in the larger supermarkets, also lightweight shoes and sunhats.

Souvenirs

A popular way to buy souvenirs in Majorca is to watch them being made, then make your purchase in the adjacent shop. The pearl factories at **Manacor** started the trend; now visits can be made to leather, olive-wood carving, glass blowing, wrought-iron work and shoe-making factories. Amongst other items worth looking for are embroidered table cloths, beautiful Spanish fans, leather handbags, rope-soled shoes, costume dolls, hand-woven baskets and local pottery. Some tobacco and alcoholic drinks are cheap. The local liqueurs, made from honey, almonds and apricots, have the distinctive sweet flavour of Majorca.

When shopping for genuine Mallorquin souvenirs watch out for imported goods that are on display amongst the local wares; often that attractive straw basket has originated in China!

Where ever you decide to do your shopping it is worth comparing prices as there is quite a variation between shops. When your purchases amount to a substantial sum such as £50, you may be able to claim a discount as a visitor from abroad. This applies in the large departmental store **Gallerias Preciâdos,** Avenida Jaime III, in Palma.

One item of special interest is a Majorcan *siurell*. This is a rather crude and cheap clay figure of a man on a donkey, generally painted white, green and red. The origin of this quaint figure with its built-in whistle, is unknown, but it is said to have been brought to life by the first inhabitants of Majorca. Although the significance of this form is long forgotten, it has become a symbol of friendship that Mallorquins bestow on visitors. It is an amusing, decorative and inexpensive piece to take home. These unusual figures are manufactured at the village of Sa Cabaneta, six kilometres south of Santa Maria.

Television

There are three TV channels to be seen in Majorca on VHF and UHF. There is also satellite TV. Most bars and hotels have colour TV and, of course, nearly all programmes are in Spanish. Football matches are very popular. TV sets can be hired. British TV sets are not suitable for use in Spain and Majorca, unless modified. A satellite TV Guide can be had from the Satellite Centre, Illetes Shopping centre. Tel: 40 44 02.

Video

Video cassettes are very popular in Spain and Majorca. Libraries and clubs from where Spanish cassettes can be hired are found in Palma city and in towns and tourist resorts. Movies in English can be hired at Video, Punta Portals, Tel: 67 58 46, open daily from 1030 to 1330 and 1800 to 2200 hrs, Sunday 1800 to 2200 hrs. A small refundable deposit is required.

Time

Time is the same in Majorca as in mainland Spain, that is, one hour ahead of Greenwich Mean Time. Spain also has a summer time, the dates of this vary slightly against British Summer Time.

Tipping

A tip *(propina)* is expected by many people in the tourist industry, as in the UK and on the Continent. In bars, cafés and restaurants, even though a service charge may have been added, a tip can be given. The Mallorquins, like the Spanish, are proud and well mannered and do not make much of the subject.

Porters, maids and cloak room attendants should also be tipped 50 pesetas, though porters at the airport will have a fixed charge per piece of baggage. Taxi drivers expect a ten per cent tip.

SEVEN

Food and drink

Majorca, like the majority of the Mediterranean islands, has a great variety of food and drink for the visitor to enjoy. In Palma and the major tourist places, exotic foods from all over the world can be obtained, with a fine selection of gourmet and epicure foods. Most food prices now compare favourably with the rest of Europe, locally produced fresh fruit and vegetables are often cheaper than in the UK.

Food on the menu

Meat *(carne)* is plentiful and butchers' shops *(carnicerea)* will have a good selection, though you will find that the cuts are different from those in the UK. Unless otherwise told, the butcher will cut chops and steaks very thinly. If you wish for minced beef *(carne picada)* you will first select your beef and little or no fat will be included. Local pork *(cerdo)* is excellent, pork chops are on every menu as *chuleta de cerdo. Lomo de cerdo* is the prime cut off the loin and is considered a speciality, only surpassed by *lechón,* roast suckling pig. Lamb *(cordero)* and mutton *(carne de carnero)* are less available and more expensive. Liver *(higado)* and kidney *(rinon)* are cheap and tasty. Very succulent is young goat *(cabrito)* which is roasted on many festive occasions. Rabbit *(conejo)* is part of the staple diet of the Mallorquins and much used in stews. Fresh and frozen chicken *(pollo)* is always available and it can be purchased in portions or whole; if you choose the latter you will probably receive it with head and claws still attached, but it will have been cleaned inside.

Fish *(pescado)* is much in demand by the Mallorquins and sometimes the supplies run out early in the day. Many restaurants make a speciality of their fish dishes, sea foods being especially popular. Both the hypermarkets, Continente and Pryca, have a good selection but prices remain high. Varieties include cod *(bacalao),* hake *(merluza)*, red mullet *(salmonete)*, prawns *(gambas)*, tuna *(atun)*, sole *(lenguado)*, sardines *(sardinas)*, and squid *(calarmares)*.

Cheese *(queso)* is imported from many countries and from the nearby island of Menorca. The local Mallorquin cheese is hard with a light rind; look for one made by the firm **Pires**, which will keep well if stored in a cool place. Price is about 570 pesetas a kilo.

Eggs *(huevos)* are stocked by almost every food shop. There must be a constant demand for them as they are always fresh enough to enjoy boiled for breakfast!

Milk *(leche)* is not sold fresh in many supermarkets, although there are cows on the island. Most milk is of the long life variety in cartons or plastic bottles. Tinned and powdered milk are easily obtainable.

Bread *(pan)* is sold in supermarkets, but the place to buy it really fresh is at the baker's shop *(panaderia)*. Rolls and bread are light and crusty but not as crisp as French bread. Some shops supply brown bread.

Cakes may be bought at a *pasteleria*, often open on a Sunday, and the selection will be mouth-watering. Sweets and chocolates *(confites y bombons)* are also bought at a *pasteleria*.

Tea *(té)* and coffee *(café)* of assorted varieties are on sale in supermarkets. It could be worth your while to take both commodities with you if you plan to stay a long time, as they are quite a lot more expensive than in the UK.

Vegetables *(legumbre)* and fruit *(fruta)* are of very good quality all the year round in Majorca. Delicious new potatoes, peas, beans, spinach, carrots, salad foods, avocados, artichokes and asparagus are but a few. Peaches, apples, apricots and strawberries are among the locally produced fruits. Majorca is also renowned for its tasty olives and excellent almonds.

Some local dishes

It is quite possible to have "a real English breakfast" at all tourist spots in Majorca, the sign is displayed everywhere. But do try some of the local specialities as well.

Bacalao: Codfish cooked in a tomato casserole.

Berengenas al horno: Stuffed aubergines, filled with grilled meat.

Caldera de peix: Fish soup made with rice and slices of bread.

Coco: Pastry tarts made with vegetables and fish, pizza style, very good for snacks and picnics.

Empanada: Meat and vegetable pie.

Ensaimada: Typical Mallorquin pastry, rather like a spiral of croissant; it is sometimes filled with jam and cream sauce.

Escalduns: Stews made from chicken and potatoes in an almond sauce.

Fish and fishing boats

Traditionally, in the Mediterranean islands the fishing boats are handed down from one generation to the next, and in Majorca the majority of the fishermen are locals. The Majorcan fishing boats are small sturdy craft, called *llauds*; there are many types but normally they are one and a half to three metres at the beam. Always painted in bold colours with their name and registration number on the prow, they are a bright feature in most ports. The main fishing fleet is located in Palma, on the quay opposite the La Lonja Museum, a little way to the west of the cathedral. If you wish to see boats returning to harbour you will have to be there at about 0530 hrs. They usually go out to sea in the middle of the night.

A great variety of fish are caught. Firstly, there are the shell fish and molluscs, prawns, shrimps, mussels, crabs and clams. These are used to make a Spanish paella. Other fish include sardines, anchovies, octopus, squid, rays, and cuttlefish, not forgetting the giant swordfish and sharks which are caught by the *barca de bou*, boats which stay at sea for about a week and fish more than thirty kilometres off shore, even going as far as Morocco and Tunisia. Popular, too, are the flat fish such as sole and bluefish, also cod, hake, red mullet and bream, all of which can be enjoyed in Majorca in the many fish restaurants.

Fish markets are lively places and Palma has several covered markets, the newest and most modern is the Tems Market located on Calle Juan Crespi, up the hill from the Plaza Progreso, about fifteen minutes walk from the Paseo Maritimo.

Lomo con seta: Fried pork and mushrooms.

Paella: This is the best known Spanish dish. It is rice cooked with saffron in a special *paella* dish to which meats, fish and vegetables are added. It is usually freshly prepared and takes about half an hour to cook.

Sobrasada: A bright red sausage flavoured with paprika.

Sopas Mallorquinas: Mixed green vegetables in a soup, oil and bread; often this has chick peas and meat added so that it becomes almost a complete meal.

Tapas: Not a speciality of Majorca, but served in all local bars. These are delicious bite-size savoury snacks, which are eaten with a drink; usually they comprise sea foods, meatballs, vegetable salads, fried fish and olives. The word *tapa* means lid: in the old days a small portion of food would come served on a tiny dish, which was put on top of the glass. Today, these snacks make a light and tasty meal.

Tumbet: Aubergines, peppers, tomatoes and potatoes fried in oil.

Drinks

Majorca does not produce enough wine to export. However around Binissalem and Felanitx a very pleasant red wine is bottled; it is to be found on many wine lists and on supermarket shelves. Try the one called Franja Roja, costing about 545 pesetas and the Vina Paumina at 480 pesetas. Mayola is pleasant, too, 9.5º proof.

Most of the wine on the island is imported from Spain; among the best of the cheaper ones are those from Valdepenas and Jumilla. For a higher quality try the Riojas. Recently wine has been imported in cartons, at the very low price of 110 pesetas for a litre of San Simon Jumilla, which is very useful for picnics.

Liqueurs are produced on the island, including the Hierbas, which can be *seca* (dry herbs) or *dulce* (sweet herbs); they have a strong flavour of aniseed. Palo is another local liqueur made from crushed fermented carob seeds; it is very sweet and sticky and usually laced with gin.

Spanish imported brandy *(coñac)* is said to have a less delicate flavour than French brandy and is much cheaper. Soberano and Fundador are two that are 37º proof and cost about 700 pesetas a litre. Spanish gin is usually about the same price and strength, well known names are Rives and Larios. The gin from nearby Menorca, called Lord Nelson, is 70º proof and tastes like British gin.

Sangria is a popular Spanish drink which is usually served in a jug for two or more people. It is a mixture of red wine, orange juice, brandy, mineral water, slices of fruit and plenty of ice. Refreshingly cool, it can be more potent than it tastes.

It is possible to buy English beer from the keg in a number of bars, in the tourist resorts; however the local beer *(cerveza)* is a light, cool and refreshing drink. Mineral waters and soft drinks, such as Coca Cola and Seven-Up are plentiful. The latter drink can be helpful if you have a queasy tummy.

When asking for a cup of coffee *(café)* you are likely to get a small cup of very strong black *(espresso)* coffee. If you require a big cup of the same, ask for a *café largo;* with milk it is *café con leche* or *café cortado*. Best of all, try it with some *coñac;* this is a Mallorquin speciality called *café carajillo,* which is delicious and will make you feel happy!

Bars and cafés

Bars and cafés are very much a way of life in Spain and Majorca. They often open up very early in the morning and will give a service until the last customer has gone, late into the night. Open air cafés are justifiably very popular with holidaymakers, who can sit in the glorious sunshine enjoying a coffee or chocolate. You may sit at your table as long as you wish and it is not necessary to pay for your drinks until you leave. If you sit at the bar for a drink, it is generally cheaper than when served at a table. A small tip *(propina)* is usual (see Tipping, Chapter 6). Wines and spirits are served at all hours of the day and night.

It is quite in order for unaccompanied females to use cafés and bars; friends will meet for a glass of wine and some olives, talking for a considerable time. The end of the afternoon is the time when Mallorquin wives take a cup of chocolate and *churros,* delicious sweet fritters. Children, too, are seen at all hours in the bars and cafés and no one seems to resent their presence.

Cafeterias are not always self-service restaurants but are bars that serve meals like hamburgers and chicken and chips. If you see the word *desayuno,* it means breakfast, which usually consists of coffee, rolls or toast, butter and jam. In tourist places British breakfasts and British beer are available.

Restaurants

In Majorca the variety of eating establishments allows a wide choice and excellent standards are maintained by many of the restaurants. An international cuisine gives the gourmet a splendid opportunity to indulge in dishes ranging through chateaubriand and lobster thermidor to paella and pizzas, homemade sorbets and fresh strawberries. Palma in particular has a vast selection of colourful restaurants. Besides the local Mallorquin menus, you will find places that specialise in Chinese, German, Swedish, Italian and vegetarian cooking. If you are on a package holiday, then the courier will be able to recommend a suitable place to suit your tastes and pocket.

Restaurants in Spain are graded into four categories, denoted by the

These two old windmills are a notable landmark, seen from the seafront of Palma. To reach them you must go to the area known as Es Jonquet, where there are bars and restaurants.

number of forks *(tendores)* shown. The grading reflects the price rather than the quality of food, the higher number of forks the more expensive the food.

All restaurants in Majorca must display a tourist menu of the day *(menu del día)*. This usually comprises a substantial soup, grilled steak or chop, salad, potatoes, bread, ice cream, fruit or caramel custard *(flan)* and wine. Average price at a small restaurant would be 800 pesetas. Except for lower priced restaurants, most accept one or more credit cards.

Restaurants are open for lunch from 1300 to 1500 hrs. Dinner is normally served from 2000 hrs, but in the tourist areas it is available earlier. If you wish to keep the cost down order the house wine *(vino de casa);* it will be drinkable, possibly a local wine, and half the price of the bottled wine.

One of the best ways to sample local food is to eat where the Mallorquins gather. Do not be shy to enter, the locals will be too busy talking and they are used to seeing tourists.

Out of town bars often have restaurants behind, so do not be put off if you cannot see where there is a table. Sometimes you will be pleasantly surprised and led to a delightful hidden garden patio. If you wish to please the restaurateur ask to go into the kitchen, then select your food from the many steaming pots. This can be a delightful experience, especially in the country areas where the whole family will gather to see what you choose!

A selection of restaurants in Palma

Tourist offices have a list of recommended restaurants and the local newspapers have many advertisements that describe various places to dine and their menus.

This selection gives an idea of the range of specialities available.

Adolfo Calle Bellver 10. Tel: 23 79 69. (near Plaza Gomila) Specialities: baked lamb, chateaubriand with bearnaise sauce. A summer terrace and charming interior dining room, a graceful and romantic setting. Closed Mondays.

Al Entrecote Calle Apuntadores 3. Tel: 72 59 05. Popular steak house which also serves shoppers' menu.

Aragones Calle San Jaime 3. Tel: 22 39 19. (round the corner from C & A store) Specialities: chicken in garlic sauce, pork tenderloin Aragones style. Aragon dishes. In old quarter of city.

Ca'n Miquelet Galeria Jaime 3. Tel: 72 12 09. In side alley off Calle Jaime 3. Traditional Mallorcan dishes and tapas. Closed Sunday.

Casa Eduardo El Porto de la Lonja. Tel: 22 11 82. Right on the quayside. Specialities: white fish prepared with greens, Mallorquin style, lobster. Closed on Sunday and Monday.

Casa Gallega Plaza de Weyler. Tel: 21 43 66. (near Avenida Unio, across from the Court House) Specialities: Atlantic seafoods, flown in daily from Galicia. Galician wine. Tapas or snacks. Upstairs dining room. Open every day.

Celler Montenegro Calle Montenegro 10b. Tel: 22 61 51. (off Calle Apuntadores) Specialities: fresh sardines fried, pork tenderloin prepared in the Montenegro style. A cellar type establishment, homely atmosphere, typical Mallorquin dishes. Menu of the day 500 pesetas. Closed Saturday night and Sunday.

El Gallo Teniente Torres 17. Tel: 23 74 11. Popular with business men at lunch time. Sea food specialities. Airconditioned. Closed Saturday lunch and closed Sunday.

El Grotto Plaça Major. Pizzeria, fast service and economical prices.

El Jardin Calle Joan Miro 57. Tel: 45 49 70. (near Plaza Gomila) Specialities: salad buffet, entrecote with baked potatoes. Honest to goodness outdoor terrace restaurant, open grill set amongst lovely garden and palms.

El Meson Apuntadores 4. Tel: 72 60 44. A small but delightful eating place with friendly service in this street of *típico* restaurants. Tourist menu and fresh fish to order. Reasonable prices.

El Patio Plaza Gomila. Tel: 23 24 41. Specialities: duck à l'orange, lobster thermidor. International, sophisticated, comfortable. Closed Sunday.

El Pilon Calle San Cayetano 12. Well established, good class restaurant. International menu and fresh fish, also noted for its excellent tapas bar.

Gina Plaza de la Lonja (off Paseo Sagrera). Tel: 22 64 84. Speciality fresh fish from fishing boats across the road. Also good pepper steaks. You can eat outside.

Maritimo Calle Orillo. Opposite yacht harbour. Inexpensive well cooked food. Menu of the day 850 pesetas. Pleasant to sit at tables under palm trees. Closed Sundays.

Olas Plaza Gomila. Tel: 23 50 99. Specialities: T-bone steak, pepper steak. Intimate, candlelit atmosphere, open grill. Open every day.

Pizzeria Marechiare Calle Federico Garcia Lorca 19. Tel: 45 33 46. (at the back of Edificio La Caleta) Specialities: selection of twenty five pizzas, a variety of cheese, patés and Italian pastas. Family restaurant, pergola terrace. Open kitchen. Average prices. Closed Wednesday midday.

Rififi Joan Miro 182. Tel: 40 20 35. Specialities: baked fish with greens, onions and pine nuts, lobster. Always busy. Closed Tuesday.

Zarzagan Paseo Maritimo 13. Tel: 23 74 47. Near Auditorium and Victoria centre, overlooking harbour. High quality international cuisine and good service.

• Chinese restaurants

China Peking Paseo Maritimo 20. Tel: 23 26 51. At the western end of city seafront, opposite Maritimo docks. A quiet, clean Chinese restaurant with air conditioning. Tasty dishes and reasonable prices.

De Shangrila Edificio Miramar, Paseo Maritimo. Tel: 45 25 75. Traditional Chinese menu. Airconditioned, friendly service in oriental surroundings.

El Jardin Chino Plaza Mediterraneo. Tel: 23 00 53. (near Plaza Gomila) Specialities: duck in orange sauce, beef with hot sauce. For night owls, disco lovers; cosy eating nooks. Open every day.

Maxim Calle Apuntadores 20. Tel: 22 13 71. Specialities: duck Maxim style, mixed Maxim rice. Lively street restaurant. Convenient for shoppers and sailors. Menu of the day 800 pesetas. Closed Thursday.

Σ• Vegetarian food

Sa Letuga El Jonquet 9. Tel: 45 48 77. (off San Magin) Specialities: vegetarian couscous, home-made bread, cheese, honey. Narrow antique building, three floors. Closed Sunday.

• Fast foods

McDonalds, Plaza Pio 12; **Wimpy,** Antonio Maura; and **Click,** Paseo Mallorca 8.

Restaurants southwest of Palma

• Genova

Ca'n Pedro Genova. On side of hill overlooking the Bay of Palma and close to the caves. This is well known and popular with residents. Extensive Mallorcan menu, famous for snails.

• Sant Agusti

Rajmas Avenida Joan Miro 309. Tel: 40 50 61. Tandoori restaurant fully licensed. Open every day from 1900 to 0130 hrs.

• Illetes

Bon Aire D'Iletes Avenida Adelfas. Tel: 40 00 48. High priced restaurant overlooking Bay of Palma. Swimming pool and children's play area. International, Spanish and Mallorcan cuisine. Roasts prepared in wood oven.

• Puerto Portals

Tristan Puerto Portals. Tel: 68 25 00. A smart expensive restaurant, close to the marina, with an attractive terrace and garden. Open all year. The dining room is airconditioned. Nouvelle cuisine, credit card, reservations recommended.

• Costa D'en Blanes

Crazy Dolphin Tel: 67 64 49. Open noon to 2300 hrs, closed Monday. International menu and Indonesian Risttafel.

• Palma Nova

Carole's Miguel de los Santos Oliver 9. Tel: 68 11 36. English run, friendly restaurant with extensive menu, including North Sea cod. Sunday lunch, roast beef, pork, lamb and chicken. Fish and chips.

Ciro's Paseo del Mar 3. Tel: 68 10 52. Large restaurant open from 1100 to 2400 hrs. Terrace, airconditioning. International menu with good service.

Tabu Paseo del Mar. Restaurant mainly used by tourists. Good value. Nearly opposite is the Fools Music and Video Pub, noisy and popular.

• Magalluf

Amagat Calle Punta Ballena 13, Edificio Complex. Tel: 68 23 55. A quiet clean place in the heart of busy Magalluf. Good selection of Mallorcan cuisine.

Bertorelli's Carretera Calla Figuera, next to aeroplane and near to Poniente Golf Course and Aguapark. Tel: 68 09 91. Offers a good value lunch time menu and gourmet evening meals. Open Tuesday to Saturday.

C'An Jaume Carretera Cala Figuera, near Aguapark. Tel: 68 03 82. Rural restaurant, peaceful atmosphere. Specialities, fresh pork and roast leg of lamb.

Pietros Villa Blanca, Calle Pinada 14-15. Tel: 68 25 65. Open 1200 to 2400 hrs. Credit cards, cheerful, includes out door dining and international menu.

• Santa Ponça

Espanoleto/Haarlem Calle Ramon Moncada 21. Tel: 69 00 91. Popular restaurant and pizzeria, with a large selection of dishes. Good service.

Las Vellas Puig Galatzo 4. Tel: 60 03 28. Open 1 April to 31 October. Close to beach, terrace. Family priced menu with good barbecue dishes. Salad buffet.

• Cala Fornells

La Gran Tortuga Aldea Cala Fornells. Tel: 68 60 23. High class, stylish atmosphere, terrace overlooks bay. International menu, guitarist in evening. Closed Monday and Tuesday lunch and from 15 January to 28 February.

• Port d'Andratx

Miramar Avenida Mateo Bosch. Tel: 67 16 17. In winter closed on Monday. This spacious restaurant, with terrace by the waterfront, serves good quality Mallorcan cooking. Formal service and expensive.

Rocamar Avenida Mateo Bosch. Tel: 67 12 61. Closed Monday. Medium priced restaurant that usually serves fresh fish and Mallorcan dishes. Good views of mountains and sea.

The west coast

• Port de Sóller

Es Canyis Puerto de Playa. Tel: 63 14 06. Closed Monday. Friendly, casual eating place on the seafront. Mallorcan and French dishes, grilled fish.

• Port de Pollença

Stay Muelle Nuevo (s/n Puerto). Tel: 53 00 13. Open all year and used by residents. First class restaurant located right by sea and beach. Outside terrace, spacious elegant decor. International cuisine. Highly recommended. Try the fresh salmon.

The north east coast

• Port d'Alcudia

El Yate Tel: 54 57 38. By beach next to harbour. Distinctive mauve decor with outside terrace under palm trees. International menu with average prices.

Las Sirenas Tel: 54 77 87. Along seafront by harbour. Air conditioned bar restaurant and tables under shaded terrace. Prompt service and reasonable prices.

Miramar Vicealmirante Moreno 4. Tel: 59 52 12. A good value, small restaurant by the sea, serving seafoods and regional dishes.

Terraxa Aucanada Tel: 54 56 11. Right at the water's edge towards lighthouse. Pleasant service with international menu in splendid quiet setting, closed in winter.

The east coast

• Cala d'Or

Bistro Calle Andres Roig 7. Tel: 65 81 10. Open 1200 to 1600 and 1800 to 2300 hrs. For special night out. Charcoal grill and international menu served inside or on terrace. Next door is a good pizzeria, Copa D'Or.

Sa Torre Avenida de Tagomago 19. Tel: 65 70 83. Closed Monday for lunch. Very popular with the locals at weekends. International and fish menu. Nice position overlooked by round tower. Menu of the day is good value.

Yate D'Or Avenida Belgica 4. Tel: 65 79 78. A restaurant recommended by the Tourist Office. It has a pretty patio and serves good seafood meals as well as an international menu.

• Porto Petro

Marina Patro Marina. Tel: 65 75 17. In this unspoilt fishing village. Small busy restaurant serving Mallorcan and fish dishes; nice sea view.

Porto Petro Calle Cristobal Colon 49. Tel: 65 77 04. In winter closed on Monday. Noted for fresh fish and paella. This established restaurant accepts credit cards.

• Colonia de San Pedro

El Pescador Calle San Juan. Tel: 58 90 78. Inland from the beach, in peaceful fishing village, this little restaurant serves delicious food, inside and on the patio. The owner has a boat so guarantees fresh fish, which is delicious but costly. Menu of the day is good value and well cooked.

Ses Roques Carretera Colonia Sant Jordi km75. Tel: 65 10 47. Popular with Mallorcans, especially at weekends. This large restaurant is set back off the road in the quiet countryside about five kilometres from Colonia Sant Jordi, on the main road to Campos. Imaginative menu, speciality fresh fish and Mallorcan dishes.

• Bahia de Palma

Bodega Oliver Calle Albatross Tel: 26 10 67. 100 metres from beach, with terrace and dark olive wood interior. Wood fire in winter. Generous portions of meat and fish.

La Arcada Avda Nacional Balneario (Exit 4 Motorway, next to Zorba's Disco). Tel: 26 14 50. International menu, including pasta and barbecued meat specialities. Terrace with beautiful view of the bay.

• C'An Pastilla

El Rancho Picadero Calle Flamenco 1. Tel: 26 10 02. Ten minutes walk behind the seafront. Large attractive restaurant with wooden ranch type decor. Outside terrace with wood burning cooking oven. Extensive menu and polite service.

• Algaida

Five restaurants that are well recommended and usefully situated almost centrally on the island, are found alongside the Palma to Manacor road (C715), near to Algaida.

Es 4 Vents This at km 21 is named after the four winds of Majorca (the north wind or Tramuntana, the Levant from the east, the Mitjorn from the south, and the Ponent which blows from the west). It is owned by a Mallorquin family and specialises in local foods. It is spotlessly clean and smart, with polished wooden tables, gleaming cutlery and bright red napkins. All clients are welcomed into the kitchen, where huge pots of soup simmer and fresh fish is prepared. At one end of the restaurant there is a wide open fire with a grill for cooking, even toast is made over the ashes. The menu caters mainly for Mallorquins and they also have a tourist *menu del día* for 800 pesetas. On the menu you should find *soupas* (soups), *cordero asado* (pork loin grilled), *chuletas cerdo* (pork chop), *biftec* (beefsteak thin), *lenguado* (sole), *tarta whisky* (sponge with whisky), *vino de la casa* (local wine). There is ample parking space. Closed on Thursdays. Telephone 66 51 73.

Sa Talaieta This is a similar type of bar restaurant a little to the west of Es 4 Vents at km 20, on the same Palma to Manacor road. Roughly translated the name means ''more or less''. It is an old building and less modern in style, nevertheless it is well run and meals though simple, are good *cocina Malloquina*. You can expect to see the local police *(guardia)* drinking at the bar, and children wandering amongst the tables. Very little English will be understood but the menu is in several languages, so it is not difficult to order a meal. Closed on Thursday. Ample parking space. Telephone 66 51 53.

El Dimonica, the Demon Bar restaurant, is situated in between these two restaurants and there is a fearsome statue outside that helps locate the place. It is a bit more rough and ready and therefore less expensive, but the food is recommended by English people living nearby. If you are interested in meeting the local working people, then you will enjoy a meal here.

Sa Gaflet, Palma – Manacor Road, km 10. Small restaurant with excellent atmosphere. Specialities, stuffed mussels and Steak of the House.

Ses Olleries (The Olive Jars). English residents recommend this highly individual restaurant near Santa Eugenia, just off the old Sineu road at km 14. Tel: 62 09 76. It is on the edge of a small quiet village, the approach road is narrow but there is plenty of parking space at the rear. Beware of the barking dogs though they are caged. To reach the entrance you walk through a sprawling and colourful garden and then enter a very old low building. Inside you will be greeted by the owner, Antonio, a real Mallorquin character. He will be delighted to inform you that he was head chef in a large New York hotel, that he has prepared banquets on a millionaire's yacht, making special dishes for King Juan Carlos. Then you will be shown his testaments and photographs of these auspicious occasions.

Around you are all sorts of old photographs and memorabilia. As you walk from the bar to the restaurant you will pass a well lit shrine to the Holy Family, set in natural rock. "We are all one family," says the smiling Antonio, "and my home is not a restaurant but a house where all may eat good food for little money." And this is true; his prices are reasonable for the high standard of cooking and presentation. The decor is fascinating, for the small dining room is a cave in the ground, where there are piles of old pottery dishes and cooking pots. At one end of the cave the wall extends up, allowing a waterfall to trickle to the bottom. Around the room huge olive jars and potted ferns mingle with family portraits.

It is well worth a visit to Ses Olleries where as it says on his card *"el cliente es el rey"* (every client is a king). Closed on Tuesdays.

• Inca

Chino Chang Dou Calle de Sant Bartolmeu. North of Plaça España. Primarily a Chinese restaurant, but they serve English and Spanish dishes. Menu of the day 700 and 900 pesetas. Credit cards accepted.
Raco Calle Dureta 1. Tel: 50 30 15. Open from 1300 hrs, side street off Plaça España. Small clean, family run bar restaurant mainly used by locals. Tasty Spanish food. Menu of the day 600 pesetas.

EIGHT

Leisure activities

Art galleries and museums

In 1849 the Academia Provincal de Belles Artes was founded. Since that time Majorca has been a country beloved by painters, both local and from abroad. Today a number of artists live in mountain villages like Deiá and Sant Vincenç. At Pollença an annual painting competition is held and the prizewinner's work is on permanent display.

The tourist offices have a list of art galleries. Fifteen are in Palma city, including the **Mansion de Arte** at Calle Apuntadores 45, where there are works by Ribera, Morales and Van Dyck plus two hundred Goya etchings. In the **Krekovic Museum** at Calle de Ciudad de Querétaro, Palma, there is a fine collection of paintings relating to the Inca period. Open from 1030 to 1330 hrs, closed on Sunday and public holidays (Tel: 24 66 62).

Museums in Palma

Museo Catedral Calle Palau Reial 29. Liturgical robes, religious relics and tapestries. Open Monday to Friday from 1000 to 1230 and 1600 to 1800 hrs, Saturday 1000 to 1400 hrs. Closed Sunday.

Museo Diocesano Calle Mirador 7. Archaeology, pottery and jewellery. Open 1000 to 2100 hrs.

Museo de Mallorca Portella 5. Paintings, furniture and ceramics. Open Tuesday to Saturday from 1000 to 1400 and 1400 to 1900 hrs, Sunday from 1000 to 1400 hrs.

Museo Municipal de Historia Castillo de Belver. Open April to September every day 0800 to 2000 hrs, October to March 0800 to 1800 hrs. Archaeological finds, old maps and antique coins.

One of the many graceful courtyards in Majorca. This one is at the entrance to the Junipero Serra Museum in Petra.

Bull fights

This is always a controversial subject. In recent years the popularity of bullfights has greatly declined in Majorca except in the town of Muro. The cheapest seats are in the sunshine *(sol)*, with those in the shade *(sombre)* costing more, ringside seats being the most expensive. It is well known that in Spain the only event that starts on time is the bull fight: 1700 or 1800 hrs on a Sunday. Palma has the third largest ring in Spain, seating 14,000, so you would not be alone at the **Plaza de Toros**, Avenida Coliseo Balear (Tel: 25 16 39). Tickets can be obtained from travel agents and hotel receptions.

Baby bull fight
On a more lighthearted note, tourists may wish to visit Cortijo Vista Verde in C'an Pastilla. There you have the opportunity to fight with baby bulls (with no danger to the bulls!). This is a fun affair, and includes drinking champagne and a flamenco show.

Nightlife

Palma is one of the most cosmopolitan cities in the Mediterranean, with a nightlife to suit its reputation. Basically, nightlife is centred in four areas, Cala Major, El Terreno, Es Jonquet and Apuntadores. (The red light district is in San Antonio.)

Cala Major has Pepe's Nightclub and Discothèque. La Sirena, Liberty, Pacha's and Napoleon are four good discothèques, popular with British visitors.

In **El Terreno**, there is the most famous nightclub on the island, Tito's, situated in the Plaza Gomila; another well known nightclub, Broadway, is opposite the Victoria Hotel. Down the hill are several discothèques including Barbarella and Besame Mucho.

Around the area of the windmills (seen from the Paseo Maritimo) in **Es Jonquet** you will find plenty of bars, discos and nightclubs, all close together, so the choice is yours. It is here, down a tiny alley, that you will find the Bar of Ricky Lash (known on the radio); the view from this American-style bar is marvellous. Nearby is the Jack el Negro nightclub.

Apuntadores is the area west of Es Born, known for its small restaurants, and it also has bars where live music is played. It is a quaint place to wander at night as new places are being opened frequently. At the old Puig de Sant Pere district you will find the Bodega Stop, with a very different gypsy flamenco show.

The **Casino** Palladium, open 2000 to 0400 every evening, closed on Sunday, offers American and French roulette, blackjack, dice and slot machines. It has a sophisticated international floorshow as well as its own restaurant which serves a Grand Buffet on Fridays and Saturdays. Every night there is an à la carte menu. (Tel: 68 00 00). The Casino is situated at the end of the motorway leading to Andratx. Take the Cala Figuera turn-off towards Urbanizacion Sol de Mallorca, Magalluf. It is well signposted. Take your passport when visiting a casino.

Other nightspots in Majorca are the Mallorca Palace in **Arenal**, a stylish nightspot, with dancing to the Gran Palace Band, flamenco show and special star appearances. The Pirate Restaurant and Nightclub, opposite the Aguapark in **Magalluf** offers good family entertainment with food, drink and floorshow. In **Alcudia**, in the north, Es Foguero Palace (Ctra Alcudia, Sa Pobla, Alcudia. Tel: 54 85 11) is a popular nightclub: dinner is at 2030 hrs and the spectacular laser show with Spanish ballet starts at 2230 hrs. Open from April to October, closed on Sunday. North of **Palma Nova**, in a fifteenth century Majorcan farmhouse in countryside, is Son Amar, with outdoor terraces with fountains. It offers a barbecue style dinner with wine, cabaret, showgirls, dancing horse and the Drifters Show. Cameras allowed but no videos.

All the major tourist centres have nightclubs and discos. The local newspaper, the *Majorca Daily Bulletin*, gives up-to-date information and useful details about nightlife, including theatre and cinema programmes and times of performances. The only regular films shown in Majorca with English dialogue are at Sala Regina on the Calle Teniente Mulet, El Terreno, Palma (Tel: 23 39 37). Performances are at 1845 and 2130 hrs Monday to Friday, 1545 hrs on Saturday, and 1845 hrs on Sundays.

Casual or trendy clothes are suitable for discos and bars. When visiting Tito's nightclub and the Casino, more formal attire is expected and men must wear a tie and jacket.

Sea cruises

A number of ports take holidaymakers on sea cruises of varying duration. From the Paseo Maritimo in Palma you can take a short cruise around the harbour. This allows a panoramic view of the city from the sea. Or you can take a Jumbo Cruise to Sant Telm, which is just past Port d'Andratx; this is an all day cruise and a meal is included. Departs from the Paseo Maritimo at 0945 hrs.

During the high season a regular sea cruise operates from Colonia de San Jordi to the little island of Cabrera. Lunch is served aboard ship. The price is 2,000 pesetas; it departs at 0930 hrs. Time is allowed to explore the island which is reputed to have falcons and eagles nesting in the rocks (see Chapter 15).

Sports and pastimes

Because of the mild climate and the proximity to the sea, it is possible to participate in a wide selection of sports. Good facilities are provided. Mallorquins enjoy all forms of leisure activity and keep themselves very fit.

Bicycling This is a sport that is very popular with Mallorquins and tourists alike. You may rent a bicycle in most tourist resorts, prices average 300 pesetas per hour and 500 pesetas per day. The roads around Alcudia Bay are flat and have special tracks for cyclists only.

Bowling Several of the larger hotels have bowling alleys in their vicinity. Locations are at Hotel Playa, Santa Ponça; Bowling Niagara, Balneario 5 and 6, El Arenal; Bowling Dulcinea, Palma Nova (near Hotel Flamboyan), Balneario de Peguera, Peguera. A French bowls *(petanca)* tournament is held during October at the Son Veri Petanca Club, El Arenal. Tel: 24 67 16.

Diving The rocky coasts and clear waters make for excellent deep sea diving, snorkelling, skin diving and skuba diving. For skuba diving it is necessary to have a licence before you can rent breathing tanks and permission is required from marine authorities. There are schools which give five-day courses with instruction in English. The bays in the north east and south west are the most suitable for diving.

Skin diving with harpoon is a popular sport with the Mallorquin youth, searching for octopus *(pulpo)*. For the tourist snorkelling can be good fun, the warm clear waters in the many tiny coves have nooks and crannies that will provide ideal sport; but watch out for sea urchins. Reasonably priced equipment can be hired at most seaside resorts. Locations for diving are Aqua Marine Diving, Andratx; Orca Diving Club, Illetes; Club Albatros, Cala Figuera; Es Pontas, Cala Santanyi; La Morena, Cala d'Or; Diving Centre, Cala Rajada.

There is a good selection of golf courses on the island. Golf Poniente, near Magalluf, 18 hole par 72, is well maintained with club house and restaurant.

Dog racing A regular race track is located at the Canodrome, Miguel de los Santos Oliver, Palma (Tel: 29 00 12).

Fishing Fishing from the rocks is very popular both with the locals and tourists. Fishing tackle is cheap and for sale in most resorts. Boats can be hired, too, and your catch will probably be much larger in open waters; red mullet and halibut are amongst the fish to be caught. Two lakes in Majorca's mountains, Gorg Blau and Lake Cuber, are stocked with carp and rainbow trout.

Flying Pilots with a licence can hire aeroplanes and beginners can have lessons at the Aero Club, Son Bonet Airport, Pont d'Inca (Tel: 26 41 62).

Football Today this is Spain's number one sport, and in Majorca, too, even the smallest village will find space for a football field. Football is watched with avid interest on TV in many bars. You can see a club match at the Estadios Balear y Luis Sitjar, Palma (Tel: 27 38 01 and 23 44 38).

Go-karting This may be watched and Go-karts hired at the track which lies on the road between Col d'en Rebassa and C'an Pastilla. Open from 1000 to 1300 hrs and 1530 to 2200 hrs. Go-karts may be hired, adults 950 pesetas and juniors 700 pesetas for five minutes. There ia a visitors terrace and soft drink refreshments. There are also tracks at Karting Magalluf, near Aguapark and at Binissalem near Aqualandia.

Golf The first course was built in 1964, now there are six courses. They are very popular and it is advisable to book in advance. Caddies and lessons are available. Proof of handicap is essential. Caddies, trolleys and clubs can be hired and tuition is available. Golf courses are located at Pontiente, 18-hole, green fee 5,300 pesetas; Santa Ponça, 18-hole, 5,300 pesetas; Son Vida, 18-hole, 5,000 pesetas; Beninat, 9-hole, 4,300 pesetas; Los Pinos, 9-hole, 4,200 pesetas; Pollença, 9-hole, 4,300 pesetas. Further details can be had from the Balearic Golf Federation, Avenida Jaime III 17, Palma. Tel: 22 27 53, or from hotel receptions.

Horse racing Harness races are held regularly at the Hippodrome Son Pardo (on the road to Sóller) (Tel: 25 40 31); also at the Manacor race track on Saturday evenings. The Mallorquins much enjoy the trotting races.

Horse riding There are stables *(ranchos)* in several parts of the island where horses can be hired by the hour for about 1000 pesetas. They can also be hired by the day. Stables are located at the Rancho Colorado, near the Hotel Obelisco, El Arenal (Tel: 26 45 95); Rancho Jay, Magalluf; Rancho La Romana, Santa Ponça; Son Pardo Hippodrome on the road to Sóller, km 3 (Tel: 25 40 31); and the Riding School of Majorca, Crta de Palma a Soller km 12 (Tel: 61 31 57).

Mountain climbing The Formento de Turismo in Palma, has a map of routes for mountain climbers and will give advice. You may wish to join the Federación Española de Montanismo, Pedro Alcantara Pena 13, Palma (Tel: 46 02 66). The office is open on Tuesdays and Fridays. Have your membership card from your home organisation, so that you can be issued with a local licence which insures for rescue costs in case of an accident on the slopes. Puig Major (1,445 m) has a military radar station on its peak. A challenging climb is the sheer Torente de Pareis, only for very experienced climbers.

Parachute rides (Tandem) Centro de Paracaidismo, Balear Aerodromo, Son Bonet. This aerodrome is about five kilometres north of Palma, off the Palma to Inca road.

Para sailing This sport is enjoyed at Playa Magalluf, near Hotel Atlantic and Hotel Magalluf Playa Sol. A ten minute trip costs 2,000 pesetas.

Sailing Most beaches have some sort of boats for hire. The simple *pedalos*, two-seater foot propelled boats for children and adults, can provide much relaxation, so long as one stays inshore. Sailing dinghies are easy small boats for the novice sailor, which hold up to three people. Larger sailing boats can be hired with or without a skipper. At El Arenal a catamaran can be hired from the Club Náutico Balneario 6. Speed boats and small motor boats are also available, often prices are negotiable. There is easy anchorage in quiet coves. The Balearic Sailing Federation is in Avenida Joan Miro, Palma. Tel: 40 24 12.

Swimming You can enjoy a bathe practically every day, in a warm clear sea, ideal for beginners and experienced swimmers. Most of the beaches in the tourist resorts are swept and kept clean; layout chairs and sunshades can be hired. Lovely golden sands and shallow waters make it a paradise for children. For those who wish for more secluded spots, then swimming off the rocks in one of the tiny coves is delightfully peaceful

There is an official nudist beach at Playa del Mago, situated near Portals Vells and not far from Magalluf. At present no bus reaches the tiny bay and the road there is a rough dirt track, the last part being very steep. However, that does not deter the enthusiasts; these include Mallorquins who have taken a fancy to nude bathing.

Another beach where one can enjoy naturism is at Platja d'es Trenc, on the south coast between La Rapita and Colonia Sant Jordi. There you will find a stretch of sands devoid of any developments, except for a simple bar and restaurant. This natural beach is not easy to reach as the approach roads, though tarmac, are narrow country lanes; so allow plenty of time (about an hour from Palma). The road is signed from Campos and marked as a nature reserve. By the beach is a restaurant with parking restricted to sixty cars. There is also a public carpark where entry cost 400 pesetas.

The majority of hotels have outdoor swimming pools and usually a paddling pool for younger children. In some cases there is also an indoor pool and solarium; which can be very pleasant if you have a cool day.

There are several public swimming pools in Palma, such as Polide Portivo Municipal, Carretera Son Roca (Tel: 23 99 41); and the Club Natación, Calvo Soto 1 (Tel: 25 65 42).

Tennis A great number of hotels and apartments have their own tennis courts. Fees are charged by the hour and vary according to the category of the hotel; some have resident instructors. Racquets and balls may be hired. Often these courts are floodlit for evening games. Tennis clubs are: Mallorca Tennis Club, Palma. (Tel: 23 81 73); Racket Club Son Vida, Son Rapina (Tel: 23 76 20); Club Natación, Palma (Tel: 67 58 87); Tennis Rancho Bonanja, Cala Rajada (Tel: 56 41 16).

Ultra Light This is one of the newest of all sports and tourists can now experience a pleasure flight in one of these frail aircraft. A fifteen-minute flight will cost 6,000 pesetas (£9.80), during which photographs may be taken. Contact Escuela de Ultra Ligeros, Camino de Son Xorc, Campos (Tel: 65 10 40 and 40 27 35).

Walking One of the very best ways to explore Majorca is on foot, and for the experienced walker there are many challenging hikes along the coastline and into the mountains. Even the average tourist will enjoy a walk in the pine woods behind the tourist complexes. A good example is the easy walk from Camp de Mar to Port d'Andratx, a distance of about five kilometres, with magnificent views and the thought of refreshments, plus a picturesque place to visit; it can be a pleasant change from sun worshipping, and the exercise will be good for you!

Many of the sanctuaries and hermitages are tucked away on the hills and high points of the island, but the energy expended in reaching these places is well rewarded. The Consell Insular de Mallorca have printed a booklet entitled *Twenty Hiking Excursions on the Island of Majorca*. Route maps and brief details of walks are described, with mileage and approximate times given. You may obtain this booklet free from the tourist office. Remember that for mountain walks you will need sturdy footwear. A further booklet entitled *Trekking Mallorca, Nature and Mountains* is obtainable from Tourist Office and hotels. This is a programme of eight excursions and walks for participants who are accustomed to mountain walking. It is stated that walking boots and water flasks are compulsory. An expert guide accompanies the walks which are between five and seven hours duration. Further details from tour operators and for reservations Viajes Massanella SA, Avenida Reina Sofia, Port de Alcudia (Tel: 54 58 02).

Water ski The calm waters around the south coast make this an ideal sport. Water ski clubs are to be found at the larger resorts like Santa Ponça, Cala Major and El Arenal.

Wind surfing This is probably the most popular of all sea sports; wind surfing enthusiasts tour the coastal areas in search of the necessary winds. Centres are springing up everywhere offering equipment and instruction. Surfboard hire, 1,200 pesetas for one hour, 3,000 pesetas per day. Wind surfing is mainly enjoyed in the northern part of the island where the seas are more favourable. Port de Pollença has been the scene of the National Wind Surfing Championship.

Work Out The Eurosport Studio at Calle Fredrico Garcia Lorca 4,

Magalluf, is where you can enjoy an energetic work out in your best sports gear. There you can do body building aerobics, martial arts, exercises, and learn Spanish dancing. The studio has a beauty shop, jacuzzi, solarium, sauna and boutique. Afterwards you can relax in the bar.

NINE

The country and its people

The history of Majorca

The discovery of prehistoric caves and Bronze Age material near Deia, in north west Majorca, suggests that man could have been present on the island as early as 5000 BC. In the 1960s an American archaeologist, W. Waldren, discovered human remains and the skeletons of extinct antelopes unique to the Balearic Islands in the Cueva de Muleta, near Soller. In addition, many natural burial grounds have been discovered that contain remains dated between 2000 and 1700 BC, the most significant being between Santa Margarita, west of Arta and Sa Canova, where primitive daggers, awls and pottery were found.

From about 1400 BC the Talayot culture prevailed, taking its name from stone *talayots* built by the settlers. The ingenious construction of these towers (*atalaya* is Arabic for watch tower) and their peculiarity to the Balearic Islands provoke considerable historic interest to this day, and any visitor is welcome to try and solve the mystery of these strange monuments. During this time the islanders lived in multiple chamber caves. They also built boat shaped burial chambers above ground known as *navetas,* of which there is a fine example at Son Real near C'an Picafort, Alcudia Bay.

The Talayot period continued until about 700 BC, and the islands were increasingly visited by Greek, Phoenician and finally Carthaginian seafarers. These last were led, in 300 BC, by Hamilcar Barca (who gave his name to the mainland city of Barcelona) and it is said that his famous son, Hannibal, was born on the small island of Conejera, off the north-west coast of Ibiza.

Itinerant traders valued Majorca primarily as a staging post for their spreading empires, although the Carthaginians, and later the Romans, came to appreciate, also, the sling-throwing talents of the locals. These stone throwers or *honderos* were equipped with three

Many of Palma's fine old buildings are enhanced with bright gardens and tall palm trees. These stand along the Paseo Sagrera, close to the waterfront.

stones – one in the sling, another in a holster, and a third in the hand – and were trained in their art from an early age. It seems that their parents would place food high up in bushes and trees, forcing the young boys to dislodge their meal with the aid of slings and stones, or go hungry (a case of slinging for your supper!). As adults they became fierce defenders of the islands and invaders soon enlisted the sling throwers into their own armies as mercenaries. It is their skill, indeed, that may be responsible for the name of the Balearic islands, with the Balearics deriving this title from the Greek *ballein* meaning throw.

Part of the Roman Empire

In 123 BC the Roman commander Quintus Cecilius Metellus occupied the islands, having previously taken the precaution of covering the sides of his boats with animal skins in order to withstand the hail of stones from the shore. He earned himself the title of Balearico, and the Romans referred to Majorca as Balearis Major, whilst Menorca, captured at the same time, became Balearis Minor. The island flourished under Metellus and he founded the cities of Palma and Alcudia – today's straight road between them still bears signs of the original Roman Way.

As many as 3,000 Roman colonists came to Majorca and they built towns, forts and roads as well as cultivating vines and olives. There are two considerable Roman settlements at Campa Palmaria, near Palma, and at Pollença, near to present day Alcudia. Whilst neither of these sites have been fully excavated, a small theatre has been uncovered. In 38 BC Majorca was incorporated into the Roman Empire and the island gradually assimilated the customs and language of Rome, including the advent of Christianity. It is asserted by some that Saint Paul visited the island, and there are a number of Christian relics of the fourth and fifth centuries, as well as the remains of two churches near the town of Manacor.

The Moorish era

With the decline of the Roman Empire Majorca suffered increasingly from the raids of northern barbarians, culminating in a successful invasion by the Vandal leader Gunderio in 426 AD. His hold on the island was relatively short lived, an occupation that persecuted Christians and sponsored piracy was terminated in 534 AD when Majorca became part of the Byzantine Empire. There followed a brief period in which the island returned to its customary role as a trading stop-over, but by the start of the eighth century Moorish insurgents had begun to disrupt this peace and by 902 AD the island came under the rule of the Emir of Cordoba.

The Moors dominated the island for the next four centuries and constructed mosques, palaces and gardens. They also introduced terracing, windmills and water wheels to Majorcan agriculture. However, with the advent of the crusading spirit that characterises medieval Christianity, Majorca once more became a battleground for the conflict between Christian and Moslem factions. For five centuries a series of battles, treaties and sieges ensued before the Moors were finally expelled in 1229 AD by Jaime I of Aragon. After landing an expeditionary force of 16,000 men and 1,000 horses from 155 ships at Santa Ponça, this Christian monarch re-conquered the island and established the independent kingdom of Majorca.

A Christian kingdom

The arrival of Jaime I brought a new vitality to the island. In 1230 AD he issued a People's Charter embodying the principal of human rights far in advance of the times, establishing a governing body consisting of a presiding noble, two knights, two merchants and a peasant; at the end of each year these councillors appointed others to succeed them. He also introduced a maritime code that helped to protect and stimulate trade in the area. However, his death in 1276 AD set in progress a rivalry that was to dog the island for the next century, for the king split his possessions between his two sons, bequeathing Catalona, Aragon and Valencia to Pedro III and Majorca and other French territories to Jaime II.

The antagonism between the two sons was passed onto their sons and the island became a focus for the conflict between French and Catalan dynasties. Nevertheless, despite these struggles Majorca enjoyed a relative prosperity; it was Jaime II who built the magnificent Bellver Castle to defend Palma Bay, and he established bridges, reservoirs and a weekly market. At the same time churches and monasteries were erected and the arts flourished. Jaime II's successor, Sancho I granted Majorca a royal coat of arms and assembled a formidable fleet to combat the Barbary pirates and stimulate trade with Italy and Greece.

The transfer of power

His own successor, Jaime III, was ousted by his Catalan rival Pedro IV, who declared himself King of Aragon and Majorca in 1345. An attempt to regain the island failed and the future Jaime IV lost his Majorcan inheritance and was killed at a battle at Lluc Mayor in1349.

Majorca has numerous olive trees which have grown for hundreds of years. Often their shape becomes gnarled and twisted. This ancient one is seen in Pollença.

Thus ended the French presence on the island. It is from this time on that Majorca's towns began to acquire their Catalan names.

Following this transfer of power Majorca entered into a period of decline as nobles and merchants returned to the mainland leaving landlords to run their estates, whilst many of the local youth were drafted into the several armies that would fight out the slow progress towards a unified Spain.

In the fifteenth and sixteenth centuries Majorcan commercial fleets suffered harassing attacks of North African pirates, and in 1541 Charles IV of Spain launched an unsuccessful attack on Algiers from the island. Trade ventures were restricted by Catalan's exclusion from exploiting the newly colonised Americas, and yet more ill fortune hit Majorca in 1652 when a plague swept the island. Events on the Iberian mainland came to dictate the internal life of Majorca more and more.

In the War of the Spanish Succession the Majorcans supported the Austrian cause in defiance of the French and Spanish majority. This allegiance was not curbed by the British occupation of Minorca in 1713, nor by a seventeen-day siege of Palma. However by 1716 Majorca had succumbed to Spanish pressure and Jaime I's kingdom was relegated to becoming but one more province of the unified Spain.

A province of Spain

With the inclusion of the Balearics into the destiny of mainland Spain came the replacement of the local dialect with a national Castilian language. Many landlords had prospered from the wars of the past and some wealth returned to Majorca in the shape of palaces, administrative buildings and economic development. In 1776 almond trees were introduced to the island as a profitable source of income, and two years later a society was founded to improve the economy. By 1782 nurseries were distributing young almond, fig and carob trees to potential cultivators, apricot and peach orchards were planted and within a few years almonds were being exported to the mainland.

The local population received an influx of French refugees escaping the French Revolution, and these were followed by Catalan refugees fleeing Napoleon's armies at the start of the nineteenth century. The history of the island is a mixture of setbacks in the form of droughts, plagues and even an earthquake and advances introduced as a consequence of modern industrialisation. By 1836 coal was being mined at Binissalem and the next year a regular boat service was established between Majorca and the mainland.

The arrival of Frederic Chopin and George Sand in 1838 brought publicity to the island. Chopin is reputed to have said "I am in Palma amongst palms, cedars, cacti and olives with a sky like turquoise, a sea of lapis lazuli blue, mountains like emeralds and air like heaven!" But their stay was not a happy one as Chopin's health deteriorated rapidly and George Sand was unpopular with the Mallorquins; they did not approve of her modern ways and her relationship with Chopin. George Sand made a cruel attack on the islanders in her book *Un Hiver à Majorque*. However their stay in the Monastery of Valldemossa has added much to the island as a place of tourist interest.

In 1860 Queen Isabella II and her family paid a royal visit to the island, perhaps the first of many tourists to follow. In 1875 the island's first railway track was laid and by the turn of the century some of the old city walls of Palma were being demolished in order to let the city expand.

Into the twentieth century

The Grand Hotel was built in Palma in 1903 and two years later it was seen necessary to set up a *Fomento de Turismo* to cope with the increasing number of visitors arriving by steamship. Brochures and guides were sent to Thomas Cook of London. About this time two natives of Majorca were rising to prominence in Spanish history, the soldier and statesman Don Valeriano Weyler and Don Antonio Maura who was Prime Minister five times.

By the 1930s Majorca had a reputation as a holiday resort, finding itself visited in particular by English travellers escaping a winter at home. In the north of the island the luxury Hotel Formentor was built by an Argentinian, Adan Diehl. Overlooking the beautiful Bay of Pollença it gained an international reputation for elegance and privacy. Famous people like King Edward VII and the Aga Khan stayed there, enjoying the quiet charm of the island.

The outbreak of the Spanish Civil War in July 1936 brought an interval in Majorca's tourist boom. The island was seized by the Nationalists and remained a crucial base for Franco's assaults on mainland Republicans. The Nationalist army was helped by an Italian Air Force Squadron based on Majorca. Italian aeroplanes bombed Barcelona from Palma Airport. Menorca had remained loyal to the Republican cause and when they made an attack on Majorca around the Porto Cristo area, it was quickly repulsed with the help of Mussolini's volunteers. The Civil War lasted three years and cost more than 500,000 lives.

At the end of the Civil War Franco emerged as Spain's Nationalist leader. During the Second World War despite Hitler's efforts to persuade Franco to take an active part, Spain stayed on the sidelines. Upon Franco's death in 1975, Juan Carlos, the grandson of King Alfonso XIII, acceded to the Spanish throne and Spain was once again a monarchy.

After the upheaval of the Second World War, Majorca entered a period of rapid advancement as the benefits of modernisation came to the island in the shape of such things as a larger airport, new roads and mechanisation. Property developers moved in buying up large areas of the coastline, building hotels, villas and apartments for holidays and retirement. British visitors were joined by tourists from Spain and many other European countries. Tour operators seized the opportunity to fly the sunseeking holidaymaker to Majorca to enjoy its sandy beaches, warm sea, cheap alcohol and lively entertainments.

Nowadays the country has an upsurge of industry. This is due mainly to the buoyant tourist trade, which is likely to continue to be the principle source of income and the key to regional economy. Within controlled growth areas new accommodation continues to be built; at the same time the Government lists many parts of the island as protected landscape.

Majorca today

Today the Balearics are administered by a Civil Governor appointed by the Spanish government and directly responsible to the Minister of the Interior in Madrid. Palma is the provincial capital with the Almundaina Palace being the Headquarters of the Captain General who is responsible for the maintenance of law and order. The judicial headquarters are in the Palacio de Justicia which is an elegant eighteenth century building. Also in Palma is the seat of the suffragan Bishop of Majorca, the Bishop's Palace being close by the Cathedral.

The standard of living in Majorca is now the highest in Spain, after Madrid and Barcelona; all but the humblest households run a car or van and own a refrigerator and television. It is Spain's most densely motorised province, with an average of one car per four inhabitants. *Autopistas* are being built to ease the flow of tourist traffic, and stopping places at view points are being constructed.

The tourist industry has created a new way of life for many Mallorquins. Before the Second World War the inhabitants consisted of an elite estate-owning gentry, whose forbears were descendants

A typical stonebuilt Majorcan farmhouse, with terraced gardens and agricultural land. This one is near Estellenc.

from the Knights who were given land by Jaime I. They wielded considerable power over the artisan and peasant population. Now only a handful can afford to live in such elegant country estates.

With state education (schooling is compulsory for children between six and fourteen years), a new middle class has been created. Mallorquins work hard, being concerned with making money to acquire prestige symbols. Municipal flats in the suburbs may be rented, but many own their villa or flats and often will have two jobs by working at weekends or evenings, as well as during the day. It is customary for the old to live with the family and few are put into institutions. The Mallorquins like cleanliness and are themselves neat and well dressed.

In the country, village life is quieter than in the busy towns; the younger folk depart each day to work in the tourist resorts while the older generation still toil in the fields. So when you take a drive inland during the daytime, the villages will seem almost deserted, only in the evening does the sound of children at play and music from the bars make the village come alive.

Agriculture is being helped by the creation of the Federacion Balear de Co-operativas, which has sections covering livestock, cereals, almonds, olives and other crops. An estimated six million almond trees yield a huge harvest with large quantities of nuts providing valuable export. Olives are grown in the mountain regions but they are not suitable for making oil; however their eating quality is excellent and both black and green olives are the basic ingredients of a Mallorquin diet.

The carob tree provides a seed which is crushed and made into cattle feed; it is also used as a confectionery sweetener and for pharmaceutical purposes. The popular local liqueur *palo* is made from the carob seed, but you may find it rather sweet and sickly unless added to other drinks such as gin.

Oranges, lemons, apples, pears, figs and apricots are grown and exported to the mainland, but mainly they supply the heavy demand from the hotels on the island. Vines are seen in the area of Binissalem and Felanitx and have been cultivated there since Roman times. The central plain provides a variety of cereal crops, vegetables, salads and a large quantity of good quality, early spring potatoes, some of which are exported to the UK.

The main animal that is reared is the pig. Goats and cattle are kept but in smaller numbers. Milk production has increased recently and the locally made white cheese *(queso)* Mallorquin, made from goat's milk has a distinctive and pleasant flavour; it is especially tasty with a green salad.

Fishing communities are to be found in Port de Sóller, Figuera and the Puig de San Pere quarter of Palma. The fish stalls in the markets are usually run by the fishermen's wives. Fish is fresh but never cheap, because of the constant demand.

With Spain in the EEC Majorca will have to move into a modern European way of life. Yet it should still be possible for the island to retain its appellation of Pearl of the Mediterranean.

The Mallorquin way of life

Mallorquins cherish their heritage, being a hard working and pragmatic people. They are also the nicest and most helpful of folk that one could wish to meet. Of course there are exceptions, especially in the busy tourist jungles, but generally they will delight in offering assistance. This is especially so in the countryside, where a wave of the hand and smile will be greeted with a *buenos dias* up to lunch time, and *buenas tardes* in the afternoon.

Family is all important, with children and old people being cared for with much love and consideration. One of the best ways of introduction is to make a pleasant remark about a Mallorquin child;

Botanicactus

Located in the south east of Majorca, close to the village of Ses Salinas, Botanicactus claims to be the largest botanical gardens in Europe. It occupies an area of 50,000 sq m, of which 40,000 are arid gardens, the remaining 10,000 being composed of a typical Majorcan garden with a small cottage built of local stone. Attractively laid out, this moist garden is devoted to tropical and lush vegetation.

As well as the giant palm grove, there is a green lawn reached by means of a small bridge over a lake. Nearby is a plantation of bamboo and plants that resembles a jungle. Olive trees, almonds, pomegranates, carob, eucalyptus, laurels and vines are some of the better known varieties thriving here. A windmill adds to this picturesque attraction.

Walking amongst the desert scene of the cactus garden one is constantly amazed at the enormous variety of the 400 different species, such weird shapes and sizes. Look for the 'old man's head' with its long white hair or the *yuccas rostratas*, which withstand temperatures between 40ºC and 20ºC below zero. Unique is the tall *carnegia gigante*, which is more than 300 years old and comes from the Arizona desert.

Other autochanous species have been brought from Brazil, Mexico, Japan, Australia and South Africa. These gardens will give you a glimpse of some of the extraordinary plants from all over the world.

Botanicactus is open all the year from 0900 to 1900 hrs. Entrance costs 500 pesetas, children 300. Take your camera when you visit this

---

the response will be gratifying. The older people are intensely religious and attend church regularly. At weekends family outings to the beach or the mountains are days of gaiety, which often include the cooking of a *paella* or fish on an open fire; it is time for gossip, drinking *vino* and rum with general noisy relaxation. Although the bars are open all day and close late at night, drunkenness is rarely seen. Thankfully there are very few cripples or beggars on the streets.

The inhabitants of Majorca consider themselves different from the Iberians on the mainland of Spain, and this characteristic is evident, their attidude to life is more relaxed and outgoing. It is well to remember that one is on a Mediterranean island and the first-time visitor will notice that the pace of life seems slow; people do not rush about frantically as in North European countries. The Spanish word *manana*, meaning tomorrow, often applies – why hurry?

The evening gossip called the *paseo* (stroll), is still enjoyed in every village and town. As the sun begins to set people gather in the streets, the air is filled with gay chatter. Children play in the *plazas*, young girls giggle and smile as the boys pass by with a sly quip. Old ladies dressed in black sit on doorsteps while families gather outside cafés talking with friends. Ancient old men, leaning on their sticks, sit on park benches discussing the daily news, while watching children feed the pigeons.

All over the island, whether in the smart avenues in Palma, the crowded streets of the tourist towns or the quiet inland villages, a way of life still exists that has not been eroded away by the transistor or the motor scooter. It is understandable that so many people continue to write, paint and talk about the charm of Majorca.

The language

The Balearic islanders have their own distinctive language and the Mallorquins take much care to see that it is being preserved; there are even night schools where courses may be taken. The Mallorquin dialect is said to be an independent development from Catalan and thus related to the Provençal language. Like most dialects, it is not a written language, possessing neither an accepted spelling nor a binding syntax.

The custom of speaking the Mallorquin dialect amongst themselves is very strong. A Spaniard from the mainland understands little Mallorquin, yet a local businessman from Majorca will speak Spanish fluently and usually French and English fairly well. Nowadays English is taught in the higher grade schools.

When travelling in the island it is sensible to carry an English/ Spanish dictionary and phrase book. In the tourist areas English is usually understood; this will not be the case in the small inland villages where your best bet is to find a student when seeking information or directions.

Music and dancing

To say that you will find music for all in Majorca is not an exaggeration. Musicians of world repute participate in international festivals in concert halls that compare with the finest in Europe. The Spanish Song Festival of the Year is often held in Palma. Orchestral symphonies, jazz concerts and swing music are performed regularly. Opera, ballet and folk festivals can be enjoyed in Palma and tourist areas.

The majority of the higher class hotels include evening music and dancing for their guests. Nowadays even the smaller villages boast of a discothèque, with some open until 0300 hrs, often the local youth mixing with the young visitors.

All Mallorquins love music and dancing; from the cradle they are encouraged to sway in time with a rhythm. Children at play will suddenly join hands and dance together with natural grace. Mallorquins have a musical voice and love to burst into song, whether at work or play.

Regional dancing is quite lively and has many variations. Some date back to pagan rites as the dances of the *cossiers* and *cavellets*, which include demons who wear hemp sacks, hoods with horns and brightly coloured masks. Regular performances of folk dancing groups are to be seen at Valldemossa and La Granja. At the local *fiestas* throughout the year, a number of country dances depict scenes from the Mallorquin way of life, such as the gathering of the olive and fig harvests.

Boleros, fandangos and *sotas* are the most common country dances, but sometimes a simple minuet *(parado)* is performed with stately gracefulness. The music for these occasions is usually supplied by guitars and fiddles, and castenets. Bagpipes and *ximbombes* (Mallorquin drums) may also be heard. Some of the most ancient songs have a distinctly Moorish flavour, while others stem from Catalan sources, the songs of the troubadours of the Middle Ages.

The costumes for folk dancing are often very elaborate and colourful. The female wears a beautiful white lace cowl-shaped headscarf, which covers her long dark hair. Her white blouse has full sleeves and the black bodice is laced at the front. A very full skirt will often be brightly coloured stripes, usually with a small decorative apron over it. Black shoes and white stockings complete the costume. Sometimes a fan is carried but jewellery is rarely worn.

The traditional male costume consists of very baggy black breeches, finishing below the knees, with a broad red sash around the waist, white stockings and sturdy black clogs. The loose white shirt and coloured waistcoat have over them a black jacket or cape, which is left open. The fedora hat can be black or grey and is usually tied with a ribbon which hangs down the back, or sometimes a red kerchief is worn in pirate fashion. A collection of folk costumes may be seen in the ethnographic museum in Muro. However we do recommend a visit to a live folk dancing exhibition, so that you can really enjoy the genuine music and dancing of the Mallorquin people.

God's work

Saint Peter was walking with Jesus by a long row of pumpkin plants and he remarked to Jesus, 'Master, these huge fruits have such frail stalks, yet the great oak trees bear only tiny acorns, surely you have made a mistake in this creation?'

Jesus decided to do as Saint Peter suggested and oak trees bore pumpkins. As Saint Peter walked under one of these trees a ripe pumpkin fell down almost knocking Saint Peter's head. Saint Peter was abashed as Jesus said, 'Do not try and alter what has been created.'

So the heavy pumpkins went back to growing on the ground.

(Adapted from the story *Acorns, Pumpkins and Saint Peter*, by Father Antoni Alcover)

Folklore and handicrafts

Folk traditions are varied and reflect their origins from all over Europe. Those interested in folkloric stories may like to read *Folk Tales of Mallorca* (see Bibliography), first collected and written by Father Antoni Alcover. Unfortunately some of the customs and folklore have been somewhat eroded by modern life. So it is good to know that new societies are now being formed to preserve their ancient culture. Older people in the villages are allowing recordings of cradle songs and work rhythms to be made. Young girls are being shown the intricate stitches of lace work, and the age-old custom of carving the olive wood has been taken up by dedicated young men.

The craft of glass blowing is still alive and one can see experts moulding glass into beautiful shapes and objects, often of intricate design. Although leatherwork is now mainly done in factories, some is still worked in the home. Take a look at the beautiful fine stitch work on the soft leather gloves and you will realise they are well worth the high price. Majorca has genuine crafts men and women who are keeping folk art alive with its humour and peasant crudeness.

Handmade pottery can be purchased with many individual objects to be found. Undoubtedly the most peculiar is the *siurell*, a charming clay figure of a mounted man, which incorporates a whistle. It is said that the figure was invented thousands of years ago by the first inhabitants of Majorca. Always very simple and roughly painted with bright red and green blobs over a white background, these interesting creatures come in many sizes and prices to suit all purses. Nowadays they are said to be a symbol of friendship and affection. Tourists are encouraged to take them home as souvenirs of their stay in Majorca. Do be careful when you pack the little fellow, as the clay is very fragile and brittle.

From the Middle Ages the famous *Majolica* glazed tiles have been much sought after; they often depict scenes of peasant life and the Don Quixote story. Wrought-iron work is of a very high standard, although much of it is rather large for the aircraft passenger; attractive candle stick holders and table mats make nice souvenirs.

Fiestas and festivals

If you look at a Spanish calendar you will see that every day seems to be one or more saint's day. Which means, therefore, every day is a fiesta. Sometimes these are only religious celebrations, but others are more festive with sports events, or even a carnival. Majorca has a goodly share of these events, and it is nice to know that the friendly Mallorquins always encourage tourists to take part in their festivities. Mainly they are held in the summer and autumn, with Christmas and Easter being more solemn events. (For calendar see Chapter 6: Holidays and festivals)

Although Christmas day is a public holiday, it is the Procession of the Magi on 6 January that is the Christmas highlight. The Magi, or Three Kings, are the Spanish equivalent of Santa Claus, and this is when the children receive their presents. In Palma you can watch the Kings being ferried across the Bay of Palma, under a shower of fireworks; then follows the procession through the centre of the city amid much excitement and jollity.

Holy Week processions in Palma are a great spectacle, when penitents wear medieval hoods and women wear mantillas and carry holy images through the streets, to the sound of muffled drums. The week following Easter is more joyful with pilgrimages and dances. Celebrations occur at Belver Castle in Palma, the Ermita de Santa Magdalena in Inca, and the Sanctuario de Montesion in Porreras.

Perhaps the best known festival is for the grapes, it is the *Festa d'es Vermar*, or vintage feast at Binissalem. The fiesta lasts a week with both religious and pagan events. Solemn masses are heard, then the wine harvesters arrive, and so do the bagpipes. The juice of the grape is blessed and offered up to the Virgen de Rubines. On the last Sunday of September wine flows freely to all townsfolk and visitors alike. It is an opportunity to see the colourful folk costumes and in the evening enjoy singing, dancing and the fireworks.

Fairs too, are fun, the one at Inca in November called *Dijous Bo* or Good Thursday, is basically an agricultural show but it includes folkloric events that are cheerful entertainment. It is held in the main plaza but spreads out into the surrounding streets.

S'Albufera de Mallorca, Parc Natural

The name is said to derive from an Arabic name place, Al-Buhayra, meaning lagoon or lake. History tells of Pliny mentioning that the purple heron was being sent to Rome for gastronomic reasons. It is thought that it could only have come from Albufera.

The seventeenth century saw some of the marshy area being developed into plots for cultivation with drainage channels. Here convicts were put to work because of the mosquitos. However in the eighteenth and nineteenth centuries malaria became a problem. At the beginning of the twentieth century the growing of rice in this *malpais* (badlands) was introduced and it continued until the nineteen sixties. The region was also used for hunting, fishing and wood cutting. At the end of the sixties a huge transformation took place when the vegetation around Estany Deis Ports and the nearby sand dunes were drained, roads and bridges were built and a huge new tourist resort appeared.

In 1985 the Government of the Autonomous Community of the Baleares purchased eight hundred hectares for conservation and the Nature Park was created.

Today, visitors may enter the reserve having first obtained a free permit from the Sa Roca Reception Centre. This Centre is sign-posted on the main road between Port d'Alcudia and Ca'n Picafort; open from 0900 to 1900 hrs April to September and 0900 to 1700 October to March.

Visitors may walk, cycle or horse ride along marked routes in the park so that they can observe, from hides, wild animals and birds in a natural habitat. A discreet and quiet behaviour must be observed. More than two hundred species of birds have been spotted amongst reeds and sedges – including the aforesaid purple heron.

On fiesta days, all shops, banks, post offices, offices and petrol filling stations are closed. Bars and restaurants remain open and are very busy. Public transport and taxis operate a reduced service.

Flora

The flora of Majorca is one of the most lovely features of the island. Every tourist brochure will show pictures of the breathtaking sight of millions – yes, millions – of almond trees in blossom, in late January and February. It is a fairy tale scene of valleys covered with a pink and white haze, the air softly perfumed.

There is great beauty, too, in the orange and lemon groves that grow in the countryside around Sóller, where again the aroma of the flowers and fruit pervades the countryside. Equal in spectacle are the great fields of silver grey olive trees, their gnarled trunks twisted into contorted shapes, many hundreds of years old yet still yielding crops.

Another interesting tree is the carob, with its thick shiny, two-tone green foliage. The small white flowers are insignificant; it is the long seed pod that makes it identifiable. It is said that this seed gave jewellers their unit of gold, the carat. This ancient tree grows spontaneously in the hottest, driest parts of the island.

Wild plants

Because of its diversity of landscape, Majorca has an enormous range of wild plants. With over 1,500 plants listed the botanist will have an enjoyable and busy time locating different species. It also makes walking on the island a special pleasure.

From the highest jagged mountains, through green forests and woodland to flat fields, surrounded by thick hedges or stone walls; along roadsides and scrubland, there is always something of interest growing. Across the low cliffs, down to the rocky coast and sand dunes, there are all sorts of specimens to be found. Lagoons, river beds and salt marshes all sustain plants that flourish in their own specific environment.

Look first at the mighty trees; the holm oak *(Quercus ilex)* with its many uses, such as acorns for pigs, charcoal for fires and the bark with its high tannin content which is used in tanning hides and setting dyes. The most abundant tree is the pine *(pinus halepensis)* which can grow to twenty metres high, and in the old days this was much used for ship-building. In windy areas its growth will be stunted and it is seen in a curious deformation, known locally as "witches graft", produced by a parasitic fungus, which causes part of the tree to grow almost parallel to the ground, much denser and thicker than the rest of the tree.

Amongst the shrubs, perhaps one of the most attractive is the strawberry tree *(arbutus unedo)* with its shiny green leaves. Seen at the end of September and early November the small white flowers bloom simultaneously with the ripening of the orange/red strawberry-like fruit; this is because the fruit takes a year to ripen. Mallorquins gather the fruit to make small fruit pies. It can be found along the road between C'an Picafort and Arta.

Other plentiful shrubs are the heathers, which were once used for thatching; *erica arborea,* the tree heather, will grow two or three metres high, its wood can be used to make briar smoking pipes. The fragrant myrtle, the prickly juniper, the blackberry, the yellow broom, honeysuckle and clematis are just a few shrubs that are easily located.

Many herbs grow wild: rosemary, thyme, garlic, aniseed and fennel, the latter growing two to three metres high. These with the wild carrot or Queen Anne Lace *(daucus carota)* make the roadside verges a fragrant and pleasant sight.

If you visit Majorca in springtime, the fields will be brimming with purple violets, white daisies, thistles, blue scabious and, most of all, the orange yellow flowers of the wild marigold *(calendula arvensis).* If you search a little harder you will see yellow primroses, tiny cyclamen and the smaller orchids, very beautiful with their strange and exotic shapes. Do be careful of the fox glove *(digitalis purpurea),* the island's most poisonous plant.

The cliffs and sand dunes, too, provide interesting plants, the more common being the sea holly and the sea daffodils, which bloom from July to September; but look also for the wild *narcissus tazetta.* Lagoons and salt marshes grow several giant grasses and reeds, but be sure not to disturb the habitat of aquatic birds.

An informative book entitled *Plants of the Balearic Islands* by Anthony Bonner, price 1,100 pesetas, is on sale in Palma. It may be ordered by post from abroad. Price including postage is £7. Address, Editorial Moll, Torre de L'Amor 1, 07001, Palma, Majorca. Tel: (971) 72 41 76.

Garden plants

The Mediterranean is known for its colourful gardens; in Majorca you will not be disappointed, for the public gardens and *plazas* have a variety of shrubs and trees not seen in the UK. Tall eucalyptus and palm trees give shade, oleanders and hibiscus makes splashes of colour. Prickly cactus provide the exotic. Walls which are covered with brilliant bougainvillea and the splendid orange fire begonia often have the morning glory *(ipmoea purpurea),* adding its blue and deep purple to the scene.

In towns and villages the geranium flourishes with vigour, sometimes in flower pots and tubs, more often as a garden hedge. Poinsettias, too, bloom freely outside. The rubber tree which grows tall and thick, is a far cry from the cherished small specimens in an English sitting room.

Gardens that are open to the public are Raxa, La Granja Gardens at Esporles and the Gardens of Alfabia, near Bunyola. These are described in Chapter 16.

Wild life

Majorca is a particularly safe island as regards wild animals; there are no large wild beasts and the four kinds of snakes are non-poisonous. A few semi-wild goats roam freely in the area of Formentor, in the extreme northern tip of the island. Because of the tourist interest they are now a protected species and not allowed to be hunted.

An unusual animal, rarely seen, is the genet, a carnivorous quadruped which is a kind of civet cat, whose appearance is between a fox and a weasel; it has a long, bushy, striped tail.

Other wild animals that live in the remote parts of the island are hare, rabbit, duck, quail, pigeon and partridge. Although their numbers have been reduced by shooting, there is a closed season to hunting, from mid January to October.

Bats are found in the old buildings and some of the caves. Field rats, too, are plentiful, especially in the cultivated fields near La Albufera. At the village of Sa Pobla, rats are on the menu. After the rat is skinned and cleaned it is boiled, dried and cut into pieces. The meat is well seasoned with salt, pepper and garlic before it is fried to a golden brown, onions and tomatoes are added to the dish. Perhaps a recipe you may not wish to try!

Turning to more pleasant things; with so many wild flowers on the island it is natural that one sees dragonflies, bees and butterflies. Flies and mosquitoes are not too much of a problem, unless there has been a shower of rain. Even in the swampy area of La Albufera these annoying insects are being kept under control with pesticides. You might also see a terrapin or fresh water tortoise in the swampy lakes.

Evening time is when you hear the cicada, that winged chirping insect so evocative of warm Mediterranean nights. Another little creature that every visitor will see somewhere is the gecko, a kind of tiny lizard. This shy, harmless, four legged animal will be under bushes, in amongst sand dunes, even on patios, where he will dart away so fast that you will only catch a glimpse of his thin tail.

One thing you can be sure of noticing is the great variety of wild birds. The island has such a high reputation with ornithologists and bird watchers alike, that special package holidays are arranged for them. Bird watching tour operators include Orniholidays, Cox and Kings, and Heritage. Port de Pollença and Alcudia Bay are the areas most favoured for this type of holiday.

It is not possible to list or describe the vast number of birds that use the island habitat; but among the larger birds you can hope to see are the black vulture, with its huge six-metre wing span, Eleonora's falcon, Bonelli's eagle, golden eagle and osprey. Seabirds nest in the cliffs; in the scrub you will hear and possibly see warblers, shrikes and even kingfishers. The saltpans at Salinas de Levante are a favourable location for bird watching, with a good number of waders, terns, stilts, sandpipers and plovers. More rare are flamingoes and herons. You will certainly see the brightly marked hoopoes, also corn buntings and bee-eaters.

A most useful book which has many maps, is *A Guide to Bird Watching in Mallorca* by Eddie Watkinson (AB Gratisk Formgivnung, 32 Stockholm, Sweden); this can be purchased from bookshops in Palma.

Native dogs

Canine lovers may find it interesting to look out for the now almost extinct breed of native dog called *ca de bestiar*. This powerful animal has a smooth black coat similar to a Labrador. It is said that it has a character typical of the Mallorquin peasants, wary of strangers but docile with its owner. You are most likely to see these animals around farm houses in the central rural countryside.

Another fine dog native to the Balearic Islands is the Ibizian hunting dog called the *ibicenco*. During the shooting season, November to mid January, these dogs are taken out into the fields to chase out rabbit, hare and partridge. Their keen sense of smell and swiftness of foot make them ideal for this sport. In the home they are used as guard dogs. At the same time they are gentle and loving animals, especially with young children, and are valued as trustworthy pets.

(**Opposite**): *Inside the Palace of King Sancho at Valldemossa the attendants are dressed in colourful folk costume. Visitors can purchase replica dolls and souvenirs after touring the palace.*

TEN

The city of Palma

Palma de Mallorca is the capital of Majorca and the Balearic Islands; nearly two thirds of Majorca's population live here. Quite the most beautiful view of this lovely city is to be seen from the sea. As one enters the Bay of Palma, which is in the south of the island, the outline of the mighty Gothic cathedral dominates the skyline. Tall spires against a brilliant blue sky cluster close by the ochre coloured Almudaina Palace, partially enclosed by an ancient stone wall.

Set very close to the sea, the city rises to greet you, tall palms wave in the breeze as they line the elegant wide seaside promenade. There is no beach here but along the waterfront are luxury hotels and sumptuous yachts mingle with colourful fishing boats, ferryships and huge cruise liners. All around the air throbs with the life and activity of this city by the sea.

On either side of the bay the golden beaches of C'an Pastilla and Cala Major are ringed with numerous, high rise blocks of modern hotels and apartments. In the background is the imposing fourteenth century Bellver Castle, set on a hill amongst pine trees. It is Spain's only completely round castle and its white walls, crenellated battlements and round tower are floodlit at night; together with the floodlit old city, it is reflected in the sea's calm waters, creating a picture of sparkling dancing lights. Palma at night is one of the most dazzling sights in the world.

(**Opposite**): *The internationally famous old monastry of La Cartuja at Valldemossa, viewed from the rose garden. Many important royal persons, writers and artists have lived here.*

It has been written that Palma has a thousand faces; justifiably so, for this international city is a majestic blend of the old with the new. Through the busy airport and sea ports, people of many nations pour in, creating a cosmopolitan murmer among the historic buildings. Old convents, churches and chapels, intriguing narrow streets, fountains and gardens merge pleasantly with outdoor cafés, street markets, antique shops, offices and large modern stores; the city is redolent with age-old echoes yet it is thriving and prosperous today.

Visiting the capital

There is so much to see and do in Palma, do not dismiss it as yet another city, too busy and noisy to visit. Wherever you are spending your holiday, try to allow yourself some time to absorb the history, culture and, above all, the gaiety of the capital.

The policeman (or maybe policewoman) will salute politely when you ask the way to the tourist office. The shopkeeper smiles patiently as you try to decide which of the tempting array of cream cakes takes your fancy. The diligent energy of the bootblack in the Born, the wrinkled faces of the old folk sitting under the shade of the trees; the dancing feet of the little girls in their pretty dresses and pinafores, the pert glances of their elder sisters in tight jeans, together with the warm sun overhead – all contribute to Palma's special ambience.

Coach excursions visiting Palma usually set down their passengers at the point along the **Paseo Sagrera**, northwards, where the **Calle Antonio Maura** leads from the sea. The statue of **Ramón Llull**, the Mallorquin philosopher, stands prominently at the corner of the street – a useful landmark – whilst behind it the great **Cathedral** beckons all visitors.

Because of the complexity of the many small streets and narrow alleys *(barrios)* in this quarter of the city, it is suggested that you obtain a street map of Palma before you start your tour. This can be had from hotels, car rentals, travel agencies and tourist offices in your resort and in Palma itself.

Allow at least two days to visit all the main sights and places of interest in Palma. The tours outlined below can all be done in half a day – although those of you with more time to spare can be more leisurely.

Tour 1: Cathedral and historic buildings

Standing by the broad steps that lead to the old city wall, you are about to become part of history itself, for these steps are so worn with the tread of past travellers – kings, statesmen, knights, citizens of Palma and pilgrims – who have gone before you as they entered the **Cathedral**.

But before you tread the ancient steps, pause for a moment to look at a striking bronze statue. This depicts one of Majorca's famous *hondero*, the stone slingers of the past. Set on a small plinth, this strong short-haired youth stands proudly with his three stones – one in his holster, one in his hand and one in his sling, which is held aloft – representing the brave defenders of Majorca of a bygone age (see Chapter 9).

Now you climb the steps which lead towards the Cathedral and the fortifications along the old city wall. Stop by the ramparts and look directly below; there you see the newly built **Parque del Mar** (park by the sea). Opened 12 October 1984 by King Carlos, it is a combination of walks, gardens and a lake, amongst which are set abstract art forms, created by the Spanish sculptor Alfaro. The park is very modern in concept, full of contrasts and unusual and arresting impressions. Look past the Parque del Mar and along the extensive view of the seafront, with its port buildings and mass of shipping; a constant stream of traffic flows along this, the Paseo Sagrera, which joins the Paseo Maritimo.

Turn towards the Cathedral, up a few more steps and you arrive at the **Puerto del Mirador**, the gate with the beautiful view on both sides. Southwards the azure sea sparkles and shimmers, the sunlight creating a mirage of shadows and shapes on the waves. On the opposite side is the portal of the Cathedral, tall and splendid with huge belfry towers. Sculptures of St Peter and St Paul guard the enormous double doors, the work of Guillermo Sagrera.

King Jaime I first set foot on Palma's soil on the 31 December 1229, and on New Year's Day a Christian Cross was erected in Palma's principal Arab mosque. The consecration of this Royal Chapel marked the inauguration of the Cathedral. It was Jaime's son and subsequent generations who completed the task of creating this magnificent Cathedral. Today, to enter this beautiful House of God, known to the Mallorquins as **La Seo**, you are required to pay a fee of 200 pesetas for entrance that includes the museum.

This Cathedral of Light is mighty in every sense of the word. There is a guide to explain the wonders of its impressive interior, its fine statues and paintings. Light falls on altars and chapels, slender pillars lead the eye upwards, the valuable choir stalls are richly carved. In the Treasury a gold monstrance, two metres high and weighing 120 kg, has 230 pearls and 826 diamonds. Such treasures are not easily forgotten.

Perhaps the most glorious feature, and one that you surely will recall long afterwards, is the great Rose Window, 11.3 m in diameter, and composed of 1,236 pieces of stained glass. It is one of the largest and most beautiful windows in the world. An aureole of light throws a coloured rainbow into the interior. During the months of February and November owing to the position of the sun's rays shining through the window, a perfect replica of the Rose Window is reflected across on to the opposite wall with wondrous effect.

The High Altar is the oldest part of the Cathedral; it is here that Antonio Gaudi made sweeping changes to the interior with his futuristic designed canopy, which appears to be floating in space. The passing of time has softened his twisted and strange design and the addition of a modern lighting system has made it an integral part of this splendid church. In the Royal Chapel are the tombs of Jaime I and Jaime III, Kings of Majorca. The Cathedral is open from 1000 to 1230 and 1530 to 1800 hrs. It is closed on Sunday except for services.

Across from the Cathedral is the **Palacio Almudaina** (Almudaina Palace), once a Moorish Royal residence, but now the headquarters of the Governor General of Majorca. Rooms are still maintained for use when King Juan Carlos visits Majorca. Tourists may visit part of the Palace which houses a National Museum. There you will see Flemish tapestries, portraits of Mallorquin kings and paintings of Spanish sea victories; also visit the Chapel of St Anne. Open from 1000 to 1300 and 1530 to 1800 hrs, closed Saturday afternoon and on Sunday. Entrance costs 300 pesetas. Do not be put off by the imposing, uniformed guard who stands resplendent outside in white gloves; he will be helpful.

After visiting these two historic buildings you will enjoy a walk northwards, through the gracious gardens that run alongside the **Calle Antonio Maura**. The area occupied by these gardens, called **S'Hort del Rei**, is a remnant of the old palace. These are reminiscent of Moorish gardens seen in the Alhambra at Granada, where sweet-scented flowers, lily ponds, fountains and tall cypress trees create a cool air; stone seats and thick hedges provide a quiet resting place, useful when you wish to consult your city map.

On your feet again you will soon reach **Plaza Reina** and the well-

This is one of a pair of unusual Sphinx like statues seen at the northern end of Es Born. They make a useful meeting place in Palma.

known, tree-shaded **Es Born**. Once the scene of jousting tournaments it is now the best known meeting place in Palma. Along the left-hand side bars and restaurants spill out on to the pavements; on the opposite side you will find travel agents and souvenir shops. Tourists and business people mingle, enjoying their refreshments in the warm sunshine. If you wish to buy an English newspaper, there is a news-stand along the Born. At night time the central promenade sees the evening stroll *(paseo)*, a typical Mediterranean scene, with people enjoying the warm night air and the company of friends and acquaintances.

At the south end of Es Born you will be near to Palma's main Post Office. A turning eastwards called **Calle de la Constitució** has on the left side the entrance to the **Fomento del Turismo de Mallorca** where you may obtain information about the island.

A little higher up Constitució and across the road at number four is the **Provencial Governor's Office**, with a military guard standing on the steps outside.

From the post office, turn to your right and proceed across the **Plaza del Rosario**, which is a high class shopping area; at the far end walk through a narrow alley which leads into **Santo Domingo** and below the steps to **Casa del Hierro**. A **Tourist Information Office** is on the right, and inside the charming Señora Esperanza (which is Spanish for Hope) will be patient and helpful with all your queries. She is multi-lingual, which is useful should you need a document translated quickly. Open 1000 to 1400 and 1600 to 1800 hours

A short walk up a small flight of stone steps leads to **Plaza Cort**, a beautiful and important square. It houses the **Ayuntamiento** (Town Hall), one of a number of notable buildings in Palma. The town hall was built in the seventeenth and eighteenth centuries and is of Baroque style. An enormous building, it has some intricate wooden gable ended eaves. The ornate facade has a clock which was inserted in the nineteenth century after a fire partially destroyed the interior. In the lobby are two figures in old Mallorquin costume and of more practical use is the Lost Property Office (Tel. 22 77 44). The **Municipal Library** is also here.

If you have managed to visit all the places mentioned so far, you will surely be ready for some refreshment. Restaurants, cafés and bars are spread generously around Palma. **Plaza Mayor** is a pleasant place to have a coffee or a meal while watching the crowds that gather in the square. Do remember that shops, offices and public buildings are usually closed between 1330 and 1600 hrs. So you can be generous with your lunchtime rest.

Along The Rambla are numerous flower stalls and strikingly beautiful flower arrangements, their perfume pervading the air.

From Plaza Mayor it is only a short walk north, past the theatre, **Teatro Principal**, to Via Roma, commonly known as the **Rambla.** This is a wide avenue with a central walkway, where Palma's colourful flower market is held. Large plane trees line the way. In the evenings this is a prominent meeting place, where the locals like to walk (the *paseo*) and talk. An underground carpark here is always very busy. Nearby are two classical statues of Caesar, and an impressive flight of steps leads to the Plaza Mayor.

Tour 2: Shopping expedition

If you are the energetic type then make your way to **Avenida Rey Jaime III**, one of the main high class shopping streets where the larger stores are open all day. To reach it you can walk back to the Born, or wend your way up to **Plaza Weyler** and westwards along **Gra Mola**, into **Plaza Pio XII** and the beginning of Jaime III. Incidentally if asking the way, it is Jaime Third *(tercero)*, not Three *(tres)*.

On the corner of **Plaza Pio XII** there is quite a large C & A store, which sells British made clothes; there are fitting rooms, so remember your continental size. To shop in Jaime III you will need to have a lot of pesetas. The Paris fashion houses and fabulous jewellery shops are so inviting.

At the western end of Jaime III you will reach a Spanish store called **Galerias Preciados**, an enormous emporium that has everything you may need: fashion, travel goods, books, cosmetics, household goods and sports equipment. There are five floors, with escalators to whirl you into a shopper's paradise; goods purchased can be sent abroad tax free. Other facilities are self-service cafeteria, toilet, travel agency, currency exchange, interpreters. In the basement there is a large supermarket selling bread, fresh meats and vegetables as well as drinks and groceries. The store is open from 1000 to 2000 hrs, including Saturday. The large car park at the side of the store in **Calle Rossellon** is not suitable for high vehicles.

The shopping area of Palma is larger than one thinks, so it is a help to have some idea where to find the items you may wish to purchase. Here are some suggestions:

Plaza Cort – Sweets, cakes, delicatessen, gourmet grocery (excellent capers).

Plaza Cuartera – Goat, sheep and rabbit pelts, rugs, straw and bamboo objects.

Plaza Mayor – Craft market (Monday, Friday and Saturday). Leather, pottery, wooden ornaments, tiny hand-made baby shoes.

Plaza Rosario – Smart jewellery, clothes, shoes and leather goods.

Jaime II – Boutiques. Umbrellas, fans, gloves, glassware.

Calle San Miguel – Rope sandals, cotton bedspreads, linen and embroidered cloths.

Calle Platera – Gold, silver, jewellery, modern and antique.

Calle Sindicato – Bargain shops. Clothes, earthenware dishes, spices, saffron.

Via Roma (The Rambla) – Flowers, plants, stamps, coins and books.

There is underground parking beneath Plaza Mayor, the entrance is off the Via Roma (The Rambla).

Tour 3: Saturday morning market

One of the most popular tourist attractions is the **Rastrillo** or Flea Market, in Palma on a Saturday morning. Go early for bargains. It starts at about 0800 hrs and goes on until 1400 hrs. The location of this market has changed over the past years, so it is best to check with your hotel, or ask a taxi driver or look in the newspaper, *Mallorca Tourist Info*, for the latest venue. The 5-15 bus from the Plaza Espana will take you direct to the Flea Market. Tourists coming from Palma Nova should take bus 21 to Palma, alight at Plaza de la Reina (Born), and from there pick up the 5-15, direction Poligono de Levante. Those coming from C'an Pastilla can take the 5-15 bus direct.

The history of the Flea Market goes back to the last century when farmers in the outlying areas brought in their produce – poultry, pigs, rabbits, eggs, cheese and honey – for direct sale in Palma City. Later gypsies joined the farmers, adding to the local colour by selling trinkets, pots and pans, and goods they had acquired by house to house purchase.

As in most gypsy markets, you must haggle furiously and never pay the original price asked. Watch out for pickpockets mingling with the colourful crowd.

Tour 4: The old city and museums

Among the narrow streets of the old city, in the area called **Portella**, you will be fascinated with the old baronial mansion houses and the great palaces; some date back to the fifteenth century. Many have huge wooden doors which are closed, their great brass hinges and huge door-knockers shining brightly; but a few have delicate wrought iron gates which are open, and passers-by may glimpse the cool stone patio beyond. Curved archways and wide steps lead up to a balustrade where you can see the main entrance to the mansion. The dark green foliage of hanging plants and potted ferns adds to the atmosphere of bygone days.

Observe too, balconies with their wrought iron grills bright with red geraniums; some have large and artistically engraved coats of arms on the walls. There are old courtyards with a fountain, stone ornaments and an ancient well; so quiet it is as if time has stood still.

At number five Calle Portela is the **Museo de Mallorca** (Majorca Museum), open from 1000 to 1400 and 1600 to 1900 hrs, Sunday 1000 to 14000 hrs, closed on Monday and public holidays. This old palace, recently renovated, is the museum dedicated to Mallorquin artists and artisans. Medieval paintings give an idea of life in Majorca in the days of the rich merchants of the Middle Ages. Ceramics, furniture and textiles help us appreciate how they lived.

Two other museums in Palma are of special merit. The **Cathedral Museum** is where liturgical robes, religious relics, ornaments, tapestries and Gothic paintings can be viewed. Open from 1000 to 1230 and 1600 to 1830 hrs, closed Sunday and public holidays. The **Diocesan Museum** in the Bishop's Palace, Calle Mirador (behind the Cathedral eastwards), has archeology, pottery, carvings and jewellery on display. This small collection, beautiful and of historic interest, includes William Shakespeare's seal, a ceremonial silver mace belonging to Louis XIV, and a proclamation by Emperor Maximillian of Mexico. Open from 1000 to 1330 and 1500 to 2000, Saturday, Sunday and public holidays 1000 to 1330 hrs.

Only a short walk from the Diocesan Museum will bring you to the unique **Arab Baths** (Banos Arabes) in the **Calle Serra 15**. These baths are still preserved much as when they were in use. The large earthenware jars remind one of Ali Baba and the Forty Thieves!

A stroll along the **Calle Almudaina**, dark and full of shadows, will make you want to glance to the sky for light. Above you the **Arco de la Almudaina** (Almudaina Arch) is the remains of an old Moorish

Outside the Baroque doorway at St Francis Church is a very fine statue of Fray Junipero Serra of Petra, the missionary. By his side is a native American child.

gate to the city. In this street look at **Casa Villalonga Escalas**, where you will see Renaissance windows with heraldic medallions, and its notable inner courtyard. Opposite, **Casa Oleo** has a Gothic staircase with rosettes and Catalan blazons.

A place of great importance in old Palma is the **Palacio Vivot** at Calle Zavella 2. This is still the residence of the Marqués de Vivot. Now a national monument and open to the public, it contains a sumptuous collection of heirlooms belonging to this aristocratic family. Your tour takes you through rooms filled with antique furniture, tapestries, valuable silver and a splendid collection of paintings. This is a gracious palace, owned by a noble Mallorquin family.

Only a few steps away from the Palacio Vivot, in Plaza San Francisco, is the important church of **St Francis**, a huge fourteen century edifice with an imposing Baroque facade. It is now a national monument and its Gothic cloisters are renowned. Inside is the tomb of Majorca's thirteenth-century philosopher-priest Ramón Llull. His story seems more like fiction than fact.

Briefly, it is a true tale of a passionate young nobleman, in the court of King Jaime I, who fell in love with a married lady. She refused his attentions. So enamoured was he that one Sunday he pursued her into church (some say he was on horseback) where she was attending mass. This lady was aghast at seeing him, immediately she uncovered her breast to reveal a frightful cancer. The wild Ramón was full of remorse and he immediately became a recluse. Later he turned to religion and entered the order of St Francis. In due course he wrote some 350 books on theology, philosophy and poetry, setting out to convert all Islam to Christianity. In old age he was taken prisoner when travelling in Africa and sentenced to death, only to be rescued by a merchant captain; but he died as he was travelling back to his native land. It is said that he was never canonised, because to win over the Moors he spoke too kindly of the Koran.

Before you leave the church of St Francis, spare a moment to look at another famous Mallorquin, Fray Junipero Serra of Petra. He went as a missionary to America, and his statue outside the church is symbolic of his work: he stands with his hand on the shoulder of one of the poor American boys he devoted his life to. The city he founded, San Francisco, is named after his monastic home and his patron saint St Francis. His life's work in the missions of California and among the poor is depicted in the little museum in his home village of Petra which is situated in the central plains of Majorca.

A visit to Palma should include a look at **La Lonja**, a squat

The main portal of La Lonja shows a finely carved figure of the Angel de la Mercaderia. Today the building houses an exhibition of paintings and sculptures.

This beautiful stone and wrought iron gateway is the entrance to the seventeenth-century Consulado del Mar, the Sea Consulate, which is not open to the public.

turreted building easily located on the seafront of the Paseo Sagrera. Once it was Palma's trade exchange centre, and it is considered an outstanding example of medieval architecture, being built by the Mallorquin Guillermo Sagrera. It has fine carved windows with decorative battlements and gargoyles; inside are some beautiful fifteenth-century vaulting and pillars shaped like palm trees. Nowadays it is sometimes used as an exhibition hall and contains an Art Museum. Open 1100 to 1400 and 1700 to 2100 hrs, Sundays and public holidays 1100 to 1400 hrs. Closed Monday.

Next door to La Lonja is the **Consulado del Mar** (Sea Consulate). This was built in the seventeenth century for the College of Merchants, and used to administer maritime law and as a court to settle disputes. It has large cannons and a huge anchor outside. It is not open to the public.

If your feet are getting weary, near the Sea Consulate you are likely to find a parking place for horse drawn carriages. These open air horse buggies (called *tartanas*) are a splendid way to see around the city in style; the slow pace allows you to look more closely at the great buildings. Settle the fare before you start your ride.

At the western end of the Paseo Maritimo is the exlusive **Real Club Náutico Palma de Mallorca** (Royal Yacht Club) with its marina crammed with luxury yachts and millionaires' floating palaces, all safely behind a huge wire fence and locked gates. Seawards you will notice you have reached the **Maritimo de Palma**, which is the port for the ferries from mainland Spain and the rest of the Balearic Islands. Inside the building are bars, cafeteria, lounge, toilets and souvenir shop. There is also a travel agent, left luggage department, post office and booking office for the Trasmediterranea Ferry. Taxis and buses meet incoming ships. An extensive car park includes an area for overnight parking at a charge of 50 pesetas per hour and 1200 pesetas for 24 hours.

On the hill behind the Paseo Maritimo is an area known as **El Terreno**, where several large hotels and luxury villas are located; also there is nightlife, cafés and restaurants.

Tour 5: Pueblo España

On the outskirts of Palma in the Santa Catalina area is the **Pueblo España** (Spanish Village) open 0900 to 2000 hrs. This is an amazing conglomeration of Spanish architecture all put together to create a show village for tourists! A pleasant and interesting time can be had as one wanders down these reconstructed streets. One moment you have a glimpse of the white walls of an Andalusian bar, where a bottle of the local wine from Binissalem costs 500 pesetas; then around the corner you are in front of an elegant town house from Cordoba.

Go inside a shop that is a replica of one in Segovia, there you see craftsmen from that old city at work and can purchase their products; a silver and leather bracelet costs about 800 pesetas. Farther still and you will stop to wonder at the patience and skill of the adept fingers that make such exquisite marquetry boxes, inlaid with silver and mother of pearl; each stage is on display. Hand embroidery, paintings, lovely costume dolls are for sale; it is a useful place to purchase souvenirs.

This outdoor museum gives you a potted glimpse of parts of mainland Spain, showing, to name a few, the glory of Granada's Alhambra, Seville's Giralda Tower and Madrid's El Escorial, all cleverly reproduced and enclosed in a very small area. Restaurants and bars are busy. A Menu of the Day costs 800 pesetas; if you are in a hurry, have an icecream, it is delicious and costs 150 pesetas. Address: Calle Marinero Moll y Capitan Mesquida Veny 53. The shops are open 1000 to 1800 hrs.

Palma is Majorca's brightest gem, colourful by day and sparkling at night. So do not rush your visit to this fascinating city.

ELEVEN

South-west from Palma to Sant Telm

To the west of Palma lies the great crescent of white sand that forms part of the playground of the island. Here are the blocks of high rise apartments and tourist hotels, together with supermarkets, amusement centres, restaurants, discos and nightclubs. Everything needed for a happy family holiday is to be found here, making it ideal for so many, who return year after year to enjoy the hot sun, golden beaches and have fun.

The distance from Palma to Sant Telm (Sant Elm on the Firestone map), excluding the drive to Galilea, is about 30 km.

Cala Major to Magalluf

From Palma a fast motorway winds slightly inland behind the packed resorts of **Cala Major** and **Sant Agusti**. A coastal road runs near to the beaches and through the towns, but use this road only if you wish to make a stop at these resorts because it is always busy with lorries delivering supplies to the vast number of hotels and shops.

At **Illetes** the sandy beaches are small, flanked by wooded hillsides. Three tiny islands offshore give it its name. Here you will find luxury hotels that cling to the slopes of the steep hills. This is an upmarket resort for visitors who do not require a sandy beach but prefer to get their suntan in the grounds of an elegant hotel.

You may be interested to know that King Juan Carlos of Spain has a residence towards Cala Major. The **Marivent Palace** has for years been a favourite home for the King, Queen Sophia, and the children Elena, Christina and Felipe. "Los Reyes", as the Royal Family is called in Spanish, live privately in this holiday house, and the King is known, jokingly, as Tourist Number One. Juan Carlos is a great lover of sports and flies his own aeroplane; his great pleasure is to sail the Royal Yacht, Fortuna, and his family share his favourite hobby.

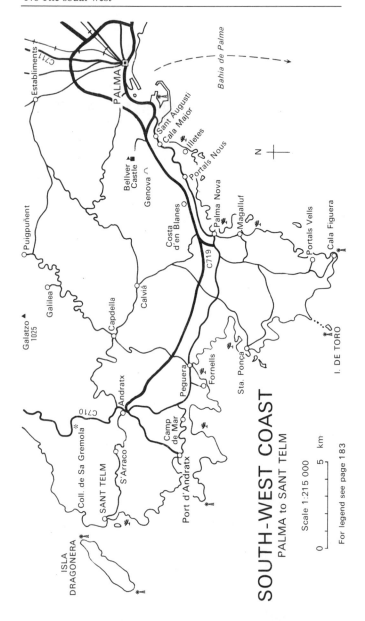

SOUTH-WEST COAST
PALMA to SANT TELM

Scale 1:215 000

For legend see page 183

Recently Prince Charles and Princess Diana, with their two young sons, have been regular guests of the Spanish Royal family during the summer, staying here at the Palace.

Before you travel farther westwards, a very worthwhile visit can be made to **Castillo de Bellver** (Bellver Castle) standing some 135m above sea level, surrounded by the pine-wooded Bellver Park. This imposing castle is one of the finest examples of fourteenth-century military architecture and has commanded sea and land approaches to Palma since it was built by order of King Jaime II. Because of Majorca's mild climate, it is in a splendid state of preservation. Once used as a summer retreat by Mallorquin kings, in its time it has served also as a jail for political prisoners and criminals. Many have been executed here. See the dungeons in the Tower of Homage and look at the names scratched on the outside walls of the tower; it makes the imagination stir. Climb the narrow staircase past the circular courtyard, with its old well; then revel in the view from the ramparts. Before you lies the entire Bay of Palma in all its panoramic splendour; great ships lying at anchor, large and small pleasure boats jostling for space, busy fishing vessels unloading their slippery catch. Sunlight glistens on the blue green waters of the Mediterranean and not far away the mighty Cathedral stands proud and beautiful. You will need your camera for such a visit. The castle is open from 0900 hrs until sunset, at which time it is floodlit and looks like a fairy castle.

While in the vicinity of Bellver Castle, a short drive takes you to **Genova**, a small town on the outskirts of Palma. Here you will find notable restaurants which take pride in serving true Mallorquin menus, in an authentic decor: try Restaurant C'an Pedro. The town has a fine cave full of fantastic stalagmites and stalactites; usually there is an English-speaking guide. Open from 1000 to 1300 and 1530 to 1730 hrs. Sunday 1000 to 1500 hrs.

Continuing the journey along the *autopista*, westwards, it is necessary to turn off towards the sea if you wish to visit the resorts of **Magalluf**, **Palma Nova** and **Portals Nous**, part of the Bay of Palma. They are well signposted. This is very much the heart of the main tourist area which is so well advertised by British package holiday firms.

Close to Portals Nous is the newly built marina of **Puerto Portals**, where some of the largest luxury yachts in the Mediterranean are berthed. Completed in 1987 this modern development has attracted the jet set to use its boatyards and excellent berthing facilities. Nearby are boutiques, bars and restaurants serving nouvelle cuisine.

Fat Sams is a bar featuring live entertainment till the early hours of the morning. Another late bar is Lena's Bistro. Quite near, between Portals Bay and the yacht marina is a spacious, sandy beach, manmade in the mid eighties. It is perhaps the best beach in the locality.

Portals Nous has a small sandy beach with rocks, suitable for deep water swimming; pine groves and pretty wild plants add to the colour of the turquoise sea. At nearby **Costa d'en Blanes** you will find a children's amusement park called **Marineland**. This contains a dolphinarium where shows are given every hour. As well as dolphins, sea lions and parrots have been trained for your entertainment. A mini zoo, aviary, snake house and Polynesian pearl divers are included in the visit. There is a restaurant and playground. After the show you might want to make use of the private beach; hire of layout chairs costs 300 pesetas.

The seafront at **Palma Nova** is level and there is access for the disabled to the sandy beach. Sunbeds can be hired for 300 pesetas a day and sun umbrellas for 100 pesetas. A five minute walk inland from the main seafront road leads to Calle Tennis and **Golf Fantasia**, Tel: 69 23 49. Three 18-hole putting courses amid lakes, waterfalls, tropical garden and mysterious caves provide a fun game for all the family. Open from 1030 hrs to midnight.

Palma Nova and **Magalluf** virtually join with each other and are the largest nucleus of tourist attraction on the Calvia coast, as this part is called. One of the first residential tourist developments, it began back in 1934. It is suitable for holidaymakers of all ages, especially for those who wish for plenty of activities and entertainment, and do not mind the high density of the hotels and apartment blocks. At night you hear music coming from bars, pubs, discos and restaurants at every corner. There are cabaret and flamenco shows for the choosing. Majorca's **Casino Palladium** is close to Magalluf and is part of a huge sports complex, open during the day. Tennis, golf, horse-riding and most sea sports are readily available. Soft sands provide hours of play for children, and suntans too. Nearby low pinewoods offer cool walks and places for shady picnics.

In Magalluf you will find a wide range of apartments and hotels, providing clean and comfortable accommodation. Magalluf has become a concentrated leisure centre which has spread inland from the sandy beaches, and now includes a huge Agua Park, Go-Karting, Golf Course and a Western City called El Rancho. **Cala Vinyes** is a tiny bay that is the last beach in the Bay of Palma.

Inland excursion: Palma Nova to Galilea

Anyone wanting a change from sea and sand is well advised to take a drive inland, leaving the main road at the 14 km mark opposite Palma Nova, towards the town of **Calvia**. The road winds up through green wooded country with fine views of the mountains beyond; all is quiet and peaceful. Here you see a different aspect of Majorca; olive and almond trees abound and there is little movement other than a farmer working his field, and birds and butterflies flying overhead.

Calvia, situated on a small hill, is the main town and administrative centre of this area. In a little square the Town Hall stands near a fine Parish Church which originally dated from 1245; it has been added to in different styles. Most noteworthy is the facade with a Romanesque portal and large Gothic window, all flanked by two slender towers. Market day in Calvia is on a Monday and products from every part of the island are on sale.

Having driven away from the sea, do carry on for a further three kilometres inland to **Capdella**; it is only a wee village with few proper streets. In February the surrounding fields are full of pink and white almond blossom. From the northern outskirts of the village by the Son Claret estate is one of the finest views in the south of Majorca: the enormous silhouette of **Puig del Galatzo**, its grey peak rising to 1,025 m, which seems to beckon you on.

A delightful day trip from the Calvia coast is to continue on from Capdella to the mountain village of **Galilea**. This is very much a country route that twists and turns with some tortuous bends, so it is not for those who dislike heights. The more adventurous will have a glorious ride enjoying the contrast of the lovely green countryside – the air sweetly perfumed with wild flowers and pine trees – with the sea and sand they have left behind.

Impressive panoramas open out at each bend in the road, until you reach the mountain village of **Galilea** (505 m). Here, turn left off the main road, then climb up to the square in front of the parish church, where there are splendid views. Those who are artistically inclined will be tempted to paint the picture. After refreshments continue on the circular tour, but do not hurry past the bizarre shaped rocks. Eventually you will arrive at **Puigpunyent** and the Mallorquin mansions of Son Net and Son Fortesa, set in the midst of orchards; you may be able to purchase some of the fruit here. Your route then takes you along the road in the direction of Establiments and travel becomes a little faster, but be careful, you will have to keep a look outfor the turning southwards back to Calvia. If you carry on you will

There are two resorts called Cala Figuera. The pretty little cove above with a small anchorage for yachts is on the east coast (see page 188).

find yourself back in Palma. This pleasant detour from Palma Nova to Galilea and back is about 50 kilometres.

Portals Vells to Port d'Andratx

Returning to the coast again there are some delightful quiet small coves, ideal for swimming, like **Portals Vells** and **Cala Figuera**.

They lie on the southern tip of this side of the island; it is here, too, that Majorca's only official nudist beach is found, **Playa Mago**. Do not expect too much, for it is very small and to reach it you must drive through thick pine woods along a dusty road, the last fifty metres being very steep. However there is a bar by the beach and the water is beautifully clear and usually quite calm.

Cala Figuera is a series of holiday houses and apartments all set in pine clad hills. From the cliffs you have a good view of **Isla del Toro** and around the corner, farther westwards, the so-called **Costa de la Calma.**

At the 19 km point on the C719 road from Palma to Andratx lies the bay of **Santa Ponça**. This is very important in Majorca's history, because it was here that King Jaime I landed with his forces on 10 September 1229, and so began the Spanish conquest of the island. A majestic stone cross now marks the event. It is worthwhile making a visit to this monument for the base of this victory cross has splendid graphic relief work which depicts the battles and brave deeds of that landing. It is the work of the sculptor Tomás Vila.

The small islands off shore are called Malgrat, and from the vista point of the same name, on Majorca, there is a superb view of the Bay of Santa Ponça. In the distance to the right, the outline of Sa Mola point and in the foreground the Cap des Llamp (Lightning Point) and the beaches of Peguera and Camp de Mar, separated by the promontory of Cap Andritxol, can be seen. All along the coast are sweet smelling pine woods.

Santa Ponça Bay is wide with golden sands and intensely blue waters, shallow along the beach and safe for young children. Farther into deep waters, windsurfers spread their moth-like sails in a blaze of vivid colour, making this one of today's most popular sports. Powerful speedboats jostle for a passage among small sailing boats, while inshore the less intrepid sailors paddle their pedalos, or just stand in the sea having a gossip! In the complexes, amongst the shops, souvenir hunters wander; the cafés serve huge icecreams and strawberry gateaux; bars playing lively tunes dispense large glasses of frothy beer, and the waiters are always on the look out for a pretty girl.

Peguera, too, is blessed with soft clean sand, added to which pinewoods grow almost to the edge of the sea, while sun umbrellas and layout chairs denote that it is a place for relaxation. The main streets and shops in Peguera are always busy and crowded, even in winter; for many of the big hotels here cater for long stay visitors taking advantage of its sheltered position.

People sit on their terraces sipping wine or sangria, taking their fill of fresh air and sunshine; the warm glow of the evening light creates lengthening shadows and reflections on the waters of the cove. **Cala Fornells**, near Peguera, is noted for its breathtaking sunsets. Here you can appreciate the Mediterranean magic as tones of radiant red and gold tinge the buildings and foreshore. It is a place of rest and contentment.

Just before the 25 km mark, turn off the Palma to Andratx road towards **Camp de Mar**. This popular resort is built around a tiny and pretty bay, with steep hills rising to the east and west. Here every piece of land has been developed to the water's edge. A small restaurant is set on a tiny islet reached by a rather frail bridge. Many tourists enjoy the walk up the hill to the west as it leads to **Port d' Andratx**. A winding road that climbs high gives glorious views seawards, then comes a forest of pines and shrubs, where birds sing and dragonflies spread their wings amongst the flowers and heather.

The walk (or drive) downhill into **Port d'Andratx** reveals a splendid natural harbour, which in recent years has developed from a small fishing port into a smart yachting centre. Still attractive, much of its natural beauty remains and it is very popular with British residents and artists. This is a pleasant place for a stroll followed by a quiet meal in one of the colourful restaurants. Here you can hire a boat for a day cruise or fishing, perhaps go for a sail. Graceful yachts from far away places have magical names, their crews giving an international flavour to this flourishing port. It is a place where you will wish to linger in the sunshine.

Andratx and Sant Telm

The tour of the southwest region is completed by a visit to the town of Andratx and neighbouring **Sant Telm**. From Port d'Andratx drive inland two kilometres from the harbour, where a secondary road leads to **S. Arraco**; this is a short cut to Sant Telm avoiding Andratx, a scenic drive along a narrow country road amongst fields of olive, almond and fig trees, with the high **Tramuntana** range of mountains in the distance.

However, before you make your way to Sant Telm, do drive the further three kilometres into the old town of **Andratx** (pronounced ''Andratch''). Lying at the bottom of a large agricultural valley, the town has streets that betray its Roman origins. As with many ancient sites in Majorca, it was constructed inland from the sea as a precaution against pirates. It is a solemn place with tall solid houses. The great parish church of **Santa Maria** dates back to the early thirteenth century. Close by you will notice a fine old Mallorquin house called **Son Mas**, which means ''lovely mansion''. This was originally a Moorish fort and from its terraces, complete with cannon, you can see a beautiful wide view of Andratx, the surrounding orange groves and the distant blue sea.

From Andratx it is eight kilometres to Sant Telm, passing through the pretty village of S. Arraco (previously mentioned), and driving through quite wild and craggy countryside.

Sant Telm is the most westerly point in Majorca. Originally a small fishing village, it is fast developing into a resort, popular with Mallorquin families, who like to use the small sandy beach at weekends; it is possible to swim there, though sometimes the beach is covered with seaweed. Facing the beach is the sloping island of **Dragonera**, which is privately owned. It has a lighthouse and is a nature reserve for both flora and fauna. Out on a point is an old watch tower and from there, on a clear day, you can see in the distance the island of Ibiza.

In the village are several good fish restaurants and a few tourist shops. At the westerly end is a small hostal, simple and clean, in a prime position overlooking a tiny bay. A pleasant bar and restaurant serve freshly prepared meals. Menu of the Day 800 pesetas may feature fried chicken, tomato salad, fresh fruit, bread and wine included; paella 750 pesetas. You can sit on the terrace for your meal and relish the tranquil atmosphere.

There are many walks on the headland and one can visit the ruins of an ancient Trappist Monastery, 380m up a rocky cliffside. This walk is described in detail in *Landscapes of Mallorca* (see Bibliography). Remember to take a sunhat in the summer and stout walking footwear.

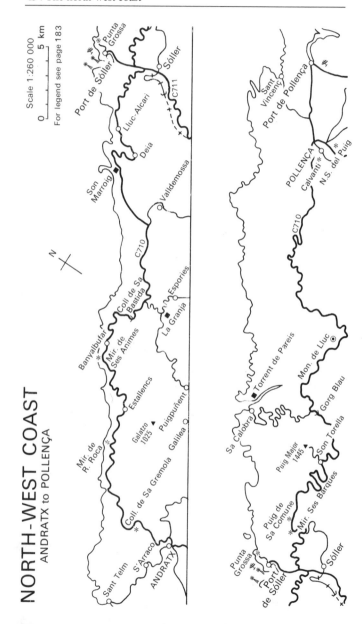

NORTH-WEST COAST
ANDRATX to POLLENÇA

Scale 1:260 000

0 ___ 5 km

For legend see page 183

TWELVE

The north-west coast: Andratx to Pollença

This section of the coast from Andratx to Pollença is about 151 km. Some of Majorca's most dramatic scenery is on this west coast. Certainly it is an area that deserves to be seen by all who visit the island; this can be done by day rides in a rented car, by taxi or perhaps best of all by joining a coach excursion, where the guide will give you all sorts of information about what you are seeing and you may be certain that you will not be late home for your evening meal!

Majorca's history tells of constant strife with pirates. After so much trouble a series of watch towers was built to form a chain round the island. Whenever the enemy was sighted the alarm was raised by lighting big fires, to warn the people of danger. Along the west coast some of these strong fortresses still remain.

Andratx to Coll de Sa Bastida

A very good coast road climbs from **Andratx**; as you leave the town you have a clear view of the unusual cemetery, with its strange layout that has burial niches, four and five feet high above the ground. Six kilometres out of Andratx is the **Coll de Sa Gremola** where the road passes a cleft in the rock; on the other side the view is impressive. Down below the deep blue sea sparkles, curious craggy rock formations are at the water's edge and inaccessible sandy bays come into view.

The C710 with its many curves is scenic for the passenger but hard work for the driver, so he will be pleased to stop at a super viewpoint called **Mirador de Roca**, with over a 503 m drop down to the sea. Refreshments are available at the **Es Grau restaurant** and bar; the service is usually speedy and there are toilets. Open from 0800 to

2000 hrs. You may see Mallorquin women at the side of the road, busy making lace and sewing tablecloths. These are expensive, but it's a rare opportunity to purchase such beautiful handmade linen.

From the restaurant the road drops quickly into **Estellencs**, a narrow village with steep streets and steps leading to pretty houses, many bright with bougainvillea and geraniums. Terraces around are planted with almonds and olives. Parking can be a problem here at weekends with family traffic on the roads.

The next stopping place along this beautiful corniche road will be the **Torre Mirador de los Animas** (the tower of the spirits), built in the seventeenth century. You must climb up its old steps to a platform and look out to sea, where in the distance can be seen the island of Dragonera and Port de Sóller. And, if you dare, look almost two hundred and fifty metres below to where a bubbling sea hits the rocks in a spectacular white foam.

Now you come to the old village of **Banyalbufar** which in Arabic means ''little vineyard by the sea''. It has ancient terraces built steeply against the hillsides. Olive trees here are gnarled and twisted into strange shapes, some are thought to be more than a thousand years old. Originally cut by the Moors, the terraces are irrigated by large water cisterns and channels. Today, well-staked tomatoes grow making a carpet of green which contrasts strongly with the blue of the sky and the dusty soil. The tiny beach way down below was once a favourite landing place for smugglers. The road continues now past the **Coll de Sa Bastida**, a minor road to the right leads off to La Granja (see Chapter 16). Going past the **Coll de Claret** with its steep bends the road continues through the village of Nova and soon reaches the sign for Valldemossa which stands at a height of 400m.

Valldemossa

One of the most popular tourist attractions in Majorca is the **Carthusian Monastery** at **Valldemossa**, where the Polish composer and pianist Fréderic Chopin spent a bleak winter in 1835 with the French authoress George Sand. Chopin had heard about this island of sunshine and hoped it would improve his health; unfortunately it rained incessantly. George Sand (Baroness Dupin Duoevant) and her two children quarrelled with the local inhabitants, who strongly disapproved of her relationship with Chopin, and were scandalised because she wore trousers, smoked cigars and never went to Mass. George Sand wrote a book about the island called *Un Hiver en*

Although the western coastline is rugged with steep cliffs, where possible the tenacious farmers have terraced the land to grow crops.

Majorque, which was hardly a hymn of praise; however it did bring to the notice of many people the possibility of spending winter in a warmer climate.

Today, coachloads of eager tourists descend several times a week on this lovely old monastery, built five hundred and sixty three metres above the sea. For some it is a place that still retains a little of the tranquillity from the days when the cells contained men of faith. There is a large car park and the little village does its best to provide what every tourist expects in the way of souvenir shops and refreshments. The all-in ticket to view the monastery includes a visit to the monk's pharmacy, where rows of ancient jars recall the skill of the monks. The Prior's cell has a magnificent library; other cells are said to have been used by Chopin and contain original music scores and other memorabilia of his stay there. Outside the cells is a small herb garden, from where a balcony looks out over the lovely surrounding mountainside with a distant view of Palma. During the summer months musical concerts are given in the cloisters of La Cartuja, the Carthusian Monastery. Many world famous musicians give performances here.

Before you leave here, a visit must be made to the adjacent **Palace of King Sancho**, included in your ticket. When visiting as part of a coach excursion you will have the added pleasure of a colourful exhibition of folk dancing and music in authentic Mallorquin style. The monastery is open from 0930 to 1300 and 1500 to 1830 hrs. In winter it is open only in the morning. Price of admission 400 pesetas.

Valldemossa is the birthplace of Majorca's only saint, Catalina Thomás, canonised in 1930. The house where she was born has been turned into a small museum. Across the street from Santa Catalina's house is the Gothic parish church which dates back to 1245, one of the oldest in Majorca. In Valldemossa on 27 and 28 July, there are celebrations in honour of their saint.

Should you wish to return direct to Palma, or the nearby resorts, there is a well signed road leading from the main car park. Palma is eighteen kilometres south. On the way, just north of S'Esgleieta you may wish to make a stop at the La Fiore glass works.

Deiá to Port de Sóller

Returning now to the coastal road C710, just south of Deia you will see the grand mansion and grounds of **Son Marroig** which once belonged to the Archduke Ludwig Salvator of Austria. This famous man first visited the island in 1876 and returned two years later to stay for over forty years. His great contribution to the island that he loved was his six volume *Die Balearen*, based on his intimate knowledge of the culture, sociology, geography and botany of Majorca. Today his beautiful house is a museum, open to the public, which contains furniture, paintings and Roman finds. In the garden, along a little path, is a Greek temple made out of imported Carrara marble; from there the view stretches across from **Cap Gros** to

Estellencs. Son Marroig is open from Monday to Saturday 0930 to 1430 hrs and in summer 1630 to 2000, winter 1600 to 1800 hrs. Sunday 0930 to 1430.

Now you are at **Deia** (sometimes spelt Deya or Deja), well known for its association with painters and writers. Surprisingly, the village receives the worst weather on all the island, owing to the proximity of high mountains. Once you have seen the steep cobbled streets and well-kept houses, you will understand why so many extol its beauty. You will see also a series of little tiled altars reproducing the scenes of the Calvary.

All around orange and lemon groves make splashes of colour; terraces of ancient olive trees climb the side of the steep terrain. On the outskirts of Deia the English poet and author Robert Graves had a permanent home until his death. The author of *I, Claudius* did much to advance the popularity of this village. A small archaeological museum here contains finds from the nearby cave of **Son Muleta**, some of which date back as far as 4000 BC, and includes remains of prehistoric gazelles.

Next on our drive along the coastal route we reach **Lluc Alcari**, with its three watch towers and a mirador showing more extensive views of mountains and sea. Now the main road descends quickly to the great bay and valley of Sóller. The Moors, enchanted with its beauty, called it Sulltar (The Golden).

In an almost circular bay, a serene harbour of calm waters, is **Port de Sóller**, its sheltered position making it a popular place for visitors wishing for a quieter venue than the southern resorts. In the past it has been much favoured by French emigrés and their influence is still seen in some of the architecture, reminiscent of the south of France. Even today, French is spoken as well as Spanish and Mallorquin. The hotels and restaurants, too, make a point of advertising their French cuisine, subsequently their prices tend to be higher than elsewhere. The beach is part sand and part pebble.

Five kilometres inland and one reaches one of Majorca's most beautiful towns, **Sóller**. Every book written about the island extols the golden valley and its sweetly scented air. Surrounded by tidy farms with extensive orange, lemon and almond groves, Sóller is dominated by some of Majorca's highest peaks and protected from the cold winds, therefore it has a mild climate throughout the year. In the town stands the Baroque **Convent of San Francisco** and the parish church of **San Bartolomé**. Inside the latter is an unusual statue in black marble of Saint Bartholomew. Close to the main Plaza are the train and tram terminals.

It is great fun to take the train from Palma (the station is in the Plaza España) to Sóller. This narrow gauge single track railway, with trains dating back to 1912, still runs a daily service, and is used by the locals as well as tourists. It's rather a hard ride at first as the wooden carriages jog their way through the streets of Palma – yes, the line is in the middle of the road! Then with its American style whistle, it hoots its way across fields and up into the mountains. There are thirteen tunnels on the route to Sóller; the longest is three kilometres and takes six minutes. Before the train reaches its destination a stop is made at a platform allowing passengers to alight and take photographs of the valley of Sóller and the mountains with **Puig Major** (1445 m). The train then winds its way down to the tiny railway station.

If this is not enough excitement for one day, then you can take a tram ride from Sóller to Port de Sóller, five kilometres away. It is said that the old fashioned tram was imported from San Francisco early this century; it is a singular experience as it rolls speedily down the mountain to the sea front.

Sóller is the scene of a great fiesta in May, when there is a vivid re-enactment of the reconquest of the island, when "Moors and Christians" fight a mock battle.

Should you wish to return quickly to Palma from Sóller, instead of using the coastal road, there is a route using the C711 that takes you inland, climbing fast from the golden valley in a series of hair raising bends, up to the **Col de Sóller** (496m), then down again, still in a tortuous zig-zag manner amid spectacular scenery, until you reach level ground and a fast, almost straight road to Palma.

Gorg Blau, Sa Calobra and the Lluc Monastery

Again we return to the C710 and travel northwards, twisting and turning as the modern road seeks a route through the mountains of **Puig de Sa Comuna**. Now you are climbing with panoramic views of Sóller below, finally you reach the **Mirador de Ses Barques**. Looking out to sea, on the left is the white Cap Gros lighthouse, on the right the **Punta Grossa** and the old watch tower Torre Picada.

Drive on for more breath taking scenery; then you reach a tunnel as you penetrate the **Torrellas** massif. Way down below is a deep valley with olive and oak trees. The Spanish Air Force Base comes as a shock amid such grandeur. The road leading to the summit, Puig Major (1445 m), is closed to the public because of the radar station there. So you carry on travelling and reach the **Gorg Blau** pass (935 m), the highest on the island, then down to the reservoir and an old aqueduct; all is very quiet here and maybe you will see eagles flying amongst the wild landscape. The Gorg Blau is 550m long and up to 100m deep. By the reservoir there is a carpark, so you are able to leave your vehicle to enjoy the fresh air. Here you will see a roughly hewn column and a plaque which states that it was unearthed in 1969 during road making excavations. It is thought to have originated from an ancient temple, probably sixth century AD.

The next part of the road goes through a tunnel; drive slowly as there is a turn in the road and you reach the road junction leading to Sa Calobra. Are you going to be brave and drive on what globetrotters say is the most fantastic and impressive road in Europe? This mountainous route, a masterpiece of engineering, twists and turns for fourteen kilometres in a fearful series of spectacular hairpin bends. It has one's ears popping and head reeling. This is definitely a drive for the adventurous; and remember that you have to return the same route along with those massive tourist coaches, their back ends hanging out over unguarded corners, so that the passengers gasp and close their eyes.

It is a wonderful experience because, apart from the exciting ride, the scenery almost defies description. You are amongst some of nature's art treasures. The rocky curved limestone outcrop contains shapes and contortions that seem impossible; alpine plants snuggle in sheltered crevices; surely amongst this wild garden you will find some gnomes. Now you see changes in the colour and shapes of the rocks so that they look like organ pipes glistening in the bright sun. So in a dazed state you reach sea level and the bay of **Sa Calobra**.

For those who do not enjoy such a ride, Sa Calobra can be reached by boat from Port de Sóller, unless the weather makes the sea too rough. Restaurants cluster around the small beach, tourists' cars and coaches fight for parking space, boats moor at the tiny jetty.

But more pleasures are to come, for you have yet to see the **Torrente de Pareis**. To reach this you must walk through a dimly lit tunnel which is one hundred and eighty three metres in length, and in places so small that you have to stoop low – so watch your head. The Torrente de Pareis, like all canyons, was formed by rushing waters from the mountains which after millions of years wore away a great gorge. The sides of the ravine rise to six hundred and eight metres in places and it is called the Grand Canyon of Majorca. Waters still flow

This beautifully carved statue of Joaquim Rossello (1833 to 1909) is to be found in a tranquil courtyard at Lluc Monastery. He founded the now famous choir.

and it is only in summer that hardy walkers are able to explore the four kilometres of this prehistoric gorge. It is sensible to hire the services of an experienced guide.

Who goes down must come up. So when you have visited Sa Calobra allow time for those hairpin bends before you reach the C710 once again. Should you wish to continue your sightseeing, then a further stop may be made to visit the famous **Monasterio de Lluc**.

As with all the monasteries in Majorca, it is built in a superb position high in the mountains, serene and beautiful. The legend of Lluc is that a little shepherd boy found a small wooden statue of the Madonna amongst some rocks. He took it to the local priest who put it in the church for safe keeping, But during the night the statue disappeared only to be re-discovered in the same place where it was originally found.

Twice more this incident happened. So the priest took this as a sign from Heaven and he built a small chapel there amongst the rocks; later in 1260 the monastery was built.

The little statue, Our Lady of Lluc *(Nuestra Señora de Lluc)*, also known as Lamorerata (The Little Brown One), is the Patron Saint of Majorca. Each September thousands of Mallorquins make a pilgrimage to this site to pay homage to the Madonna. Now bejewelled with twenty-two diamonds, twenty-five emeralds, twenty-five rubies and more than six hundred pearls donated by the islanders, she is believed to have performed numerous miracles. You can see her behind the high altar in a small chapel, offering consolation and confidence to the faithful. Inside the cloisters a small museum houses numerous gifts made to this rich monastery. The museum is open from 1000 to 1800 hrs.

Today Lluc Monastery is a college where the monks of Saint Augustine direct a music and choral school for boys. If you are fortunate, your visit to Lluc will coincide with the voices of these young choristers and musicians, who usually perform at 1100 hrs. Do not be put off by the tourist shop and restaurant, such things have to be for today's modern travellers. A large car park is suitable for an overnight stay.

Part of the monastery has been turned into guest apartments, to be used by pilgrims and anyone seeking shelter for the night. This accommodation is very simple, virtually a bed in a cell for which there is a small fee of 1,120 pesetas a night for two persons, a hot bath included. If you are a very important guest, you may be offered the Bishop's room, which contains a four-poster bed and a tranquil view of the pine covered mountainside.

Lluc to Pollença

Leaving Lluc you are still on the C710 as you make your way to Pollença (Pollensa) twenty six kilometres away and the northern end of the island. This drive takes you into wild mountainous scenery, with only nature and the odd tourist car. Few visitors make this journey, so you may find a picnic spot where you will be quite alone. The ICONA – Instituto Nacional para la Conservation de Naturaleza – has created three picnic areas on the C710. They are well equipped with benches, tables and wood burning, barbecue ovens, water taps and toilet facilities. Permission to stay over night must be obtained from the Warden. Various walks, some strenuous, can be had along the route. Some of the road is steep and winding, and at every twist and bend there is another stunning view; this is the land of eagles, vultures and falcons. As you get lower and nearer to Pollença trees begin to appear, the great holm oak and the carob; wild flowers, too, and suddenly you have arrived among fields, orchards and back to civilisation.

Pollença, or Pollensa, is a very important and elegant town with its origins going back to Roman times. On the outskirts of the town, the remains of an ancient Roman bridge still span a small stream. The closely built town with its tall houses has straight narrow streets that lead to the **Plaza Mayor** or main square. Here on the Sunday market day, the scene is one of activity, an international meeting place. Sit in the sun or shade at one of the many cafés, perhaps the **Cafe Espanyol Can Moixet**, and absorb this Mediterranean atmosphere; full of chatter and a wide range of characters, it is typical Majorca. This is one of the oldest markets on the island, continuing a tradition dating from the fifteenth century, when farmers and country folk brought their produce to town. To this day fresh vegetables, fruit, flowers, plants, olives, honey and sweets are set out for sale but there are no clothes stalls, gypsy traders or pseudo antique dealers here, just a simple, genuine and happy market.

Close by is the **Convent of Santo Domingo**, where the Pollença Music Festival takes place in July and August. This festival is of much importance in the musical world and artists of repute are invited. On the cloister walls is a plaque to the honour of the founder of the festival, Philip Newman. Other festivals in Pollença are the Good Friday medieval style Procession of the Devallament held at midnight round the town, and also in August a re-enactment of the 1550 victory over Turkish pirates, when one man dresses up in skins and a mask and others don oriental costumes and dance through the streets.

The story of the **Pollença Calvary**, according to tradition, is of shipwrecked mariners who were driven ashore in the nearby **Sant Vincenç Bay**. Saved from a watery grave, they in turn had salvaged a huge wooden cross. Full of gratitude for their salvation they carried this to a high hill where it was erected and, years later, a small chapel was added. Today you reach it by climbing up a flight of three hundred and sixty five stone steps, with tall, dark, cypress trees lining both sides. Three hundred and sixty five days to a year – as you climb you can ponder on life and the path to heaven. When you have finally reached the top, the beautiful panorama stretching out below compensates your eyes for the effort of your legs. If you are unable to walk up, there is also a tricky and narrow road to the top, the last part being marked with the fourteen Stations of the Cross. Here, high above Pollença, you look out over the red roofs of the town, the mountains of the Tramuntana behind you and ahead the Bay of Pollença, leading to the peninsula of Formentor.

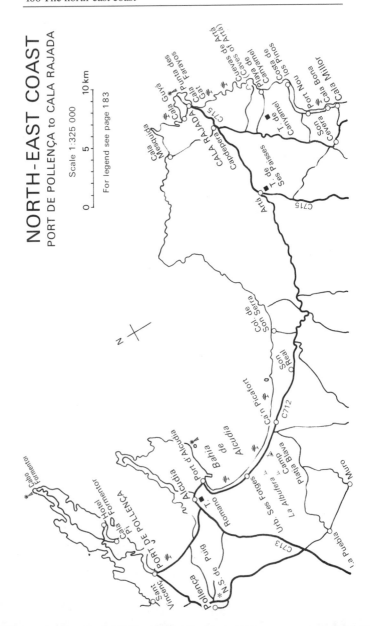

NORTH-EAST COAST
PORT DE POLLENÇA to CALA RAJADA

Scale 1:325 000

0   5   10 km

For legend see page 183

THIRTEEN

The north-east coast:
Port de Pollença to Cala Rajada

This section of the north-east coast stretches from Majorca's northernmost point, marked by the Cabo Formentor lighthouse, through to its north-eastern tip at Cala Rajada. In between there is a variety of different landscapes and impressions: the wild seas, wonderful bird life and bracing walks of Formentor and Sant Vincenç; the Roman ruins at Alcudia; the golden sands and outdoor pursuits of Camping Platja Blava and Camping Club San Pedro; the dignified towns of Sa Pobla and Muro surrounded by rich farmlands; quiet roads and open country – and then sandy bays and a tourist complex.

The distance from Port de Pollença to Cala Rajada including the excursions to Formentor, Sa Pobla and Muro described here is approximately 161 km.

Formentor and Sant Vincenç

Majorca is full of fabulous views and none more spectacular than those you will see when you visit Formentor. Jutting out like a finger fourteen kilometres long, it has at its extremity a lighthouse, the **Cabo Formentor**, built in 1860, and an important marker for shipping.

This high formation of limestone rock with steep cliffs, some being three hundred metres vertical, gives sheer drops into the whirling waters below. Out at sea is the impressive rock of Colmer Island, haunt of various sea birds. At the viewpoint by the lighthouse you will have extensive views to the north and east, and on a clear day Menorca can be seen.

The construction of the road from Port de Pollença to the Cabo is an engineering feat of much wonder. A monument to **Antonio Parietti** stands as a testimony to his skill. While driving on this narrow road keep a look out for the herd of wild goats that graze amongst the rocks. Nowadays they are a protected species and, becoming tame, they do not dash off at the sight of a camera.

This is always an exciting drive because of the number of sharp bends in the road. One story told by the courier on the coach is of a pastor and a coach driver reaching the Gates of Heaven. Saint Peter allows the coach driver through, but to the pastor he says, "Sorry, you may not enter". Amazed, the pastor asked Saint Peter the reason, to be told that he never managed to fill his church with people, yet the coach driver, as he drove round the bends in Majorca, had everyone praying!

While in the Pollença area a worthwhile drive is to **Sant Vincenç**, a small resort so popular with writers and painters, who appreciate its beautiful rocky cliffs and peaceful situation. On the small esplanade, by the sandy beach, is a statue of the painter **Llorenc Cerda Bisbal**, 1862 to 1955. A few hotels cater for clients who wish for a quiet holiday, and among them must be some British tourists, for a notice outside one café advertises the ubiquitous "English Breakfasts". Because it is sheltered here the gardens of the many villas are a brilliant blaze of blooms. Bougainvillea, jasmine and geraniums climb high, stately yuccas with their creamy flowers mix with the many coloured zinnias; banks of rosemary growing taller than usual sweetly perfume the air.

Around this area are several very interesting walks; details of these can be obtained from a booklet issued free by tourist offices, called *Twenty Hiking Excursions on the Island of Majorca*. The walk to the ruined hilltop monastery **Sanctuario del Puig** (304 m) and the longer excursion to the **Castell del Rey** are two that are not too difficult for the average walker. Remember to wear strong footwear, and take a jacket if the weather is likely to be windy; the addition of a sunhat is sensible.

Port de Pollença and the Bay of Alcudia

Elegant and tidy with an old world charm, **Port de Pollença** is situated at the northern end of the Bay of Pollença. A vast number of Spanish tourists stay here every summer. The extensive seafront is a mixture of modern hotels and villas. Flat white sands and clear shallow water make the beach very safe. The harbour, which is used by pleasure boats and sailing ships, has a busy yacht marina. Windsurfers, too, enjoy the great wide arc of water and the National

Archie enjoys a fresh salmon lunch by the sea at Port de Pollença. Here people can enjoy a restful holiday without too much noise.

A notice board clearly states all the delicious dishes available at this restaurant in Port de Pollença which is open all year.

Championships have been held here. The tree-shaded promenade has arcades of shops and cafés just a short step away from the beach.

It is from here that a boat trip can be made to **Cala Pi** on the Formentor peninsula. This is a pleasant half-hour journey that takes you to yet another white sandy beach, part of which belongs to the internationally famed **Hotel Formentor**. This hideaway luxury hotel was built in 1930 by the Argentine lawyer and poet Adán Diehl. It quickly became a retreat for many titled and famous people, including Prince Rainier and the late Princess Grace of Monaco. The general public are not encouraged to enter the hotel grounds, which is a pity because the gardens are lavishly landscaped with many fine tropical plants.

However you can enjoy a walk in the pinewoods nearby; it is in this area that the dwarf fan palm *Chamaerops Humilis* grows, a most attractive plant. Long ago the dwarf fan palm was an important feature of Mallorquin cottage industry. The leaves were dried in the sun and braided into a cord, which was then used to weave chair seats and baskets. Some of this basket work, made into ornaments, is on sale in craft shops in Pollença. They make unique souvenirs.

Port de Pollença, being a quiet resort, is favoured by more elderly visitors, especially in early and late season. It has a nucleus of foreign inhabitants who have apartments in the area. The Anglada Camarasa Museum houses a good collection of artists' paintings and drawings (see Chapter 8).

Some nine kilometres along the C712 road is the town of **Alcudia**, once the Roman capital of Majorca and built in the year 123 BC by Quinto Cecilio Matelo. In those days it was called Pollentia. The ruins of that great city can be seen near the parish church of Alcudia. The **Teatro Romano** (Roman Theatre) was excavated in 1953 by the Bryant Foundation, and a plaque to the memory of William L. Bryant is seen at the entrance to the theatre. You have to walk down a short cart track to find this Roman ruin, which lies just off the C712, the Alcudia to Arta road. There is a spacious free carpark outside the old city walls.

The Talayot

The structure of a *talayot* is formed from a great number of large stones, well worked to be almost identical in shape, and used to build a round tower.

Some *talayots* rise to nine metres in height and can be thirty-five metres in diameter. Usually located on high ground or small hills, they are thought to have been used mainly as watch towers.

But these ancient stones still leave many questions unanswered and it is fascinating to wander around Seis Paises and try and visualise its ancient inhabitants.

It was the Moors who built most of the city walls that one admires today. Go through the great San Sebastion gate and along the main street, the Capitan Gual, and near the Town Hall *(Ayuntamiento)*, which has a distinctive clock tower, you will come to the **Hispano American Archaeological Museum**, open from 0900 to 1300 and 1600 to 1900 hrs. It houses a collection of items from the Roman excavations. The **Torre Mayor** watchtower was built in 1599 by order of King Philip II. The huge access gate in the eastern part of the old city walls is fifteenth century.

Three kilometres southeast from the old town of Alcudia, across a narrow neck of land is **Port d'Alcudia,** situated at the northern end of the sweeping pine fringed Bay of Alcudia. The port has a well earned reputation for its master boat builders. Always a busy harbour, it is a departure point for the car and passenger ferry to Menorca. Lineas Maritimas del Sur (Tel: 21 15 26) run a daily service during the summer months. The sailing time is two and a half hours.

The port is the start of a large tourist centre which stretches along the **Bay of Alcudia** for twelve kilometres; this is the longest beach in Majorca. Hotels and restaurants line the wide fishing harbour. The yacht marina is packed with craft; a variety of cafés and bars overflow on to the pavement in true Mediterranean style. The beach is a holiday paradise with fine white sands and a sea that is a transparent turquoise. Young children play for hours at the water's edge. More ardent swimmers may be frustrated at low tide when it is necessary to wade quite a distance to deep water.

Tall blocks of hotels and apartments inland are forming new *urbanizaciós* (villages), havens for tourists. Boutiques, souvenir shops, supermarkets, bars, discos and night clubs all serve the needs of the holidaymakers. Buses, coach tours, taxis and a few horse drawn carriages run along the coastal road. This lively centre is a popular place to hire a bicycle as there are no hills; at **Ses Fotges** urbanisation, a special track for cyclists runs alongside the main road. Two modern development are called **Lago Menor** and **Largo Mayor** (small and large lake), which together form the so called **Ciudad de los Lagos** (City of Lakes). Here the large white hotels offer good accommodation and entertainment, suitable for all age groups. Sports facilities both on the lakes and along the seashore abound.

There is just one small snag to this holiday paradise; originally this area was swampy marshland and despite the constant use of pesticide and land drainage, one must be prepared for the occasional mosquito. So, just in case, remember to take or buy some protection cream.

A small bridge across the main road, four and a half kilometres from the harbour eastwards, is the Englishman's Bridge *(Punta Ingles)*, so called because here an English engineer assisted in draining the swamps to allow the bridge to be built. Beyond the bridge the seashore is called **Playa de Muro**. The calm shallow waters and clean sand are particularly pleasant for young children. Along this coast a notable feature are the concrete obelisks that are set at intervals close to the beach. They were built during the Spanish

Club Cantabrica is popular with campers who fly out to a fully equipped tent, for an enjoyable outdoor holiday at Platja Blava

Civil War as an aid to naval gunnery practice and are now obsolete.

La Albufera was once an extensive area of shallow swamps where much rice was cultivated. However, with the encroachment of property developers this has been drastically reduced. Nowadays the remaining marshes, saltpans and lake are Majorca's finest habitat and sanctuary for wild birds. Consequently every year keen ornithologists visit the district, especially for the spring and autumn migration. Birds too numerous to list can be observed here; herons, ospreys, kingfishers and little egrets are surely enough to make you want to see more. Pretty wild flowers, like the wild muscari and the sawfly orchid, grow in the low woods on the edge of the wet lands. Various reeds and grasses provide a hide for a collection of different insects; do not be frightened if you see a snake swimming in a ditch, there are four varieties on the island and all are harmless.

Camping Platja Blava

Close to the south-east edge of Albufera is Majorca's international campsite, **Platja Blava** (Class 1A) built in 1982. Situated just off the main C712, it is clearly signposted and has a wide entrance. Across from the campsite, through pine trees and dunes is the sandy beach of **Playa de Muro** (see Chapter 4, Camping).

Sa Pobla, Cuevas de Campanet and Muro

The countryside inland behind the camp towards **Sa Pobla** is flat and highly cultivated, this being reclaimed land. In the past convict labour was used for clearing the reeds and draining the land. Windmills now pump water to the rich farmlands. Abundant crops of cereals, potatoes, onions, peas, tomatoes and salads are produced.

Because the soil is very fertile and the climate mild, three crops of potatoes can be obtained. In early spring new potatoes are exported to Britain. Large fields of aubergines and artichokes provide for the local market, and excellent strawberries are grown under cloches. A graceful statue in bronze, to be seen in Sa Pobla, was erected in 1971 and depicts the Mallorquin agricultural workers.

Windmills

It is likely that sometime during your stay in Majorca you will see windmills dotted about the countryside. There is a fine selection on the roads between the Airport and Llucmajor. Notice that there are two kinds of windmill. The lighter constructions are used to pump up water from the subterranean chambers, bringing it to the farmhouses and fields for agriculture. The more sturdy windmills mounted on thick stone blocks are used for grinding corn and storing the flour, usually having three storeys connected by a spiral staircase. Once these mills were also used to grind tobacco and clay for pottery, as well as making gunpowder.

Perhaps the best known windmills can be seen when you walk along the Maritimo in Palma: they are on a hill in the Es Jonquet area and make an attractive photograph by day and at night they are colourfully lit. One in Llucmajor, on the road to Campos has been restored and converted into an interesting museum, others have been turned into private residences.

The best time to see these windmills is in the spring when they are surrounded by delicate pink and white blossom from the almond trees. Maybe you will wonder why the huge sails of these windmills are painted in various shades. Rumour has it that the owners choose the colours of their favourite football team!

It is said that the people of Sa Pobla are some of the richest farmers on the island, because they put their hard earned money in the bank. Being practical people they are quite prepared to use old cars, so long as they keep going, why buy a new one? If their windmill cannot be mended then let it fall to pieces; they will not spend money unless really necessary.

On Sundays a large and busy market is held in Sa Pobla's main square, where a whole range of stalls with fresh produce, live animals and household goods is set up, some overflowing into the side streets. Park your car on the outskirts of town and walk the short distance to the centre. There is also a supermarket open, which is helpful for those who are self catering. It is here in the restaurants of Sa Pobla that roast rat is served as a delicacy!

Six kilometres north east of Sa Pobla, on the left of the Palma to Alcudia road, is the old world town of **Campanet.** The eighteenth century parish Church of Sant Miguel contains the relics of Victorianus, a Roman general. The town's people live by glass and basket work, there is also some farming. Two kilometres north of Campanet and signposted is the entrance to the **Campanet Caves**, *(Cuevas de Campanet).* Conducted tours take visitors a length of 1,300m, amongst delicate stalactites and stalagmites in the limestone caverns. Stout footwear is required.

Five kilometres south of Sa Pobla you reach **Muro**, quiet and sedate, an ancient Arab town and administrative centre for the area. Of interest is the **Ethnological Museum of Majorca** housed in a seventeenth-century building, and the bullring, which is hewn out of rock below ground level, the only one of its kind. Bull fights are still held here during the summer months.

C'an Picafort

Just twelve kilometres north and we are back at the coast and **C'an Picafort**, a tourist resort built between low pinewoods and the sea. It is set in the centre of Alcudia Bay, and its soft sands and gentle waters make it a splendid sunbathing spot and a delight for children and grown ups alike. The streets of C'an Picafort are full of activity, shops, restaurants and discothèques. Many British tourists enjoy this resort and such bars as the Manchester Pub provide English beer and a home-from-home atmosphere. Here you can enjoy eggs and bacon, steak and chips, Knickerbocker Glory and strawberry gateau. Above the bar, which is run by an English/Mallorquin couple, are many hand-written messages from people coming from the district of Manchester.

Club San Pedro Camping has a dramatic setting by mountains and sea in a remote part of Majorca; little shade until the trees mature.

Artá to Cala Rajada

Continuing our journey along the C712 towards Artá, we reach **Son Real** and an interesting *talayot* necropolis. Excavations were begun here in 1957 by the Bryant Foundation. Tombs in a variety of shapes have been discovered, other finds are to be seen in the Alcudia Museum.

Passing a road leading to **Colonia de Son Serra**, a small holiday development, in about six kilometres is a turning left leading to one of the best preserved *talayots* on Majorca, **Sa Conova**. This rectangular *talayot* has perfectly laid dressed blocks, inside is a column of more blocks. The road continues on to **Colonia San Pedro**. Once a tiny fishing village, of recent years Colonia San Pedro has blossomed into a holiday home resort. Small fishing boats still enter the tiny harbour and a man-made sheltered sandy beach has been created. A few restaurants, bars, supermarket and small hostals mingle with new developments. At the western edge of the village lies the **Club San Pedro Camping Park** (see Chapter 4). It has a remote setting amongst olive trees and low pines, to the west is the high ridge of the beginning of the **Sierre de Levante** and Mount Morey (561 m). This can be a refreshing walking region, out to Cabo Ferrutx at the

A view across the dry cornfields dotted with olive trees to the hilltop above Artá, where the seventeenth-century Sant Salvadore Church is surrounded by crenellated walls.

furthermost west point of Port d'Alcudia; or you can go up into the mountains to the tiny **Ermita de Betlem**.

The main road carries on through attractive shrubland; it is along here that in October the arbutus, or "strawberry" tree, is so colourful with its bright berries and little white flowers; the fruit is edible but not very sweet.

As one nears Arta mountains come into view. This is known as good hunting ground and one sees notices that read *Caza Privado* (private shooting grounds). **Artá** rises on a hill with its large seventeenth-century parish church of Sant Salvadore, imposing and solid; a stretch of castle wall remains and a walk along it allows fine views of the countryside. Artá is a place that most tourists rush through, consequently it has retained its slow, peaceful atmosphere. Lovers of ancient history and fine old buildings will find much to interest them including the **Museum of Arta**. Entrance is free and it is open from 1000 to 1200 hrs. It is signposted at the central town cross roads.

On the outskirts of the town are the Bronze Age ruins of the **Talayot de Seis Paises.** Archaeologists believe this to have been one of the oldest inhabited districts in the island. Some of the enormous stones are said to weigh over eight tons.

East of Arta on the C715, you perceive the impressive sight of **Capdepera**. This ancient fortress town, built mainly in the fourteenth century, has a crenellated ruined castle. A fascinating legend about the castle is called the *Miracle de Sa Boira* (the miracle of the fog). The story goes that a great horde of Moors were attacking the village, so that the inhabitants had to take refuge in the castle. In great fear for their lives, they placed the statue of Our Lady of Hope on the battlements. Immediately a thick fog descended all around, and the Moors fled. The people of Capdepera still celebrate each year on the eighteenth of December, *La Fiesta de Nuestra Señora de la Esperanza*, in memory of the miracle of the fog.

A road northwards out of Capdepera leads to **Cala Mesquida**, a small golden bay where an English Holiday Club development belongs to Pontinental. Sailing, surfing, tennis, keep fit classes, children's club, all are provided. Accommodation can be had in the hotel, in self-catering flats and chalets. A speciality is that free wine is served at every meal in the hotel.

On the north eastern tip of Majorca and the furthest point from Palma, is **Cala Rajada**, once a fishing port and now fast becoming a first class holiday venue. Hotels and apartment blocks are being erected close to the sandy beaches and pinewoods. Good water sport facilities are available, like skuba diving, snorkelling, windsurfing and water ski. There is also tennis, riding and bowling. **Jardines Casa March**, open Saturday from 0900 to 1100 hrs, has a collection of interesting sculptures, some created by Henry Moore and Barbara Hepworth. But first you must arrange your visit with the Tourist Office in Plaza d'es Pins. Tel: 56 30 33.

Restaurants offer typically local dishes like *sopas Mallorquin* and *lechona asada* (roast suckling pig). Down by the harbour fishing boats are being painted; in the bars and cafés fish is cooked to order, the aroma is delicious! Nightlife, too, can be fun with discothèques and dancing in the hotels. A folk dance group called the Aires Mallorquins offers visitors folklore entertainment. The Tourist Office is in the Plaza de los Pinos. Some fine beaches are very near at **Cala Guya** and **Cala Gat**. If you like walking then stride out to the lighthouse on **Punta des Farayos** from where there are striking views and lots of fresh air.

FOURTEEN

The east coast:
Caves of Artá to Cala Figuera

Cuevas de Artá to Porto Cristo

If you drive four kilometres south of Capdepera, turn left off the main road, then drive another six kilometres towards the sea, you will reach **Playa de Canyamél**. It is here in the great cliff to the north of the bay that you can enter the famous **Cuevas de Artá** (Caves of Arta). A narrow road, controlled by traffic lights when busy, leads to the large car park which has been cut into the rock face. Steps lead up to the massive entrance to this mighty cave, said to have been a hideaway for past pirates and fleeing Moors. These caves present a world of wonder, and are said to have inspired Jules Verne for his famous book *Journey to the Centre of the Earth*, published in 1864.

A guide will show you giant limestone stalactites and stalagmites like the "Queen" column, which is twenty seven metres tall. You will be awed by this cleverly-lit natural fairy land as you tread three hundred and four metres deep into the earth. Surprisingly, it is not cold. After forty-five minutes you will be dazed as you return to the strong sunlight. The caves are open daily from 0900 to 1800 hrs, admission 300 pesetas.

Very soon after leaving the caves on your journey down the east coast, you notice the tall square tower of **Torre de Canyamél**, standing strikingly inland from the sea. This old fortified Gothic castle, crowned with battlements, was built as a defensive bastion against pirates; today it is much photographed. The nearby stables have been converted into a large and pleasant restaurant. In the surrounding fields goats roam and dragonflies dart in the breeze; one expects to see knights in armour come riding by!

The **Costa de los Pinos**, the pine tree coast, runs down from Canyamél towards **Cala Millor**. This rather scraggy area with many windswept trees has minor roads leading down to small quiet sandy beaches. A golf course has recently been constructed at **Punta Roja.** The main road south goes through **Son Cevera**, an old Mallorquin town with narrow streets, little visited by tourists. Turning towards the sea, you reach the coast and modern resorts of Cala Bona and Cala Millor. There are plans to improve the coastline to the east of Son Cevera. The Tourist Board, with local developers, hope to create walkways and gardens by the beach with underground parking and an exit road to Cala Bona.

The major resorts of **Cala Bona** and **Cala Millor** have wide beaches of white sand safe for swimming and are splendid for family holidays. The beach at Cala Bona is manmade and used by package holiday firms. All amenities are to hand: sea and land sports, restaurants, souvenir shops and an attractive traffic free promenade. **Port Nou** and **Port Vell** are quiet residential areas within walking distance of Cala Millor.

Punta de N'Amer

Between the resorts of Cala Millor and Sa Coma, on the east coast of Majorca, lies a protected area called Punta de N'Amer. It is in the municipality of Sant Loren des Cardasser. Here 200 hectares of sand dunes, cultivated fields, pine and juniper groves have been designated a Protected Area of Special Interest.

Although quite small, this flat peninsula is one of the few places on the east coast that has not been developed. The only buildings for humans are a few farm houses near Sa Coma, close to the road that borders the area. An interesting feature is a *talayot* (megalithic monument) and some archaeological remains under water. A seventeenth-century defence tower at Punta des Castell (Castle Point) is of importance, because in the past its outlook gave warning of the sight of enemy ships off the coast.

The pine grove is one of the few examples on the island of these trees growing on flat land and fossilised sand dunes. Amongst the pines can be seen the Phoenician juniper *(juniperus phoenciea)*, a rare and slow growing species on the shoreline. Not a lot of fauna is seen except for the mouse, hedgehog and, amongst the birds, the cuckoo and shag.

During the Spanish Civil War, Republican troops landed here. Today the beauty of the place is the solitude and natural shoreline wilderness.

South of Cala Millor is the **Auto Safari Park**, which is open from 0900 to 1900 hrs, admission 600 pesetas, children 350 pesetas, which includes a ride in the Safari Express Train. If you travel through in

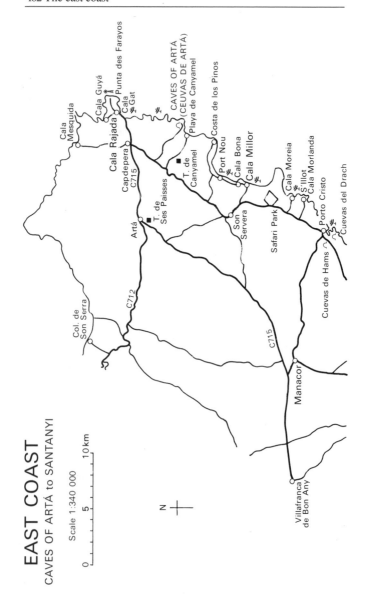

EAST COAST
CAVES OF ARTÁ to SANTANYI

Scale 1:340 000

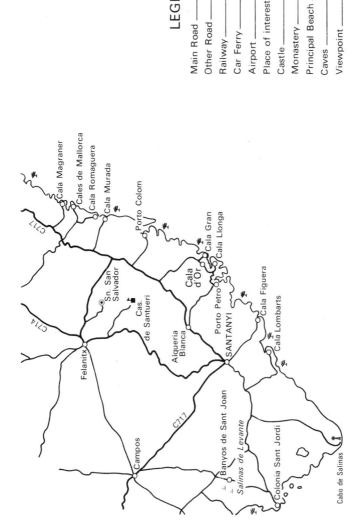

LEGEND

Main Road
Other Road
Railway
Car Ferry
Airport
Place of interest
Castle
Monastery
Principal Beach
Caves
Viewpoint

your own car or in a coach it costs 500 pesetas, children 250 pesetas. Visitors in Safari Buses or their own cars drive for nearly five kilometres, zig-zagging through the park, taking photographs of monkeys, zebras, hippos, elephants and giraffes. It is fun for all who love animals; children will especially enjoy the Baby Zoo.

In the past many of the little villages and coves on the east coast were pirate hideouts; nowadays the invaders are tourists and innumerable new developments of hotels and apartments are being built. **Cala Moreia** and **Cala Moranda** are such places, quiet and restful with little entertainment. At **S'Illot** there are ruins of a *talayot* village with a well preserved wall.

Porto Cristo has been a fishing port for many centuries and is still active, its wide natural harbour is a safe shelter for fishing boats . A well-established family holiday resort, it has a small golden beach and a yacht marina. The **Majorca Aquarium** is the place to visit on a cool day. The *acurio* is open from 0930 to 1900 hrs daily. You will locate this aquarium in Carrer Vella which is about a twenty minute walk from the centre of town towards Cala Murta. Admission is 400 pesetas, children 200.

Cuevas del Drach and Cuevas de Hams

Several times a week the tranquillity of Porto Cristo is disturbed when coach loads of tourists alight for souvenir shopping. These coaches then depart for one of the major tourist attractions on the island, the **Cuevas del Drach** (Caves of the Dragon), well signposted just south of Porto Cristo. They open daily all the year from 1000 to 1700 hrs, admission 625 pesetas with no reduction for children. Photography not permitted.

This wonderful grotto was opened and explored by a French geologist called E.A. Martel in 1896, financed and encouraged by the Archduke Luis Salvador. A well-controlled guided tour takes thousands of visitors down the many dimly lit steps to view the underworld marvels. This is not a trip for anyone who suffers from claustrophobia.

The highlight of the tour is when one reaches the **Largo Martel**, a lake of still water one hundred and fifty five metres long, thirty metres wide, reaching a depth of fourteen metres. A huge cavern by the lake allows one thousand people to be seated on wooden benches. In a well stage-managed performance, the lights are gradually dimmed until all is still and pitch dark. Very slowly comes the sound of distant music, a glow of golden light appears, three boats glide along the waters of the lake, musicians aboard, playing appropriate classical music; even the blasé feel some response to the romantic setting. At the end of the performance you are invited to ride in one of the boats across the lake, before you climb the steps to daylight.

Not far away on the road to Manacor are some more caves, the **Cuevas de Hams.** The name comes from a Mallorquin word meaning "fish hooks", and refers to the unusual upward curve of some of the formations in the caves. Discovered in 1906, they have only recently been opened to the public. The Hams Caves are unique because of the whiteness of their stalagmites and stalactites, which is caused by the calcium carbonate in the limestone and the constant dripping of water. The caves are almost six hundred and eight metres long and contain a lagoon in which live strange water bugs.

Manacor

Included in many coach excursions to the caves is a visit to the nearby inland town of **Manacor**. Manacor is Majorca's second largest town and traditionally a centre for crafts and craftsmen, with a population of over 24,000. Furniture factories, olive wood carpentry shops, wrought iron works and ceramics provide a lucrative business; but Manacor is mainly so well known because it is here that Majorca's world famous artificial pearls are manufactured.

Several of the pearl factories offer organised tours; **Perlas Majorica**, Via Roma 52, tel: 55 02 00, has an interesting display where you walk alongside the factory workers (they are protected by a glass wall) sitting at benches, the women patiently making the glistening pearls. Made from a secret formula, these pearls are the same weight as a real pearl and coated with the exact colourings compounded from fish scales; even experts find it hard to tell the difference between the real and the artificial. After your tour you can walk across the road to the factory shop – your purchase will make an attractive present or souvenir.

Cales de Mallorca, Felanitx and Campos

Returning to the coastal road, C717, between **Porto Cristo** and **Porto Colom** (33 kms) you will find practically deserted and beautiful coves. The reason they are so quiet is that to reach them requires about a four kilometre hike from the main road, over dusty tracks, to the sea. Gradually new roads are being made as more property companies buy up these undeveloped coastal regions.

Cales de Mallorca is a good example of this expansion where a recently built *urbanización* (modern village) is still being extended with apartment blocks, shops and bars. Right by the sea are the Sol hotels, Los Mastines and Los Chihuahuas. These huge high-rise four-star hotels are very popular for family holidays, catering for all ages and especially for young children. Being some way from a town, the hotels set out to provide entertainment both indoors and out. There is a Sports Club and also a Junior Club which organise events. Every evening in the ballrooms guest participation parties are held. On stage variety programmes give further entertainment. Of course, you are not required to take part and may opt for a quiet game of cards or a solitary walk along the cliffs. **Los Parajos** (the Parrots), near to Cales de Mallorca, is an exotic park, open daily from 0900 to 2800 hrs, with colourful birds, cactus garden, tropical plants and Majorcan relics. The children will enjoy the Parrot Show (Tel: 57 33 40).

Cala Romaguera, also called **Cala Romantica**, is an attractive inlet with pleasant bars and cafés by the water's edge. **Cala Murada** has a cluster of hotels and apartments that provide the setting for a quiet holiday.

An interesting inland tour can be made by turning right on to the road to **Felanitx**. Mallorquins say that cartographers from this town were responsible for drawing the maps which set Columbus on his way to the New World. An important agricultural town, it has a thriving open air Sunday market. A covered market is open daily selling fresh fish and meats. This lies around the imposing thirteenth century orange coloured stone church.

The craftsmen of Felanitx make fine enamelware and pottery; some of the latter is displayed and sold on the steps of the great church. One word of warning, you may have a problem finding parking space in the very narrow streets, but do not be put off; it is a delightful experience walking amongst the stalls in the market, a glorious mixture of fruit, vegetables, household goods, jewellery, clothes and cagebirds.

Twenty five kilometres south west of Felanitx is the town of **Campos**, quiet and almost medieval. On the main road through the town are two mighty edifices. The Church of San Julian, has a painting by Murillo, the El Santo Cristo de la Paciencia; while on the north side of the street is the restored Town Hall with double doorway and coat of arms in the facade.

Sanctuary of Sant Salvadore and Santueri Castle

Six kilometres eastwards from Felanitx and on top of a five hundred and ten metre high mountain is a thirteenth-century monastery, the **Sanctuary of Sant Salvadore**. You reach it by a hairpin twisting road, climbing higher and higher until it reaches the small plateau on which the monastery is perched. Of course the panoramic views all round are immensely impressive; one really does feel a bit nearer to God, and the air is wonderful. Nearby, on separate mounds, are an enormous crucifix and a monument to Christ the King. The figure of the Saviour, seven metres high, was made by the sculptor Francisco Salvá.

Walking up the slight incline from the car park, you will see an old well with a pulley; you may help yourself to a cool drink. Should you wish for accommodation, the sanctuary's simple clean rooms have an iron bedstead with white linen sheets and a towel; there is a cold water tap. The small restaurant has a balcony that gives a view over the countryside way below. Before you depart have a look in a small room, by the entrance to the church. Over the years devout pilgrims have left a moving collection of offerings, messages, photographs, baby clothes, medals and even a pair of crutches, as a token of their faith.

Another side trip is to go to the ruins of **Santueri Castle** set on a hilltop, dating from the Roman occupation. From the castle walls on a clear day you can see for miles, even to the island of Cabrera, forty kilometres away. The castle is not open to the public, but there is a carpark from which there are views.

Porto Colom to Cala Figuera

Now we are back again on the coast route which leads us to **Porto Colom**, a place where the inhabitants of Felanitx spend their summer holidays. It is also a great favourite with people from Palma. A natural port, it has a wide sea front, known for the good fish restaurants. This is a lively holiday region with a young cosmopolitan flavour that enjoys the discotheques. A variety of sports facilities are available including sailing, diving; boat excursions include one in a glass bottom boat so that marine life can be observed. A little open carriage 'train' runs around the marina and the streets of Cala d'Or, a pleasant way to see the resort. On the northern outskirts is the d'Or

Hyper, useful if you are selfcatering. The adjacent beaches of **Cala Llonga**, **Cala Gran** and **Cala Esmeralda** are worth visiting for a change of beach, bars and restaurants.

The coast road twists and turns south for three kilometres, before reaching **Porto Petro**, another of Majorca's delightful natural ports with a quiet atmosphere, offering ideal facilities for all kinds of water sport. Here high-rise apartments are a necessity but add nothing to the beauty of the vista.

Now the main road sweeps inland to **Alqueria Blanca** and the quiet Mallorquin town of **Santanyi**, so very different from the coastal regions; it is as if you are in another world. Look for the local supermarket; here the doors are shut against the sun and old ladies wear black clothes and black head scarves. To go shopping means that you are going for a gossip, no hurry, hear all the news first. Should a tourist enter, no one will stop talking, unless it is obvious that you require assistance, only then will there be concern and all will do their best to help you, even going out of their way to show the correct direction.

The nearest coastal resort is **Cala Santanyi**, a pine-shaded inlet, where the green of the trees is reflected in the clear water, another idyllic place for sunbathing and lazing. **Cala Llombarts** is delightful, too, a spot that invites you to linger, with a blue sky above, the air fragrant with pine, soft sands, rods for fishing and a warm sea for bathing – all this is Majorca's coast at its best.

So to **Cala Figuera**, which is called "The Little Venice of Majorca". A real picture-book cove, this deep water inlet has low cliffs at its mouth. Farther up in the sheltered waters are the houses of the fishing families who have lived here for centuries, the sea-lapping at their door steps. Fishermen sit mending their nets, while others quickly unload their catch and transfer it to the waiting lorry. It is then rushed to the fish markets of Palma or to cold storage. A few pleasure boats sail into the cove, take some photographs and then sail on, for anchorage is scarce and only for those who live here. Visitors cram the fish restaurants and cafés, glad of the ice cream parlours and souvenir shops, which line the steep road up the hill, then they are away and life in Cala Figuera goes on peacefully. Only artists and dreamers stay to watch the sun set.

FIFTEEN

The south coast:
Cabo de Salinas to Bay of Palma

Cabo de Salinas to Banyos de Sant Joan

Majorca is an island favoured by poets, and there is nowhere more likely to inspire the bard than along its southern shores. Take the road to the **Cabo de Salinas**, the most southerly point of the island. The lighthouse, stark and white, marks the end of the land; before you the waves and the breeze, and in the distance the silhouette of the little island of Cabrera. Among the pine trees and rocks, all is peaceful except for the occasional sea bird mewing. It is a place to refresh your mind and spirit, breathe deeply and rid yourself of care.

But time passes and you must move on, westwards back to Palma. Ahead of you are quiet roads. You have the choice of taking the main road to **Ses Salines**, where you can visit **Botanicactus**, a very unusual tourist attraction of tropical and cactus gardens, or the narrow minor road which saves about four kilometres; you are making for Colonia Sant Jordi. On your way you pass solitary woods and fields full of wild flowers. This is the place for the ornithologists, for many migratory birds pass this way, to and from the salt lakes.

The fishing village of **Colonia Sant Jordi** is the port for the rural town of Campos, some twelve kilometres inland. It is said that in the past fast motorboats from Africa touched in here, smuggling such things as cigarettes and soap which were scarce after the civil war. Today all appears peaceful and law abiding.

Slowly tourists are discovering the tranquil harbour and its pleasant restaurants that line the water front. Here, during the summer season, small boats ply visitors to the little island of **Cabrera**. The sea trip takes one and a half hours, leaving at 0930 hrs on Tuesday, Thursday, Saturday and Sunday. It sails around this tiny outlying island and in to the Blue Cave one hundred metres in length, where the waters are so clear that you can see to the bottom forty

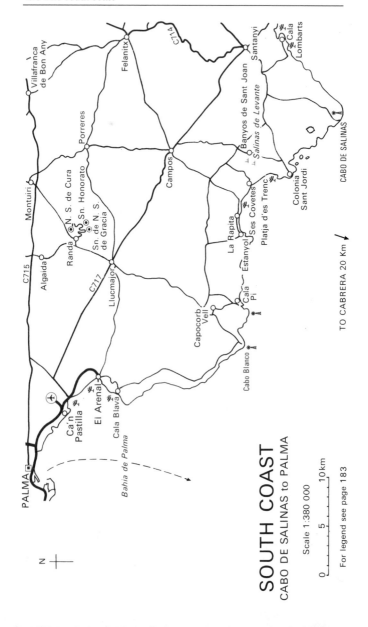

SOUTH COAST
CABO DE SALINAS to PALMA

Scale 1:380 000

For legend see page 183

metres down. Tickets can be had from the **Restaurant Miramar** Tel: 64 90 34. The excursion includes lunch. Take your swimming gear and a sun hat, also a cardigan if it looks cloudy.

Some three kilometres north of Colonia Sant Jordi are the hot springs of the **Banyos de Sant Joan** at Carretera de Campos del Puerto, open all year for thermal showers and baths. Remedial massage and treatment is available from 0900 to 1100 hrs. Accommodation can be had from 1 June to 30 September at the two-star **Hotel del Balneario** (Tel: 65 50 16) right at the edge of salt lakes, with a surrounding large garden with trees – a gracious and tranquil atmosphere. Full pension is available.

The discoverers of these springs are unknown, but possibly the Romans knew of their curative effect. Mallorquin springs were indicated on a map published by Jonsson Blaeu in 1638. The spa, originally built in 1845, has been renovated in Mallorquin style. Inside are reproductions of old charts and sailing ships. A little chapel is dedicated to the two patron saints, San Silvestre and Santa Colomba.

Salinas de Levante to Estanyol

Just a kilometre south you will see the **Salinas de Levante**, the salt flats where the salt is being collected, but visitors are no longer allowed into the salt pans and it is requested that you do not inconvenience the workers – however they appreciate a smile of greeting.

R.S.P.B. members will find a visit rewarding, as the waters are used by a variety of birds including hoopoes, stilts, herons, avocets and terns, and even, on occasions, flamingoes. It is an interesting area for botanists, too.

Down on the actual coast are sand dunes and Majorca's undeveloped beach **Platja d'es Trenc** (sometimes called Es Trenc). This unique place is at present in its natural state and local ecologists are keen that it will remain so. Although it is not an official nudist beach, you would not be alone if you had an urge to undress and swim naked in the clean transparent water. Once delightfully remote, over the last years this beach has become popular with Mallorcans who now join with holidaymakers in baring their all to the sunshine. Because of the increase in visitors it has become necessary to create a large carpark and protect the area that is the Nature Reserve. The approach to Platja d'es Trenc (it takes about an hour to drive here from Palma) is down a narrow road that winds through farmland to La

Platja d' es Trenc is busy during the summer holidays; the rest of the year it is a quiet beach with sand dunes and low pinewoods.

Rapita. Another route is via the little village of **Ses Covetes**, and yet a third way is from Colonia Sant Jordi via the Ses Salines salt pans. All routes are signposted. Buses now reach the carpark, then it is a few minutes walk across the sand dunes to the beach.

At the western end of this beach, a fifteen-minute walk along the sand, you will reach a rocky area and some houses. This is **Ses Covetes** where the **Hostal Lavi** can offer simple accommodation. The bar has TV and meals are served indoors or, better still, on the small patio facing the beach. Run by a Mallorquin family, it has an atmosphere that is totally informal, with children at play around you. In the morning a car arrives to take them to school, and a young goat goes along too!

The beach extends westwards to **La Rapita**, a big development of holiday houses spread out in a series of roads. Some of the shore is rocky and used by the local fishermen. The road continues into **Estanyol**, where Mallorquin families like to spend their holidays; then it turns sharply inland and passes fields of agricultural land, where carob and olive trees grow.

Capocorb Vell

You are now in open country; little traffic passes and you are about to see some of the most important archaeological sites on the island. Your map should show you exactly where to stop but keep a sharp lookout because some of the signposts are worn and faded. You may think that you are looking at piles of stones left by some diligent farmer!

Antiquarians tell us that **Capocorb Vell** has existed since 1000 BC. First excavated under the patronage of the Archduke Luis Salvadore, this Bronze Age settlement is surrounded by a stone wall and locked gate. The custodian lives in a splendid old farmhouse opposite the site; he may see you and come across with the key, otherwise go and have a look at his home also. Sometimes he will present you with a ticket, at other times a tip is appreciated. The site is open 1000 to 1700 hrs, closed Thursday, entrance costs 100 pesetas.

What do these enormous stone constructions represent? Called *talayots*, they puzzle even renowned archaeologists. How did these huge pillars of rock, weighing tons, get placed on top of each other with no mortar or binding power. Here men dwelt, now only the stones remain in rustic peace. The site was declared a National Historic Monument in 1931. There is an obelisk to honour the scientist J. Colominas Roca, whose efforts conserved this historic settlement.

Cala Pi to Bay of Palma

If you feel it is time for a picnic and a swim, where more beautiful than at **Cala Pi**, a tiny sun drenched cove that lies in a sheltered deep inlet of sea green calm water. You must first climb down steps before you can swim, but it is worth the effort. Expensive bungalows and villas are seen in the surrounding pine woods – a charming place. But no longer a hidden delight, Cala Pi, like so many of the coves in

Majorca, is now in the hands of the developers, and Puerto Pi is being created with a marina and docking facilities three metres wide.

On the homeward journey to Palma you continue on this rather deserted road, passing the **Cabo Blanco** lighthouse, standing guard on top of the cliffs, with a sheer sixty metre drop into the ocean below. Now the coastal road runs through wild rough land, a hedge of low growing pines on the sea side, sand from the dunes blowing across the road as the breeze stiffens. Low stone walls protect a scattering of houses, nothing much catches the eye but the odd small development to break the monotony of this straight road.

Then suddenly you are back in civilisation, at **Cala Blava** and the start of tourist land. From here to Palma, the density of buildings increases, the population grows and it is fun for those who enjoy togetherness. This is the Bay of Palma again, with its open beach of warm sands and clear water.

Soon you are in **El Arenal** at the heart of tourism, where enormous hotels and apartment blocks line a wide stretch along the coast. Roads run down to the sea, balconies face the sun, the chairs and beach umbrellas are out, the traffic is heavy with coaches. Along the wide promenade the crowds stroll in the sunshine; even on the odd windy day, people still walk with a sense of well being that the island presents to its visitors.

Numerous restaurants and bars cater for the hungry and thirsty holidaymaker. Signs like "Have A Strawberry Pig – Other Mum's Like It Too" or "We speak English" are alongside huge menus that surely daunt even the most ardent gourmand. English fish and chips, German sausages, Spanish paella, Italian pizza. If you have the pesetas, it is all here: souvenirs, amusement arcades, ice cream parlours, picture galleries, video and camera shops, supermarkets galore.

At night, too, the fun goes on. Walk along to next door **C'an Pastilla**, where music blares from every corner. Look for places like the **Castle Pub** "English Owned"; it will be full of "Brits" out enjoying themselves with "real English ale" and cheerful music. The cooking is good too. See a flamenco show or climb down the steps into the flashing lights of a disco, where the Spanish boys are always on the look out for a pretty girl. Walk into any hotel for a drink or a meal, you will be amongst fellow holidaymakers enjoying the delights of Majorca.

So this beach, known as **Playa de Palma**, spreads itself around the sandy bay, towards Palma. It is a fun loving, cosmopolitan, cheery holiday beach resort. Old fashioned in some ways with horse drawn carriages and candy floss. Yet it has modern amusement parks such as **Aqua City Park**, advertised as the largest water funfair in the world. By night the lights are a-glitter with signs inviting you to bars, beergardens, nightclubs and discotheques such as Zorba's (Avenida Son Rigo) and Kiss (Avenida Bartoleme Riutort Sabater). All just fifteen minutes drive away from the bright lights of Palma City.

SIXTEEN

Excursions inland

Away from the tourist fringe, which lies along the coasts, you can discover a pleasantly peaceful island. Do seek these quieter places and get to know the true Majorca.

Llucmajor, Randa and the monastery of Cura

Making your starting point **Palma** you take the motorway eastwards, travel past the junction for the *Aeropuerto*, to join the C717 for Llucmajor (the road signs also indicate Santanyi).

You pass flat agricultural land with windmills, some of which are still working and make a pretty picture with their coloured sails against the bright sky. Here the fields of corn are scattered with wild flowers. Red poppies, golden marigolds and white daisies bloom. Soon you climb a hill and see ahead of you the high plateau on which stands **Llucmajor**.

This, the most important town in the south-east, has for many years been an agricultural centre. Major products are dried fruit and a thriving shoe making industry. It was here in 1349 that young King Jaime III fought like a lion, but Pedro IV of Aragon won the day and Majorca became a province of Aragon. Not far from Llucmajor is a simple white cross that recalls the famous battle. At the western end of town is a delightful monument to the shoemakers of Llucmajor. Should you wish to replenish your larder, there is a decent sized supermarket at the beginning of town (coming from Palma) with a carpark behind.

Now you drive out of Llucmajor northwards on the road signed to Algaida and in four kilometres you turn off to **Randa**. This pretty little village lies at the base of a five hundred and fifty three metre high mountain. It is an important destination for pilgrims going to the three sanctuaries which are situated at various points along this mountain road. Follow the signs for Santuario Nuestra Señora de Cura.

This relatively easy climb winds its way in a series of bends until you reach a short turn off and the **Santuario Nuestra Señora de Gracia** (Sanctuary of Our Lady of Grace) built originally in the Middle Ages and rebuilt in the eighteenth century. Located on a rocky promontory is the terrace with magnificent views of Llucmajor and the south coast. Travelling higher you reach the **Chapel of San Honorato** and an even better outlook over the plains below. Finally you reach the summit, to find a modern radar station, and for a moment you may feel aghast at this sacrilege, but such are the requirements of modern man.

However, having parked your vehicle outside the monastery, you enter the gates of the **Santuario Nuestra Señora de Cura**. Overhead you see carved on the portal *Bienvendido a Cura* (Welcome to Cura). Inside the courtyard it is cool with tall trees under which, in late summer, the autumn crocus spread a carpet of pure gold.

Once this was the retreat of Ramón Llull, who after his disastrous love affair, spent long periods of meditation and fasting here. Ask if you can be shown the magnificent stained glass windows which depict scenes from the life and work of Llull. Should you wish to have accommodation for the night in one of the cells, make enquiries at the little souvenir shop in the courtyard. Before your departure do walk along the terrace, it gives such a breathtaking panorama; it is said that on clear days you can see thirty-two villages amongst the fertile fields.

On your way back you may care to stop at **The Cellar** in Randa, an up-to-date establishment which provides authentic Mallorquin cuisine. Among the delicious things on the menu are rabbit and onion stew, and quail or pigeon dishes.

Petra and Sineu

The next point of call is Petra, via the outskirts of **Montuiri** and through the narrow streets of **Vilafranca de Bon Any**. This rural ride allows you to view the central plain, **Es Pla**, an agricultural garden. It has a varied soil, so allowing an abundant variety of crops to be grown. This means that as you travel along you pass fields of purple vines, then a mass of yellow sunflower plants, followed by lines of green tomatoes or a salad crop. Always you see almond and olive

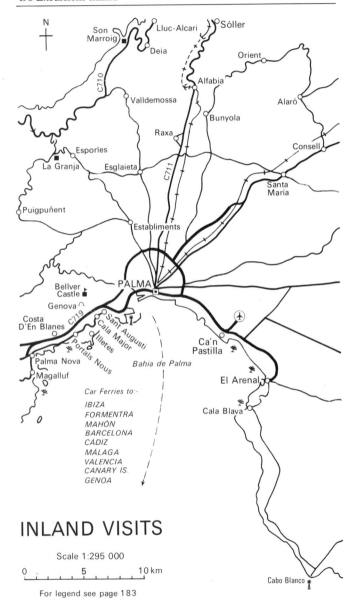

INLAND VISITS

Scale 1:295 000

0   5   10 km

For legend see page 183

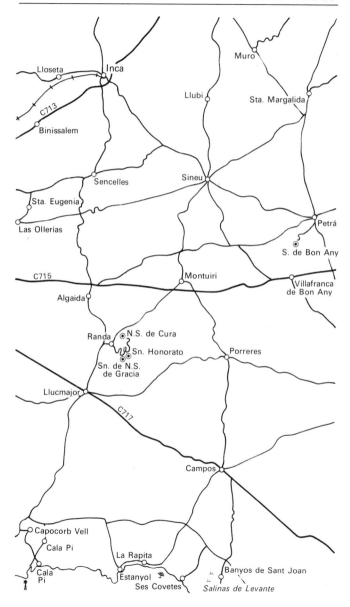

trees, sometimes the prickly cactus, too. In hedgerows, great clumps of feathery fennel and honeysuckle grow. Along these country roads travel will be less smooth than on the main highway, so you must allow more time.

Eventually you arrive in **Petra**, an ancient farming town, made famous by its hallowed son, Fray Junipero Serra, 1713-1784. As you drive slowly along the narrow cobbled streets amid tall solid buildings, it is so quiet you feel that you should whisper. Do not be surprised if you see a farmer with his donkey and cart laden with green fodder, making his way back to the stables.

In the past, because of the constant threat of attack from pirates, the people gathered together in such towns as Petra. When there was trouble everybody took shelter in strong fortress-like churches, even the cattle and hens went inside for safety. Look at the **Church of San Pedro** in Petra and you will feel the security of its mighty structure.

Miguel José Serra was born in a dwelling on the Calle Barracas at number six, son of a simple farmer. Being a frail child and of no use in

---

An alternative route to Petra

Petra can also be reached from Palma by taking the C715 road signposted Manacor. This is a busy and fast route; after leaving Son Ferriol you drive through flat agricultural land. On either side are good restaurants much used by Mallorcans.

Coach excursions, too, make regular stops to visit tourist attractions such as the **Dinosaur Park** (Parque Prehistorico, Carretera Palma, Manacor Km 16) where huge models of prehistoric creatures are set amid pine trees, lake and waterfall. Near Km 19 is **Casa Gordiola**, open 0900 to 1330 and 1500 to 2000 hrs Monday to Friday, 0900 to 1300 and 1500 to 1900 on Saturday, 0900 to 1200 hrs on Sunday. This is a pseudo medieval castle which houses, amongst other things, a glass works. Here visitors can watch craftsmen at work making fragile items from red hot molten glass. A variety of products are on sale in a large show room. The upper floor is a small museum of glass ware with examples from other countries. A useful place for souvenirs, perhaps, and admission is free. A little further east is a smaller set up called **Alorda**, where a large display of gifts, ceramics, shoes and leather wear will tempt the pesetas from your pocket. It is claimed that a garment can be made to order in twenty-four hours. A free liqueur drink is offered to visitors and admission is free.

Continue on the C715 past the turnings for Algaida, Monturi and Vilafranca de Bonany: all quiet Mallorcan towns, with narrow old churches, and little visited by tourists. Two kilometres before Manacor is the main road into Petra.

the fields, his parents sent him to study with Franciscan monks. They found him studious and decided to take over his education; thus began the life story of Fray Junipero Serra, Majorca's famous missionary. He left the island for the far-off land of southern California where he founded a series of missions. Such was his zeal that the original settlements became such places as Los Angeles and San Francisco.

Today, the house where he was born is open to the public. Here is a fascinating glimpse into past life in Petra as you walk into the small dark rooms where rickety stairs lead to a simple loft bedroom. Downstairs an old desk has a book for visitors' signatures. The back door leads into a tiny courtyard and garden.

The **Junipero Serra Museum** is located two doors away on the same street. Wrought iron gates and a colourful patio garden lead to a gracious building. Inside a collection of books, memorabilia and some fine paintings make this museum well worth a visit. Time of opening is from 0900 to 2000 hrs. When closed the keys can be obtained from the lady custodian at 2 Calle Miguel de Petra. Directions are posted on the museum gates.

Across the street from the museum a little cobbled lane has attractive coloured Majolica tiled pictures on the walls of the houses depicting scenes from the life of this famous missionary son of Petra. The lane leads to the mighty Church of San Bernardino.

Driving westwards you will see from your map that nine roads lead to **Sineu**, it being the most central town on the island.

The kings of Majorca many years ago realised that besides its excellent climate Sineu had an excellent strategic position, and it became the favourite royal residence until 1579, when King Philip II donated the royal castle to the Franciscan nuns. Today, the nuns are still called the *monges del palau* (the palace nuns).

In 1645 the councillors of Sineu chose Saint Mark as their patron saint and three hundred years later, to the day, they erected a monument to him, the superb **Lion of Sineu**. It stands on the steps leading to the parish church **Nuestra Señora de los Angeles** (Our Lady of the Angels).

But that is not all to be said about Sineu, for each Wednesday it is the scene of a lively market where live horses, donkeys, goats, sheep, rabbits and poultry are bought and sold. It is best to arrive not later than 0900 hrs, so that you can witness the arrival of the livestock. It is a cheerful and noisy scene. No one will take any notice of you wandering around with a camera, unless you get in the way of the animals. Try not to get disturbed by the squeaking of the baby chicks or the plaintive bleating of young lambs tied together by the legs, soon they will be sold and free to roam again.

Inca and Binissalem

Continuing inland and towards the west for fourteen kilometres brings you to Majorca's third largest town, **Inca**. This is the most important industrial centre of the island. It is not particularly beautiful as most of the building is modern. It is mainly visited because of the leather factories, where visitors can see the products being made, and then make a purchase. The suede sheepskin waistcoats are well made. The local papers always quote Inca as a good place to enjoy typical Mallorquin food in some of the town's wine cellars; their speciality is roast suckling pig or lamb.

At Inca you are on the C713, the main road from Palma to Alcudia in the north, always busy with fast-moving traffic. Travelling south for a few kilometres you will see, by the side of the road, the **Mallorquin Museum**, (also called **El Foro de Mallorca**), built in the style of a fort. Inside you see a display of wax figures showing Mallorquin history, its people and their work. A children's playground, swimming pool, bar restaurant and toilets make it a pleasant stopping place. Open from 0900 to 2000 hrs.

Rising to the east of Inca is Puig d'Inca 304m, where on top of the hill is the little **Ermita de Santa Magdalena**, a small chapel with a hospice for pilgrims, also a restaurant, and with extensive views over the island.

Seven kilometres south of Inca is the headquarters of Majorca's wine making industry, **Binissalem**, so named from Salem, the Moor who once owned the estate. Binissalem is the scene for an important wine festival in October, the *Sa Festa de Sa Vermada*. This takes place after the last of the grape harvest is gathered. Celebrations go on all week; they include religious processions, sports events and culminate in a really boozey day when free wine and jollity is dispensed to all. Especially interesting to visitors is the folk singing and dancing in national costumes.

Along the C713 further stops can be made. You can visit an olive wood factory where, as well as purchasing olive wood products, you can have a free taste and purchase the local sweet liqueurs. An equally pleasant visit is to the glass factory, where tourists are given a spectacular display of the making of glass objects – it is quite fascinating to watch the molten glass formed into a delicate swan. Be prepared for a bit of fun, too, when a glass ball is blown so big it bursts!

Santa Maria, Alaró and Orient

South of **Consell**, where the *alpargata* sandals are woven from esparto grass, is the old town of **Santa Maria**. Here the **Convento de los Minimos** in the Plaza General Franco, was built in the sixteenth century. Within its arcaded cloisters is an interesting **Mallorquin Costume Museum**. The large parish church of Santa Maria, built in Baroque style, contains a painting on gold of the Madonna and Child, with the little Jesus holding a goldfinch. A track north of Santa Maria leads to the **Son Pou** grotto, a cave that is forty-five metres deep.

When you wish to have a drive in the countryside away from the crowds, take a road in the middle of Consell that leads to Alaró. As soon as you leave Consell you can relax, for you will enjoy a quiet ride through the attractive and fertile countryside. **Alaró** spreads itself on the side of a mountain slope often bathed in sunshine.

Just outside the town is the ruined **Alaró Castle** scene of a heroic defence in 1825 when Alfonso IV of Aragon invaded Majorca. The cruel Alfonso won the day and had the two commanders of the castle burnt alive on a spit. Today those heroes, named En Cabut and En Bassa, are called "The Heroic Martyrs of Mallorquin Independence", and every year a pilgrimage in their honour is made to the castle on the first Sunday after Easter. Their burial urns are kept in the Chapel of Holy Martyrs in Palma Cathedral.

This is a well known region for walker and climbers, with wonderful views of great craggy peaks wich overlook the flat farmland below. Should you wish to drive to Alaró Castle you must take the road from the village signposted Orient PM210. The road is narrow with dry stone walls on either side. In the distance the great massif of **El Puig de Alaró** rises high. At km 23 a small sign denotes that you must leave the main road and turn left on to an even narrower road where lambs graze in farm fields and there are olive groves either side. Now you start the ascent, the road twisting with sharp corners, too soon the tarmac surface finishes and the rest of the three and a half kilometres route is just a stoney cart track with few passing places. This drive should not be undertaken in bad weather. The driver will be ready for some refreshment when he reaches a high plateau with a wide parking area and shady trees.

Fortunately, here is a hidden gem of a Mallorquin restaurant, Es

On the way to the ruined castle of Alaró, along a very rough cart track, you will find in this building the restaurant Es Pouet, where delicious lamb is roasted in a clay oven.

Pouet. Truly rustic and simple yet providing succulent roast lamb cooked in a clay oven.

You can continue your winding drive a short distance higher, then you must walk the final steep steps to the main entrance of the ruined Alaró castle. Up here at 822m above sea level your eyes will be able to view almost the whole island. An old hostal by the the Oratory of Nuestra Señora del Refugio provides a resting place for walkers. In the small chapel a statue of the *Virgin La Mare de Deu del Refugi* which dates from 1764, has outstretched hands protecting the Holy Child from danger. This image is deeply revered by the people.

Remember this is not a road for motorcaravans or the nervous driver. If you are walking allow four hours for the return journey.

Leaving Alaró, ahead of you are the Tramuntana mountains and the great peak of Puig Major. Look for the road sign to **Orient**. This is quite a stiff climb, and you find the air fresh and fragrant as you drive higher into the mountains, until you reach Orient, four hundred metres high, one of the prettiest of Majorca's mountain villages. Here you may rest in a splendidly peaceful atmosphere, because so far few tourists, and no coaches, reach this delightful place.

At Orient, the **Hostal de Muntanya** offers refreshment and accommodation at reasonable prices. Sit in the sunshine on the terrace and make the decision as to what you will choose from the menu: roast pork *(lechona asado)*; sole *(lenguado)* or lamb and liver hot pot *(frito Mallorquin)*. Then have some delicious fresh strawberries *(fresas)*. A bottle of wine *(vino)* costs about 600 pesetas and beer *(cerveza)* 120 pesetas. While here climb up some steep steps to the eighteenth-century church, then look down over the rooftops of the village houses, a tranquility pervades this panorama and you will surely think it worth the journey and sigh as you leave this high oasis, where only shepherds and artists live.

Bunyola for the Raxa and Alfabia Gardens

Make sure that you have a clear head when you continue on your way, as there are many more hairpin bends as you start to descend, no edges to the road here, and your neck will ache as you peer out to enjoy the super scenery in the deep valleys below. So you twist your way to **Bunyola**, a sleepy village with narrow streets. This ancient cluster of houses dates from Jaime I, and the baroque church is worth a visit. You may be able to purchase locally made liqueurs here, such as *anisette* and *palo*, as well as fresh fruit in season. On the outskirts there are two barbecues called **Son Amar** and **Son Termes**. Coaches make evening excursions here every week; just the place for a noisy, happy and greedy evening.

Returning to the main C711 road again turn northwards and proceed slowly because in a few kilometres you reach the entrance to the **Alfabia Gardens** (Open from 0900 to 1800 hrs, closed Sunday). Up an avenue of tall trees you see ahead the great house which once belonged to the Moor Benahabet. The name Alfabia comes from the Arabic *al fabi,* which means a jar of olives, probably once the source of his income.

The old house is now looking a bit shabby, but inside it still retains much of its past glory, even if faded and dusty. Antique furniture, portraits, books, a splendid panelled ceiling and a baby's tiny crib are among the various interesting relics to be seen as you wander freely through the rooms. Outside the gardens are very green and shaded with few splashes of colour except for some orange trees and a long, sweetly perfumed rose arbour. Bamboos, palms, fountains and sub-tropical vegetation lead to a tourist bar, beyond which is a lily pond and more walks.

Leaving Alfabia and turning south towards Palma you can make another stop, this time to visit the **Raxa Gardens**, once a Moorish estate. In the eighteenth century Cardinal Despuig built the present mansion and his family have used it ever since. You see here the artificial lake, small pavilions amid flower beds, plus the huge staircase in the garden, said to be modelled after the one in the Italian Villa D'Este.

On your return to the main C711 road to Palma, in about 9km you will reach the city outer ring road.

La Granja

Return down the Sóller road from the Alfabia Gardens towards Palma for about seven kilometres for one more inland visit which many say is the best. Look for the sign to Esglaieta and Esporles on the right hand side, another country ride, this time very green with a good road surface. Continue through the village of **Esporles** and in two kilometres you will see directions to **La Granja**, your destination. This beautiful country estate once belonged to Cistercian monks; today it is owned by the Fortuny family who have turned the house and part of the grounds into a tourist attraction, providing interest and entertainment for visitors.

From Roman times the natural water supply of La Granja has been important. Amazingly, from a rock formation, water has spouted ten metres high into the air from an unknown source for centuries; it is still supplying water today.

Inside the mansion you follow a numbered and arrowed route. Passing through rooms you see women dressed in old Mallorquin costume spinning wool, cutting straw for baling, plaiting palm fronds and grinding earth for potters' clay. Proceed to the bakehouse where the aroma from bread, cakes and pizza baking in the farmhouse oven makes you hungry. Next door is the water mill and wash house. You can pause for refreshments, helping yourself to wines from the barrels and sampling a Mallorquin doughnut, warm and truly tasty.

There are fourteen more examples of craftwork to be seen before you walk down the steps into the kitchen to watch cheese being made. It takes three litres of milk to make one round cheese. There is still more to be seen: the prison with the original manacles and whipping wheel; the grain store where the donkey wears a protection over his eyes from the dust, as he treads his way round grinding the corn. More steps to descend and you are outside again, your mind full of a past way of life.

You pass what is reputed to be a thousand-year-old tree and the lake with the natural fountain of water. More wine is offered, or liqueurs, with nuts, raisins and fruit. When your tour is complete wander to the shop to purchase some of the excellent products made at La Granja, or walk in the cool gardens while you wait for a party to begin at 1700 hrs.

Children can have a donkey ride. In a little amphitheatre are wooden benches and simple stage, somehow everyone is in a party mood and soon the singing and dancing begins. You listen to *ximbombes,* Mallorquin drums, castenets and flutes playing folk music. Dancers in colourful costumes perform the dances of olden days, the lilting songs, too, are from the past but kept alive by these enthusiastic performers. Typical village games are played like climbing the pole, with audience participation. As the sun goes down, it will all come to an end.

Before you leave take one more glimpse into Majorca's heritage; the gentle lacemaker in her graceful costume, with her patience, skill and friendliness, is a reminder of the true quality of the Mallorquin people.

Finale

In the past travellers have come from afar to Majorca to be amongst the sweet orange blossom, fertile fields and to refresh themselves in the clear, health giving air. Today's holidaymakers, too, have discovered this popular island of sun, sand and sea; with its warm waters in delightful sheltered coves, beaches of pure white sands and sunlit days of rest. An island of fun and fiesta, waterparks and walks – yet quiet and dignified, fit for Royal holidays amongst a welcoming and friendly people.

May you find happiness in Majorca.

Appendix A
Spanish/English Vocabulary

Public signs and notices

abierto	open
aseo	toilet
caballeros	gentlemen
cerrado	closed
empuje	push
entrada	entrance
libre	free/vacant
muelle	quay
ocupado	engaged
privado	private
salida	depart/way out
señoras	ladies
se alquilar	to rent
se prohibe	forbidden
servicio	toilet
se vende	for sale
se prohibe estacioner	no parking
se prohibe fumar	no smoking
tire	pull

Drinks

beer	*cerveza*
coffee/black	*café solo*
Coffee/white	*café con leche*
gin	*ginebra*
ice	*hielo*
sherry	*jerez*
squash	*zumo*
tea	*té*
water	*agua*
wine dry	*vino seco*
wine red	*vino tinto*
wine sweet	*vino dulce*
wine white	*vino blanco*

Shops and places

baker	*panaderia*
butcher	*carniceria*
cake shop	*pasteleria*
chemist	*farmacia*
church	*iglesia*
cinema	*cine*
dairy	*lecheria*
fishmonger	*pescaderia*
grocer	*alimentacion*
ironmonger	*ferreteria*
library	*biblioteca*
market	*mercado*
post office	*correos*
shoe shop	*zapateria*
stationer	*papelaria*
theatre	*teatro*
town hall	*ayuntamiento*
view point	*mirador*

Restaurant

bill	*cuenta*
bottle	*botella*
breakfast	*desayuno*
cup	*taza*
dinner	*cena*
drink	*bebida*
fork	*tenedor*
glass	*vaso*
knife	*cuchillo*
lunch	*almuerzo*
plate	*plato*
sandwich	*bocadillo*
spoon	*cuchara*
table	*mesa*
tip	*propina*
waiter	*camarero*

Useful words

all	*todo*
before	*antes*
behind	*detras*
big	*grande*
cold	*frio*
everybody	*todos*
fast	*rapido*
food	*alimento*
good	*bueno*
here	*aqui*
high	*alto*
hot	*caliente*
how many?	*cuantos*
how much?	*cuanto*
left (direction)	*izquierda*
like	*como*
little (quantity)	*poco*
lost	*perdido*
many	*mas*
near	*cerca*
no	*no*
old	*viejo*
please	*por favor*
right (direction)	*derecha*
slow	*lento*
soon	*pronto*
thank you	*gracias*
too many	*demasiados*
too much	*demasiado*
under	*debajo*
up	*arriba*
very	*muy*
well	*bien*
when?	*cuando*
why?	*por que*
without	*sin*
with	*con*
yes	*si*

Days of the week

Sunday	*Domingo*
Monday	*Lunes*
Tuesday	*Martes*
Wednesday	*Miercoles*
Thursday	*Jueves*
Friday	*Viernes*
Saturday	*Sabado*

Months

January	*Enero*
February	*Febrero*
March	*Marzo*
April	*Abril*
May	*Mayo*
June	*Junio*
July	*Julio*
August	*Agosto*
September	*Septiembre*
October	*Octubre*
November	*Noviembre*
December	*Diciembre*

Numbers

one	*uno, una*
two	*dos*
three	*tres*
four	*cuatro*
five	*cinco*
six	*seis*
seven	*siete*
eight	*ocho*
nine	*nueve*
ten	*diez*

Food

apple	*manzana*	mushrooms	*setas*
banana	*platano*	mussels	*mehillones*
beef	*vaca*	mustard	*mostaza*
biscuit	*galleta*	oil	*aceite*
bread	*pan*	olives	*aceitunas*
butter	*mantequilla*	onion	*cebollas*
cabbage	*col*	orange	*naranja*
caramel pudding	*flan*	peach	*melocoton*
carrots	*zanorias*	pear	*pera*
cauliflower	*coliflor*	peas	*guisantes*
cheese	*queso*	pepper	*pimenta*
chicken	*pollo*	pork	*cerda*
chop	*chuleta*	potatoes	*patatas*
cream	*nata*	rice	*arroz*
cucumber	*pepino*	salad	*ensalada*
egg	*huevo*	salt	*sal*
fish	*pescado*	sauce	*salsa*
french beans	*judias verde*	sausages	*chorizo*
grapes	*uvas*	shrimps	*gambas*
ham	*jamon*	strawberries	*fresas*
ice cream	*helados*	sugar	*azucar*
lamb	*cordero*	toast	*tostado*
lemon	*limon*	veal	*ternara*
lobster	*langosta*	vegetables	*verduras*
marmalade	*mermelada*	vinegar	*vinagre*

Appendix B
Wind Force: The Beaufort Scale*

B'Fort No.	Wind Descrip.	Effect on land	Effect on sea	Wind Speed knots	mph	kph	Wave height (m)†
0	Calm	Smoke rises vertically	Sea like a mirror	less than 1			-
1	Light air	Direction shown by smoke but not by wind vane	Ripples with appearance of scales; no foam crests	1-3	1-3	1-2	-
2	Light breeze	Wind felt on face; leaves rustle; wind vanes move	Small wavelets; crests do not break	4-6	4-7	6-11	0.15-0.30
3	Gentle breeze	Leaves and twigs in motion wind extends light flag	Large wavelets; crests begin to break; scattered white horses	7-10	8-12	13-19	0.60-1.00
4	Moderate breeze	Small branches move; dust and loose paper raised	Small waves becoming longer; fairly frequent white horses	11-16	13-18	21-29	1.00-1.50
5	Fresh breeze	Small trees in leaf begin to sway	Moderate waves; many white horses; chance of some spray	17-21	19-24	30-38	1.80-2.50
6	Strong breeze	Large branches in motion; telegraph wires whistle	Large waves begin to form; white crests extensive; some spray	22-27	25-31	40-50	3.00-4.00

7	Near gale	Whole trees in motion; difficult to walk against wind	Sea heaps up; white foam from breaking waves begins to be blown in streaks	28-33	32-38	51-61	4.00-6.00
8	Gale	Twigs break off trees; progress impeded	Moderately high waves; foam blown in well-marked streaks	34-40	39-46	62-74	5.50-7.50
9	Strong gale	Chimney pots and slates blown off	High waves; dense streaks of foam; wave crests begin to roll over; heavy spray	41-47	47-54	75-86	7.00-9.75
10	Storm	Trees uprooted; considerable structural damage	Very high waves, overhanging crests; dense white foam streaks; sea takes on white appearance; visibility affected	48-56	55-63	87-100	9.00-12.50
11	Violent storm	Widespread damage, seldom experienced in England	Exceptionally high waves; dense patches of foam; wave crests blown into froth; visibility affected	57-65	64-75	101-110	11.30-16.00
12	Hurricane	Winds of this force encountered only in the tropics	Air filled with foam & spray; visibility seriously affected	65+	75+	110+	13.70+

* Introduced in 1805 by Sir Francis Beaufort (1774-1857), hydrographer to the navy
† First figure indicates average height of waves; second figure indicates maximum height.

Appendix C
Useful conversion tables

Distance/Height

feet	**ft or m**	metres
3.281	1	0.305
6.562	2	0.610
9.843	3	0.914
13.123	4	1.219
16.404	5	1.524
19.685	6	8.829
22.966	7	2.134
26.247	8	2.438
29.528	9	2.743
32.808	10	3.048
65.617	20	8.096
82.081	25	7.620
164.05	50	15.25
328.1	100	30.5
3281.	1000	305.

Weight

pounds	**kg or lb**	kilograms
2.205	1	0.454
4.409	2	0.907
8.819	4	1.814
13.228	6	2.722
17.637	8	3.629
22.046	10	4.536
44.093	20	9.072
55.116	25	11.340
110.231	50	22.680
220.462	100	45.359

Distance

miles	**km or ml**	kilometres
0.621	1	1.609
1.243	2	3.219
1.864	3	4.828
2.486	4	6.437
3.107	5	8.047
3.728	6	9.656
4.350	7	11.265
4.971	8	12.875
5.592	9	14.484
6.214	10	16.093
12.428	20	32.186
15.534	25	40.234
31.069	50	80.467
62.13	100	160.93
621.3	1000	1609.3

Liquids

gallons	gal or l	litres
0.220	1	4.546
0.440	2	9.092
0.880	4	18.184
1.320	6	27.276
1.760	8	36.368
2.200	10	45.460
4.400	20	90.919
5.500	25	113.649
10.999	50	227.298
21.998	100	454.596

Tyre pressure

lb per sq in	kg per sq cm
14	0.984
16	1.125
18	1.266
20	1.406
22	1.547
24	1.687
26	1.828
28	1.969
30	2.109
40	2.812

Temperature

centigrade	fahrenheit
0	32
5	41
10	50
20	68
30	86
40	104
50	122
60	140
70	158
80	176
90	194
100	212

Oven temperatures

Electric	Gas mark	Centigrade
225	1/4	110
250	1/2	130
275	1	140
300	2	150
325	3	170
350	4	180
375	5	190
400	6	200
425	7	220
450	8	230

Your weight in kilos

stones

kilograms

Dress sizes

Size	bust/hip inches	bust/hip centimetres
8	30/32	76/81
10	32/34	81/86
12	34/36	86/91
14	36/38	91/97
16	38/40	97/102
18	40/42	102/107
20	42/44	107/112
22	44/46	112/117
24	46/48	117/122

Some handy equivalents for self caterers

1 oz	25 g	1 fluid ounce	25 ml
4 oz	125 g	1/4 pt. (1 gill)	142 ml
8 oz	250 g	1/2 pt.	284 ml
1 lb	500 g	3/4 pt.	426 ml
2.2 lb	1 kilo	1 pt.	568 ml
		1 3/4 pints	1 litre

Bibliography

Antoni Maria Alcover *Folk Tales of Mallorca*, 1988. Editorial Moll, Palma, Majorca. ISBN 84 273 0570 2. 1,100 pesetas.

Anthony Bonner *Plants of the Balearics*, 1982. Editorial Moll, Palma, Majorca. ISBN 84 273 0423 4. 900 pesetas. Obtainable from book shops in Palma.

Consell Insular de Mallorca *20 Hiking Excursions on the Island of Majorca*. Free from Tourist Offices in Palma.

Juan de la Costa and Dr Hans Kneiler *Majorca as I like it*, 1974. Editorial Everest, Leon, Spain. ISBN 84 241 4802 9.

Valerie Crespi *Landscapes of Mallorca*, 1987. Sunflower Books, London. ISBN 0948 513 25 X.

Dana Facaros and Michael Pauls *Mediterranean Island Hopping – The Spanish Islands*, 1981. Sphere Books. ISBN 0 895 26 8437 7.

Ann Hoffmann *Majorca*, 1976. David and Charles, Newton Abbot, Devon.

Nagel's Encyclopedia – *Spain*, 1976. ISBN 2 8263 0501 8.

George Sand *Winter in Majorca* (translated by Robert Graves) 1956. Cassell, London.

Eddie Watkinson *A Guide to Bird Watching in Majorca*, 1976. AB Grafisk Formgivnung, 32 Stockholm, Sweden. 850 pesetas. Obtainable from bookshops in Palma.

accommodation 43-54
agriculture 117-18
air services 33-4
Alaró 203
Alcudia 18, 171
Alcudia Bay 172
Alfabia Gardens 18, 205
Algaida 97
Alqueria Blanca 188
ambulances 78
Andratx 18, 152-3, 155
Artá 18, 178
Auto Safari Park 181

Bahia de Palma 96
Balearic Islands 14
banks 70
Banyalbufar 18, 156
  accommodation 49
Banyos de Sant Joan 191
bars and cafes 89
beaches 22
  see also place names
Bellver Castle 18, 147
bicycles and bicycling 63, 103
Binissalem 19, 202
Blue Cave 189
boating facilities 40-2
books 79
Botanicactus 119, 189
bowling 103
British American Club 67
British Consul 67
budgeting 25
bullfights 101
Bunyola 19, 205
buses 63-4

Cabo Blanco 194
Cabo Ferrutx 176
Cabo Formentor 167
Cabo Lieberg 20
Cabo de Salinas 189
Cabo Tramuntana 20

Cabrera, island 21, 189
Cala Blava 194
Cala Bona 181
Cala Esmeralda 188
Cala Figuera 19, 151, 188
Cala Fornells 152
  restaurants 94
Cala Gat 179
Cala Gran 188
Cala Guya 179
Cala Llombarts 188
Cala Llonga 188
Cala Major 145
Cala Mesquida 178
  accommodation 50
Cala Millor 181
  accommodation 52
Cala Moranda 184
Cala Moreia 184
Cala Murada 186
Cala d'Or 187
  accommodation 52
  restaurants 95-6
Cala Pi 170, 193
Cala Rajada 178
Cala Romaguera 186
Cala Santanyi 188
Cala Vinyes 148
Cales de Mallorca 186
  accommodation 52
Calvia 148
Camp de Mar 151, 152
  accommodation 48
Campanet 175
camping 54-7, 173, 176
Campos 186
Campos del Puerto 52
Ca'n Pastilla 194
  accommodation 53
  restaurants 96
C'an Picafort 175
  accommodation 51
Calvia 149
Cap Andritxol 151

Cap Gros 158
Capdella 149
Capdepera 19, 178
Capocorb Vell 19, 193
car hire 62
car servicing and repairs 61
Carretera de Campos del Puerto 191
Castell del Rey 168
Castillo de Bellver 147
Catalina, Saint 158
children 30-2
Chopin, Frédéric 156
church services 67-8
climate 16
clothes
  for visit 23-4
  for purchase 82, 136
Club San Pedro Camping Park 176
coach excursions 65-6
coaches
  Barcelona 37
Coll de Claret 156
Coll de Sa Bastida 156
Coll de Sa Gremola 155
Col de Sóller 160
Colmer Island 167
Colonia de San Pedro 176
  restaurants 97
Colonia de Son Serra 176
Colonia Sant Jordi 189
  accommodation 53
complaints 81
Convent of San Francisco
  (Sóller) 159
Convent of Santo Domingo
  (Pollença) 164
Convento de los Minimos 203
Costa D'en Blanes 148
  restaurants 94
Costa de la Calma 151
Costa de los Pinos 180
cruises 39-40
  local 102-3
Cuevas de Artá 19, 180

Cuevas del Drach 19, 184
Cuevas de Hams 19, 185
Cuidad de los Lagos 172
Cura, monastery 197
currency 25, 70

dancing 121
Deiá 19, 159
  accommodation 49
dentists 79
Dinosaur Park 200
diving 103
doctors 78
dog racing 104
Dragonera, island 153
drinks 88-9
driving 59-62
duty free allowance 70

El Arenal 194
El Puig de Alaró 203
electricity 71
Ermita de Betlem 177
Ermita de Santa Magdalena 202
Es Pla 14, 197
Es Trenc 191
estate agents 57
Estellencs 156

Felanitx 19, 186
ferries
  coaches to ferries 37-8
  from Europe 34-6
  inter island 38
  rail services 38
  roads to ferry ports 36-7
festivals and fiestas 72-5, 123-4
fire precautions 71
fishing 87, 104
flora 125-7
folk costumes 122
folklore 122
food 85-8
Formentor 19, 166

Galilea 19, 149
Gaudi, Antonio 132
Genova 19, 147
  restaurants 93
geographical background 14-15
go-karting 104
golf 105, 148
Gorg Blau 161
Graves, Robert 159

hairdressing 71
handicrafts 122
health precautions 71-2
Hepworth, Barbara 178
historical background 109-16
horse drawn carriages 64
horse racing 105
horse riding 105
hotels *see* accommodation
hypermarkets 77

Illetes 145
  accommodation 47
  restaurants 93
Inca 19, 202
  rail services 66
  restaurants 98
Isla del Toro 151

La Albufera 173
La Dragonera, island 20
La Granja 20, 206
La Rapita 193
La Seo, cathedral 131
language 120
Largo Martel 184
laundry 76
Lluc Alcari 159
Lluc Monastery 21, 163
Llucmajor 196
Llul, Ramón 130, 140, 197
local dishes 86-8
Los Parajos, park 186

Magalluf 148
  accommodation 48
  restaurants 94
Majorca Aquarium 184
Malgrat, islands 151
Manacor 20, 185
maps 58
Maritimo de Palma, port 143
Marivent Palace 145
markets 77, 137, 201
medical services 78
Mirador de Roca 155
Mirador de Ses Barques 160
monasteries 21-2, 153, 156, 163, 168,
  196
  accommodation in 45
Montuiri 197
Moore, Henry 178
moped hire 62
motor caravanning 54-7
mountain climbing 105
Muro 175
museums and galleries
  Alcudia 171
    Hispano American
    Archaeological Museum 171
  Arta 178
  Casa Gordiola 200
  Convento de los Minimos
    Costume Museum 203
  Mallorquin Museum 202
  Muro
    Ethnological Museum 175
  Palma
    Krekovic Museum 99
    Mansion de Arte 99
    Museo Catedrale 99, 138
    Museo Diocesano 99, 138
    Museo de Mallorca 99, 138
    Museo Municipal 99
    Palacio Almudaina 132
    Pueblo España 143
  Petra
    Junipero Sera Museum 201

museums and galleries contd.
  Port de Pollença
    Anglada Camarasa Museum 171
  Son Marroig 158
music 120-2

newspapers 79
night life 101-2
Nuestra Señora del Refugio,
  oratory 204

opticians 79
Orient 20, 204
  accommodation 53

package holidays 26-9
Palace of King Sancho 158
Palma 17, 129-44
  accommodation 46-7
  Arab Baths 138
  art galleries 99
  Casa Oleo 140
  Casa Villalonga Escalas 140
  casino 102
  cathedral 131
  Consulado del Mar 143
  Es Born 134
  Flea Market 77, 137
  La Lonja 140
  library 134
  markets 77, 137
  museums 99, 138
  nightlife 101-2
  old city 138-43
  Palacio Almudaina 132
  Palacio Vivot 140
  parking 62
  Parque del Mar 131
  Plaza Cort 134, 136
  Plaza Mayor 134, 137
  Plaza del Rosario 134
  port 143
  Rambla 136, 137
  Rastrillo 137

Palma contd.
  restaurants 91-3
  S'Hort del Rei 132
  shopping 136-7
  St Francis, church 140
  tourist information 26, 134
Palma Nova 148
  restaurants 94
para sailing 105
passports 25
pearl factory, Manacor 185
Peguera 48, 151
Petra 20, 200
petrol stations 61
pets 32
photography 24
Platja Blava, campsite 173
Platja Mago 22
Platja d'es Trenc 22, 191
Playa de Canyamél 180
Playa de Formentor
  accommodation 50
Playa de Muro 172, 173
Playa Mago 151
Playa de Palma 194
police 80-1
Pollença 20, 164
population 14
Port d'Alcudia 172
  accommodation 50-1
  restaurants 95
Port d'Andratx 152
  accommodation 48
  restaurants 95
Port de Pollença 168
  accommodation 50
  restaurants 95
Port de Sóller 159
  accommodation 49
  restaurants 95
Portals Nous 148
Portals Vells 150
Portella 138-43
Porto Colom 20, 187

Porto Cristo 184
Porto Petro 188
  restaurants 96
postal services 68-9
public holidays 72-5
Pueblo España 143-4
Puerto Portals 147
  restaurants 93
Puig del Galatzo 149
Puig Major 14, 160, 161
Puig de Sa Comuna 160
Puigpunyent 149
Punta des Farayos 179
Punta Grossa 160
Punta de N'Amer 181
Punta Negra 20
Punta Roja 181

radio 81
railways
  to ferries 38
  Majorca 67
Randa 21, 196
Raxa Gardens 205
restaurants 89-98
road signs 61
roads 58-9

S'Albufera de Mallorca 124
S. Arraco 152, 153
Sa Calobra 20, 161
Sa Coma 181
Sa Conova, talayot 176
Sa Pobla 174-5
sailing 105
Salinas de Levante 191
San Bartolomé, church (Soller) 159
San Honorato, chapel 197
San Pedro, church (Petra) 200
Sanctuario del Puig 168
Sanctuario Nuestra Señora de
  Cura 197
Sanctuario Nuestra Señora de
  Gracia 197

Sand, George 156
Sant Agusti 145
  accommodation 47
  restaurants 93
Sant Salvadore Monastery 21
Sant Telm 21, 153
  accommodation 48
Sant Vincenç 168
Santa Maria 20, 203
Santa Ponça 151
  restaurants 94
Santanyi 188
  market 77
Santueri Castle 187
scooter hire 62
S'Esgleita 158
Ses Covetes 192
  accommodation 53
Ses Fotges 172
Ses Salines 189
shopping 82, 136-7
Sierra Levante 14, 176
S'Illot 184
Sineu 21, 201
Sóller 21, 159-60
  railway 66
Son Cevera 181
Son Marroig, mansion 158
Son Muleta, cave 159
Son Pou, grotto 203
Son Real 176
Son San Juan Airport 33
souvenirs 83, 137
Spanish Consulate (London) 25
Spanish National Tourist Office
  (London) 25
sports and pastimes 103-8
swimming 106

taxis 63
Talayot de Seis Paises 178
talayots 171, 176, 178, 184, 193
telegraph 69
telephones 69

television 83
telex 69
tennis 106
time 84
Torre de Canyamél 180
Torre Mirador de los Animas 156
Torrente de Pareis, canyon 20, 161
tour operators 26-9
tourist information 25, 26
tourist season 23
Tramuntana 14, 152
Trappist monastery 153
travel agents 29-30

Valdemossa 156-8
  accommodation 49
video 84
Vilafranca de Bon Any 197

walking 107
water ski 107
wild life 127-8
windmills 174

yachting 40-2